DECOLONIZATION AND FEMINISMS IN GLOBAL TEACHING AND LEARNING

Decolonization and Feminisms in Global Teaching and Learning is a resource for teachers and learners seeking to participate in the creation of radical and liberating spaces in the academy and beyond. This edited volume is inspired by, and applies, decolonial and feminist thought – two fields with powerful traditions of critical pedagogy, which have shared productive exchange.

The structure of this collection reflects the synergies between decolonial and feminist thought in its four parts, which offer reflections on the politics of knowledge; the challenging pathways of finding your voice; the constraints and possibilities of institutional contexts; and the relation between decolonial and feminist thought and established academic disciplines. To root this book in the political struggles that inspire it, and to maintain the close connection between political action and reflection in praxis, chapters are interspersed with manifestos formulated by activists from across the world, as further resources for learning and teaching.

These essays definitively argue that the decolonization of universities, through the re-examination of how knowledge is produced and taught, is only strengthened when connected to feminist and critical queer and gender perspectives. Concurrently, they make the compelling case that gender and feminist teaching can be enhanced and developed when open to its own decolonization.

Sara de Jong is Lecturer in Politics at the University of York, UK. Her research on the politics of unequal encounters in a global world has been published in several journal articles and in the monograph *Complicit Sisters: Gender and Women's Issues across North–South Divides* (2017).

Rosalba Icaza is Associate Professor in Global Politics, Gender and Diversity at the Institute of Social Studies, Erasmus University of Rotterdam in the Netherlands. Her research focuses on decolonial feminism and global politics, and her essay 'Social Struggles and the Coloniality of Gender' was recently published in *The Routledge Handbook on Postcolonial Politics* (2018).

Olivia U. Rutazibwa is Senior Lecturer in European and International Development Studies at the University of Portsmouth, UK. Her research centers on decolonial thinking and international solidarity. She is the co-editor of *The Routledge Handbook of Postcolonial Politics* (2018) and associate editor of the *International Feminist Journal of Politics*.

Teaching with Gender

The series is a collection which has a longstanding tradition of publications of theoretical reflections and case studies that address the pedagogical, conceptual and political dimensions of teaching and learning about gender. First linked to its predecessor, the ATHENA network, the *Teaching with Gender* book series is now coordinated by ATGENDER – the European Association for Gender Research, Education and Documentation. A wide range of international scholars have contributed to the edited volumes in this series, offering teaching tools and seminar exercises that give students and teachers valuable sources for the teaching and studying of gender and sexuality.

www.routledge.com/Teaching-with-Gender/book-series/TWG

Teaching Gender: Feminist Pedagogy and Responsibility in Times of Political Crisis
Beatriz Revelles Benavente and Ana Maria González Ramos

Decolonization and Feminisms in Global Teaching and Learning
Sara de Jong, Rosalba Icaza and Olivia U. Rutazibwa

DECOLONIZATION AND FEMINISMS IN GLOBAL TEACHING AND LEARNING

Edited by Sara de Jong, Rosalba Icaza and Olivia U. Rutazibwa

AT**GENDER**

LONDON AND NEW YORK

First published 2019
by Routledge
2 Park Square, Milton Park, Abingdon, Oxon OX14 4RN

and by Routledge
711 Third Avenue, New York, NY 10017

Routledge is an imprint of the Taylor & Francis Group, an informa business

British Library Cataloguing-in-Publication Data
A catalogue record for this book is available from the British Library

Library of Congress Cataloging-in-Publication Data
Names: Jong, Sara de, editor. | Icaza, Rosalba, editor. | Rutazibwa, Olivia,
    editor.
Title: Decolonization and feminisms in global teaching and learning /
    edited by Sara de Jong, Rosalba Icaza, Olivia U. Rutazibwa.
Description: Abingdon, Oxon ; New York, NY : Routledge, 2019. | Series:
    Teaching with gender | Includes bibliographical references.
Identifiers: LCCN 2018015251 | ISBN 9780815355939 (hardback :
    alk. paper) | ISBN 9780815355946 (pbk. : alk. paper) | ISBN
    9781351128988 (ebook)
Subjects: LCSH: Decolonization. | Feminism. | Higher education.
Classification: LCC JV152 .D43 2019 | DDC 325/.3082—dc23
LC record available at https://lccn.loc.gov/2018015251

ISBN: 978-0-8153-5593-9 (hbk)
ISBN: 978-0-8153-5594-6 (pbk)
ISBN: 978-1-351-12898-8 (ebk)

Typeset in Bembo
by Swales & Willis Ltd, Exeter, Devon, UK

MIX
Paper from
responsible sources
FSC
www.fsc.org   FSC® C013056

Printed and bound in Great Britain by
TJ International Ltd, Padstow, Cornwall

CONTENTS

CONTRIBUTORS

Jess Auerbach was part of a team setting up the Social Sciences degree at the African Leadership University. She was trained in South Africa, the UK, and the USA, and has undertaken research in Lusophone Africa and in Brazil. Students in the founding class of the Social Science program at ALU come from 16 African countries and collectively speak 29 languages. They opted to major in social science out of a desire to contribute towards a more equitable world. Jess also acknowledges the contribution of her colleague Janice Ndegwa, from Kenya, in the formulation of these commitments. Jess has now left ALU and is working on these commitments with the think tank Mauritius Forward based in Port Louis, and with the Center for Indian Ocean Studies in Africa at the University of the Witwatersrand in Johannesburg, South Africa.

Sara de Jong is a lecturer in Politics at the University of York, UK. She is the co-chair of ATGENDER, the European Association for Gender Research, Education and Documentation. Her wider research includes the politics of NGOs in the fields of migration, gender, and international development, and she has been published in *Social Inclusion, International Feminist Journal of Politics, Journal of Ethnic and Migration Studies,* and *Identities: Global Studies in Culture and Power.* She is currently particularly interested in the role of brokers in colonial and contemporary unequal encounters as mediators of migration, conflict, and international development. She recently published the monograph *Complicit Sisters: Gender and Women's Issues across North–South Divides* (2017) and co-edited an open access special issue on 'Decolonising the University' for the *Dutch Journal on Gender Studies* (2017), together with Rosalba Icaza, Sophie Withaeckx, and Rolando Vazquez.

Batallones Femeninos is integrated by Obeja Negra–Lady Liz–Kiara–Murder–Bawa–Dilema–Candy–Xirena–Xibakbal–Luna Negra–Yazz–Polyester Kat. They define themselves as a collective project of hip-hop and artivism by women in Mexico. Batallones Femeninos was born in Ciudad Juarez, Chihuahua, Mexico – the world capital of feminicide – in 2009. Their members are border women, students, artists, single mothers, workers, and housewives united by music, and their Facebook page can be accessed at www.facebook.com/pg/BatallonesFem/ about/?ref=page_internal. Batallones' songs are free to download at https://soundcloud. com/batallonesfemeninos.

Marta Fernández is an adjunct professor at the Institute of International Relations, Pontifical Catholic University of Rio de Janeiro (IRI/PUC-Rio), Brazil, which awarded her PhD. She is the Director of IRI/PUC-Rio, and has been teaching on international relations theory and postcolonial/decolonial studies. Her current research deals with Brazil's engagement in peacebuilding operations, development, South–South cooperation, postcolonial and decolonial perspectives and racism.

Andréa Gill is a professor and research practitioner at the Institute of International Relations of the Pontifical Catholic University of Rio de Janeiro (IRI/PUC-Rio), Brazil. She graduated in Social and Political Thought from Western University and the University of KwaZulu-Natal, has a master's in Political Science from the University of Victoria, and a PhD in Political Science and Cultural, Social and Political Thought from the University of Victoria. Areas of interest include postcolonial and decolonial studies; race, gender and class relations; urban politics; international relations and globalization; Brazilian social and political thought.

Rosalba Icaza is a decolonial feminist and International Studies scholar with 15 years of research and teaching experience on gender and development, international political economy, and research methodologies. Rosalba is member of the Transnational Network Other Knowledges (RETOS) and collaborates with the Universidad de la Tierra (UNITIERRA) Oaxaca, Mexico. Her recent publications include "Social Struggles and the Coloniality of Gender," for the *Routledge Handbook on Postcolonial Politics*, and "Diversity or Decolonization? Researching Diversity at the University of Amsterdam" (with Rolando Vazquez) for *Decolonizing the University* (Pluto Press). She is also co-editing (with Xochitl Leyva) *Cuerpos en Rebeldía y Resistencia* (CLACSO). She is Associate Professor in Global Politics, Gender and Diversity at the International Institute of Social Studies (ISS), Erasmus University of Rotterdam (EUR).

Roselyn Masamha is a Zimbabwean lecturer in Learning Disabilities Nursing in the UK, with a clinical practice background in forensic learning disabilities nursing. Roselyn has a keen interest in educational research with a focus on approaches to international student education largely influenced by her own experiences as a migrant student. Her current doctoral research is concerned with the impact of competing perspectives of teaching and learning for international student nurses. Central to this research is an analysis of the politics of knowledge production, African identity, race, migrant status, and media representations within a UK nursing education context.

Sara C. Motta is a mother, critical theorist, priestess of the feminine divine, poet, and popular educator who currently works in the Discipline of Politics at the University of Newcastle, New South Wales. She has published widely in academic and activist journals. Her most recent book, *Constructing 21st Century Socialism in Latin America: The Role of Radical Education* (Palgrave Macmillan, 2014), explores the role of the pedagogical in the re-visioning of emancipation. Her upcoming book,

Liminal Subjects: Weaving (Our) Liberation, is a decolonial feminist non-manifesto of liberation and will be published by Rowman and Littlefield in 2018.

Sereana Naepi (Nakida, Natasiri) is Associate Director of All My Relations, an Indigenous Research centre at Thompson Rivers University, and is completing her PhD at the University of British Columbia. Sereana's work explores the way in which structures within universities hinder the success of all learners and staff. As part of this work, Sereana has mentored Indigenous students for over 10 years in both Aotearoa and Canada.

RETOS stands for "Red Trasnacional Otros Saberes" (Transnational Network Other Knowledges). It is an articulation of academics, academic-activists, artists and artist-activists involved in various movements, organizations, and groups existing throughout the Americas/Abya Yala that are concerned about epistemic racism, land-grabbing, and intersectional forms of violence. RETOS works through nodes of committed people based in: Brazil; Colombia; Chapel Hill, USA; Chiapas, Mexico; Peru; Puerto Rico; and the Netherlands. RETOS members coordinate the working group Bodies, Territories and Resistances at the Social Sciences Latin American Council (CLACSO). They also founded the autonomous and cooperative publishing house Editorial RETOS, which in 2005 published the highly acclaimed three-volume *Prácticas otras de conocimiento(s): Entre crisis, entre guerras*. The RETOS website can be found at www.encuentroredtoschiapas.jkopkutik. org/index.php/es/

Olivia U. Rutazibwa is senior lecturer in European and International Development Studies at the University of Portsmouth in the UK. Her research centres on ways to decolonize thinking and practices of international solidarity by recovering and reconnecting philosophies and enactments of dignity and self-determination in the postcolony: autonomous recovery in Somaliland, Agaciro in Rwanda, and Black Power in the US. She has published in *Postcolonial Studies, Ethical Perspectives, Journal of Intervention and Statebuilding*, and *Journal of Contemporary European Studies*, and is the co-editor of *The Routledge Handbook of Postcolonial Politics* and associate editor of the *International Feminist Journal of Politics*. She is the former Africa desk editor, journalist, and columnist at the Brussels-based quarterly MO* magazine and author of *The End of the White World. A Decolonial Manifesto* (in Dutch, EPO, 2018).

Robbie Shilliam is Professor of International Relations at Johns Hopkins University, Baltimore, USA. He is author of, among others, *The Black Pacific: Anticolonial Struggles and Oceanic Connections* (Bloomsbury), and co-editor of *Race and Racism in International Relations: Confronting the Global Colour Line* (Routledge), *Meanings of Bandung: Postcolonial Orders and Decolonial Visons* (Rowman & Littlefield International), and *The Routledge Handbook of Postcolonial Politics*. He is co-editor of the book series *Kilombo: International Relations and Colonial Questions* for Rowman & Littlefield International.

Sixteen Participants of the "Crossing Borders" Conference in Lesbos, Greece, July 2016, included activists, academics and activists-academics from different regions of the world with common concerns about the use of refugees and migrants' lives by the conference organizers.

Xochitl Leyva Solano is a Barefoot Feminist. She is a member of anti-systemic networks as well as those practicing co-labor and decolonizing research. Researcher and professor at the Center for Higher Research of Social Anthropology (CIESAS), in San Cristóbal de Las Casas, Chiapas (México), Professor Leyva has published in Maya, Spanish, English, French, and Finish across different continents. In the last three decades, her work has been with women and youth in communities in resistance. Among the books she has co-edited are *Human Rights in the Mayan Region* (Duke University Press) and *Encuentros Antropológicos: Power, Identity and Mobility in Mexican Society* (ILAS).

Asha Varadharajan is Associate Professor of English at Queen's University, Kingston, Ontario, and the author of *Exotic Parodies: Subjectivity in Adorno, Said, and Spivak* (University of Minnesota Press). Her writing and public speaking engage the broad sweep of postcolonial, cosmopolitan, global, secular, rights, migration, and development debates. Her most recent essays have appeared in the *Puritan Literary Magazine, Cultural Studies, College Literature, Kunapipi, University of Toronto Quarterly, TOPIA, CSSAAME,* and *Modern Language Quarterly,* and she has contributed chapters to books on human rights, biopolitics, and intercultural discourse. The most fun she has had lately was writing her entry on Eric Idle for the *Dictionary of Literary Biography,* and the most flattered and chuffed she has been was when, in 2017, her students nominated her for the W.J. Barnes Award for excellence in undergraduate teaching.

Elena Vasiliou is a PhD candidate in Gender Studies at the University of Cyprus (2014–2018). Her academic background is in psychology (Panteion University Athens) and her research interests include: queer theories, post/decolonial theories, and critical prison studies. Elena worked as an instructor at the Nicosia Central Prison Education Program between 2010 and 2015. She took part in a number of local and European projects as researcher. Her activist background includes mental health advocacy and LGBTQ issues. She is an amateur triathlon athlete.

Françoise Vergès has a BA in Women's Studies and Political Sciences from the University of California, San Diego and a PhD in Political Theory from the University of California, Berkeley. She holds the "Global South(s)" Chair at the Collège d'études mondiales in Paris, France, and has directed the scientific and cultural program for a museum in Reunion Island (2002–2010) and been the president of the French Committee for the Memory and History of Slavery (2009–2012). As an anti-colonial feminist, curator, educator, former journalist, and political theorist, Vergès has authored documentaries and written extensively on memories of colonial slavery and colonialism, Aimé Césaire, Frantz Fanon, museums, and processes of creolization. Her most recent publications include "A Sound Like a Rumor" in *Kader Attia. RepaiR* (2014), *Les Armes miraculeuses* (2014) and *Le Ventre des femmes* (Albin Michel). She co-wrote the Manifesto Atelier IV (in this volume) with fellow scholars/activists Gia Abrassart, Bénédicte Alliot, Kader Attia, Paola Bacchetta, Jean-François Boclé, Odile Burluraux, Jephthe Carmil, Gerty Dambury, Myriam Dao, Lucie Dégut, Alexandre Erre,

Fabiana Ex-Souza, Nathalie Gonthier, Yo-Yo Gonthier, Antoine Idier, Marta Jecu, Léopold Lambert, Carpanin Marimoutou, Myriam Mihindou, Laura Huertas Millan, Kat Moutoussamy, Frédéric Nauczyciel, Pier Ndoumbe, Pascale Obolo, Yohann Quëland de Saint-Pern, France Manoush Sahatdjian, Melissa Thackway, Mawena Yehouessi and Mikaëla Zyss.

Wanelisa Xaba is a Black Radical feminist activist, decolonial writer, and thinker. She started her activism at 15 years as a children's rights activist, engaging policy-makers from the Department of Social Development regarding intervention for orphaned and vulnerable children. In her undergraduate career at University of Cape Town (UCT), she was part of a collective called Conscious Conversation, which partnered with the vice chancellor and transformation offices to facilitate discussion about race, justice, and restitution. She is the founding member of the South African Young Feminist Activists, and was a junior researcher, guest lecturer, and tutor for the African Gender Studies at the UCT. She also pursued a master's by research at UCT, which focused on undergraduate students' experiences of Blackness and how Black students navigate institutions of higher learning. She documented LGBTIQ hate crimes in South Africa with Iranti-org, and was named one of the *Mail & Guardian* and *Guardian*'s 200 Influential Young South Africans. She currently conducts workshops on decolonization and is interested in using decolonization for the intervention of violence against women, girls, and the LGBTIQ community.

ACKNOWLEDGMENTS

First and foremost, we would like to express our gratitude to our students who so often remind us of the value of teaching in higher education, even under challenging or restrictive circumstances. Thanks for asking critical questions, for your patience when we get things wrong, for calling us out, and for keeping us on our toes. To the Vietnamese student asking which war was meant when referring to the "Vietnam War," the student challenging stereotypical representations of "African" women in "canonical" introductions to development studies, the student reminding all her peers that Haiti was the first anti-colonial revolution and Black republic, the Mixteca-Mixe indigenous student defining indigeneity not as an "identity", but as a way of being and sense the world . . . We treasure the moments of collective insight in the classroom as well as your gestures of appreciation.

We are particularly thankful to our teachers in and outside of schools and universities, for their inspiration and dedication.

Rosalba Icaza also wants to thank UNITIERRA-Oaxaca and her friends and colleagues in RETOS, who support her pathway to an understanding of learning as a co-creative process. She is particularly grateful to the late Enrique Brito Velazquez, Xochitl Leyva Solano, Gustavo Esteva, Valiana Aguilar, and Angel Ku; and her teachers-friends and comrades in struggle.

Sara de Jong also wants to thank Wendy Harcourt for encouraging her to think about decoloniality in relation to the (post-)colonial, Sophie Withaeckx, Rosalba Icaza, and Rolando Vazquez for being co-editors of the special issue on "Decolonising the University" for the *Tijdschrift voor Genderstudies (Dutch Journal of Gender Studies)*, as well as Karim Murji, Parvati Raghuram, Lisa Tilley, and Olivia Rutazibwa for an inspiring "Engaged Scholarship" seminar on Decolonising the University, supported by the Strategic Research Area Citizenship & Governance at the Open University.

Olivia U. Rutazibwa would like to extent her gratitude first and foremost to Sara and Rosalba, for including her on this journey and their affective and intellectual generosity and support amidst the everyday challenges of this activism/profession. Additionally, she thanks – apart from her family and friends – her students and immediate colleagues at the University of Portsmouth for providing a safe and stimulating space to try to think and do decoloniality: Ann Matear, Ben Garner, Tony Chafer, Tamsin Bradley, and Emmanuel Godin in particular; her colleague-friends who have generously introduced/inspired her thinking on decolonizing IR and IDS: Robbie Shilliam, Felwine Sarr, Meera Sabaratnam, Lisa Tilley, Ajay Parasram, Rolando Vazquez, Gurminder Bhambra, Mark Griffiths, Sabelo Ndlovu-Gatsheni; and scholar-bureaucrat/activist-warrior Andrea Cornwall for showing how to translate critical thinking into practice.

We are grateful to the Global Development Studies section of the International Studies Association (ISA), and British International Studies Association (BISA) Colonial/Postcolonial/Decolonial Working Group, for providing us with a vibrant space of exchange and for organizing the annual workshop in 2016 where the three editors found themselves in the same room for the first time. We also would like to thank ATGENDER, the European Association for Gender Research, Education and Documentation, for the editorial support and the opportunity to publish this edited volume in its "Teaching with Gender" book series.

The anonymous reviewers of the book manuscript provided us with immensely valuable feedback and heartening encouragement. We would like to thank Alexandra McGregor and Kitty Imbert from Routledge for their faith in this project and their support, and Sierra Kane for her editing and proofreading assistance.

Finally, as editors we are immensely grateful to the authors in this volume, some of whom we had the pleasure to work with for the first time, some of whom have been long-term companions on decolonial feminist paths. Its beauty and urgency is wholly due to their craft(wo)manship, commitment and willingness to share their insights, politics, and experiences so generously.

INTRODUCTION

Decolonization and feminisms in global teaching and learning – a radical space of possibility

Rosalba Icaza and Sara de Jong[1]

This book aims to be a resource as well as a toolbox for teachers and learners seeking to participate in the creation of radical and liberatory spaces in the academy and beyond, recognizing that "the classroom remains the most radical space of possibility in the academy" (hooks, 1994, p. 13). While mindful of power differences, critical pedagogy both understands teachers as learners and students as co-responsible with their teachers for the creation of a communal space of learning. This edited volume is inspired by and presents two fields with powerful traditions of critical pedagogy – decolonial and feminist thought – which have been in productive exchange as well as tension with each other.

We understand feminisms as interrogating and challenging gender divisions and hierarchies in societies. Feminisms in plural is to acknowledge the plurality of points of departures and geo-genealogies of thought that have informed practices and struggles committed to undo violence and inequalities emerging from the intersections of race/ethnicity, class, gender, sexual orientation, age, body ableness, and so on (Harcourt, Icaza & Vargas, 2016).

Decolonial thought and practice concerns itself with understanding our historical present as a modern/colonial configuration (Vazquez, 2015). In other words, there is no modernity without coloniality, and this later has been understood as

> long-standing patterns of power that emerge in the context of colonialism, which redefine culture, labor, intersubjective relations, aspirations of the self, common sense, and knowledge production in ways that accredit the superiority of the colonizer. Surviving long after colonialism has been overthrown, coloniality permeates consciousness and social relations in contemporary life.
> *(Mendoza, 2016, p. 114)*

Both fields share a deep commitment to pedagogy and treat it as core to their praxis, rather than as unrewarding housework or as an unwelcome distraction from the 'real work' of research. Pedagogy is concerned with the various modes of teaching and learning. Critical pedagogy understands learning and engagement with knowledge as political, and part of struggles for emancipation and liberation. The engagement with and interest in pedagogy that decolonial and feminist thought share with one another is rooted in the critique of knowledge production (and its understanding of knowledge as political) that is fundamental to both.

Feminist and decolonial politics of knowledge and learning

Feminist thought has uncovered Knowledge with a capital K's false claim to neutrality and objectivity and revealed its male-centric perspective. Decolonial work has shown that the Enlightenment-based form of knowledge is rooted in the violent project of colonialism and the erasure of other epistemes (Castro Gómez, 2007; Lander, 1993; Mignolo, 2010; Walsh, 2013, 2015). More recently, decolonial thought has interrogated the extent to which academic canons have made invisible the modern/colonial divide and brought forward pedagogies – of positionality, relationality and transition – to encourage awareness of the importance of working toward epistemic justice (Icaza & Vazquez, 2018). It is precisely through the pedagogy of positionality that feminisms and decoloniality encounter each other. In particular, this pedagogy deploys concepts of Black feminism and decolonial feminism to explore ways of teaching that are not centered in reproducing the norm but in enabling the recognition of difference as a ground for knowledge (Icaza & Vazquez, 2018).

Both feminist and decolonial work have highlighted the connections between the personal and the political, theory and activism, in a commitment to praxis (e.g. Lugones, 2010, p. 746). As bell hooks explains, "my commitment to engaged pedagogy is an expression of political activism" (1994, p. 203). Both traditions of thought – as well as authors bridging the two and those drawing on postcolonial theory, which shares the impulse of decentering knowledge, albeit from a different angle (Bhambra, 2014) – have sought to create space for marginalized perspectives by displacing the hegemonic (Arashiro & Barahona, 2015; Trinidad Galván, 2016). In foregrounding alternative voices, they have created space for different repertoires and registers of expression. They thereby challenge the mind–body split and attend to the affective dimension of thinking and learning (cf. Motta, 2017).

Feminist and decolonial engagement also share an uneasy and ambivalent relation to the institutional context of the university. Neither part of established disciplines, they have recognized the way in which disciplines can discipline, exclude, and constrain thought by adhering to a monolithic and monocultural disciplinary canon and strict regimes of scholarly recognition. Since the political struggles that feminist and decolonial thought emerges from cannot be fixed in disciplinary boxes, they have both embraced trans- and interdisciplinary modes of engagement. As Trinh Minh-ha states, interdisciplinarity is not a simple adding of different disciplines together, but instead "it is to create in sharing a field, that belongs to no one, not even to those who create it" (1991, p. 108) and, in so doing, it questions the notions of specialization, expertise, professionalism, and discipline. The academy is considered a site, which can nourish but also stifle critical thought and reproduce dominant frameworks as well as colonial patriarchal oppressions. The composition of its staff reflects structures of domination rather than the diversity of society, with white males occupying the most senior positions (Parker, Smith & Dennison, 2017). Classrooms have been both spaces of refuge and learning as well as of further marginalization and alienation (Adriany, Pirmasari & Satiti, 2017; Autar, 2017). Therefore, decolonial and/or feminist thinkers have sought to intervene in the academy from the margins but are also conscious that the institutionalization of their critical perspectives carries the risk of co-optation.

The structure of this book reflects the above synergies between decolonial and feminist thought in its four parts, which respectively offer reflections on: the politics of knowledge production; giving voice to marginalized perspectives; the constraints and possibilities of institutional contexts; and finally, the relation between decolonial and feminist thought and established academic disciplines.

Feminisms and decolonization in productive tension

Many feminists of color and decolonial feminists have both expressed their commitment to feminism, decolonization, and liberation pedagogies, and have illustrated through their work the productive synergies between these interrelated struggles. They have also made visible the ambivalences, tensions, and conflicts in and between each of these bodies of thought. For instance, in her book *Teaching to Transgress: Education as the Practice of Freedom*, US American feminist of color bell hooks dedicates a chapter to Paulo Freire in the form of an internal critical dialogue between herself, Gloria Watkins, and her pen name, bell hooks. Trying to find a language to acknowledge her indebtedness to Freire's work and honor their friendship while engaging critically with "not only the sexism of the language but the way he (like other progressive Third World leaders, intellectuals, critical thinkers such as Fanon, Memmi, etc.) constructs a phallocentric paradigm of liberation" (1994, p. 49), without succumbing to a binary language that either embraces or denounces him, hooks writes that "Paulo's work has been living water" for her (1994, p. 50). As living water, his writing quenched her thirst even if it contained some dirt. Following this metaphor, hooks argues that the quest for purity and unwillingness to engage with "contaminated" thought is a luxury that those on the margins, like her, could ill afford.

While feminist of color Philomena Essed does not employ the notion of decolonization herself, she politically endorses the work of people who use that umbrella to alter the curriculum, increase the number of faculty of color, and challenge the dominance of whiteness (Withaeckx & Essed, 2017). At the same time, she worries that "if everything goes under the umbrella of decolonization, what may happen is that gender and sexuality is pushed aside, and that men take over", repeating many earlier examples in which "black women start movements or take more risks than men to get the ball rolling, only to be pushed aside by men who are eager to be the spokesperson" (Withaeckx & Essed, 2017, p. 281).

In her article "Toward a decolonial feminism", María Lugones seeks to "complicate [decolonial thinker Anibal Quijano's] understanding of the capitalist global system of power, but . . . also critique his own understanding of gender as only in terms of sexual access to women" (2010, p. 745) by thinking through the coloniality of gender, the modern-colonial enforcement of the binary gender system. Lugones' analysis of the imposition of a binary gender system has productive resonance with transgender studies. As Muñoz poignantly states, referring to the fact that a notion of gender is a provisional and temporal construction fluctuating through histories, cultures, geographies and political settings, "to transgender the curriculum . . . is to decolonize gender" (in Muñoz & Garrison, 2008, p. 301).

Lugones' work is, however, not only a feminist critique of decolonial thought but also a decolonial critique of feminist thought. This comes through particularly in exposing white feminism's core conceptual framework and political reference point, i.e. the categories "Woman" and "Gender", as colonial impositions. And, while Lugones seeks to build coalitions from different marginal and fractured places, she explicitly denounces the kind of hegemonic sisterhood offered "over and over by white women in consciousness-raising groups, conferences, workshops, and women's studies program meetings [seeing] the offer as slamming the door to a coalition that would really include us" (2010, p. 755). In a similar vein, while Indígena scholar Sandy Grande acknowledges the "invaluable contributions" of feminists to critical pedagogy, she concludes from a review of several publications on feminism and pedagogy, that they remain largely "whitestream" (2003, p. 329), focused on white middle-class women's liberation rather than an emancipation of all women which is necessarily interconnected with decolonization.

Our foremothers, our points of departure

This book therefore takes as its point of departure the tensions and conflicts as well as the possibilities and synergies that the interrelated projects of constructing decolonial feminist pedagogies, gendering decolonial learning, and decolonizing feminist teaching bring. It will show that the call to decolonize universities – addressing how knowledge is produced and taught at universities and for whose benefits – is strengthened when connected to feminist and gender perspectives, and at the same time it will demonstrate that gender and feminist teaching can learn and grow by incorporating a decolonial approach.

This book thereby seeks to contribute to critical analyses of higher education concerned about its contemporary crisis marked by the dispersion of a neoliberal style of governance and the emerging antagonistic forces within them:

increased student fees, rising levels of students and institutional debt, increased performance management within and across institutions through the imposition of teaching and research metrics; a lack of transparency and accountability for managers to the students and academics who labor inside the universities; the corporatization of the university and the diminution of its potential social agenda beyond the market; historic pedagogic practices that emerged from inside the public, liberal university and which are bound up with colonial power.

(Hall & Winn, 2017, pp. 1–2)

It is precisely these foundations of the university as a modern/colonial institution that the contributions of this book unpack in their accounts as what sustains and reproduces coloniality in/by universities. In this way, this book also contributes to recent critical attempts at debating decolonization and the future of universities (Bhambra, Nisanciouglu & Gebrial, 2018; Grosfoguel, Hernandez & Rosen, 2016; Icaza & Vazquez, 2018; Santos, 2017). Nevertheless, as this book focuses on teaching gender and research practices and critically engages with feminist approaches, it makes a concrete contribution to feminist debates on universities, and higher education in general, as spaces full of potentials to transgress coloniality.

One of the outcomes of this book has thus been its constitution as a space of encounter for Chicana and Black feminism, postcolonial theory and decolonial interventions, which in many contexts "seem to run along parallel tracks [. . .] in spite of the seeming affinities" (Carrillo Rowe, 2017, p. 526). For instance, in Asha Varadharajan's chapter in this volume, "'Straight from the heart': a pedagogy for the vanquished of history", queer-feminist critical-race, postcolonial scholar Sara Ahmed's work on failed or non-performatives of anti-racism is put in conversation with Tuck and Yang's now classic essay "Decolonization is not a metaphor" (2012).

Unsurprisingly, perhaps, each of us as editors, as well as our authors, has had different entry points to thinking about the relation between colonialism and contemporaneity and intersectional oppressions. For Rosalba Icaza there is a before and after in feminist theorizing with the publication of Chandra Talpade Mohanty's (1984) "Under Western eyes: feminist scholarship and colonial discourses" and of María Lugones' "The coloniality of gender" (2008). Whereas Mohanty's work will open a whole area of criticism on feminist work in the so-called Third World and later on transnational activism, the ideas of Lugones will shake the very historical foundations of the notion of gender in feminist theorizing (Icaza & Vazquez, 2016). On the one hand, Mohanty questions the epistemic privilege of White Western Feminism and its complicity with the erasure of the struggle of other women, particularly of colonized women. On the other, María Lugones, while coinciding with Mohanty's critique, radicalized the importance of non-Western feminism. For her, the critique should not end in the acknowledgment of the struggles and conditions of oppression of women of color within the realm of feminism; in other words, it is not a matter for seeking recognition within the field of feminism. María Lugones shows how the experience of oppression and the struggle of colonized women should be a cornerstone of a radical critique of the whole edifice of Western modernity (Icaza & Vazquez, 2016). In particular, decolonial feminisms provide us with practices of liberation and healing where 'gender' is not taken for granted as an always existing category, but it is understood from its underside: coloniality (Icaza, 2018; Lugones, 2008; Mendoza, 2016).

Nonetheless, Rosalba Icaza's first encounter with feminist decolonial praxis occurred via her engagement with indigenous and Afro-descendant people's struggles for land, life and hope in Abya Yala (now the Americas) (Icaza, 2018). As she stumbled with her own modern/colonial gaze, as a highly educated woman she realized

> the horizon of possibilities that are imposed on us as female academics from the "South" and "educated" by the academia of core countries in the geopolitics of knowledge . . . Condemned to deny our origin and relationship to those "other" women, for many of us to be *desraizada* (un-rooted) became a sign of emancipation and freedom.
>
> *(Icaza, 2015, p. 5)*

From that painful and embodied unlearning, this editor has come to understand decolonial feminisms as a praxis-debate that is re-rooting her to both the everyday small actions of healing as resistance and to the affirmation of the possibilities of being teacher-researcher otherwise that exist in the encounter of indigenous, Afro-descendant, Black, Chicana, Lesbian, Mestiza, trans and anti-racist struggles across the world (Mendoza, 2016).

For Sara de Jong it was initially the work of feminists of color and postcolonial theory, particularly the feminist postcolonial work of Gayatri Chakravorty Spivak and Trinh T. Minh-ha, which offered a new language – and therefore new perspectives – to understand structural injustices. Postcolonial theories signaled the need (and hope against all odds) for developing what would be called a constructively complicit critique (Spivak, 1999, pp. 6–7; cf. de Jong, 2009). Both Spivak and Minh-ha have been outspoken in their interest in and commitment to alternative forms of teaching and learning. Filmmaker and literary theorist Trinh T. Minh-ha, who has described herself as remaining "utterly inappropriate(d)ly 'other'" (1992, p. 156) – one of the instances of her inspiring, playful use of language – when she navigates hegemonic contexts, has challenged the idea that her films should "teach" something, instead hoping to encourage a mutual engagement of "reflective and critical ability" (Minh-ha 1991, p. 109). Spivak alludes in several publications to her engagement in rural education in India, alongside her position at Columbia University. While she notes that there is no formal relation between the two sites of teaching, other than that the latter is a salaried job that sustains the former, "the initial non-relationship between Columbia and the village work . . . has been transformed to the extent that it feeds the former intellectually now" (2011, p. 118). Spivak describes her pedagogical intervention in the metropolitan site of Columbia University as one in which she seeks to "rearrange [her students'] desires noncoercively" (2004, p. 532), encouraging them to suspend their belief in their centrality and indispensability, instead "unlearn[ing their] privilege as a loss" (Spivak, 1990, p. 9). She later changed the latter notion into the imperative to "learn to learn from below" in order to move away from the potentially narcissistic impulse that the unlearning of privilege as a loss could produce (Andreotti, 2007, p. 69).

This editor encountered Spivak both through her writing and through the critical pedagogy initiative Open Spaces for Dialogue and Enquiry (OSDE), coordinated by Vanessa Andreotti at the University of Nottingham's Centre for the Study of Social and Global Justice, which translates Spivak's work into concrete pedagogical resources (Andreotti, 2007). This was one of the many moments in which the university revealed itself as a highly ambivalent place: enabling the critical interrogation of imperialist structures through the learning about and facilitating of critical pedagogy seminars, while simultaneously building replicas of its UK campus in Malaysia and China where it could charge international student fees (cf. Heinemann & do Mar Castro Varela, 2017).

For the third editor, Olivia U. Rutazibwa, growing up as a visible minority (second-generation Rwandan girl) in the 1980s and 1990s in Flanders, Belgium, explicit engagements with issues of race and racism, colonialism and feminism, came remarkably late in life. Personally, holding on to dignity and pride was expressed through a desire to "rise above it". In a "white (man's) world" context, this meant buying into the color-blind phantasy and the possibility of escaping racism by "working hard" and aiming for invisibility through integration and assimilation. Similarly with feminism, embracing it at that time felt like a defeat, rather than empowerment – buying into the myth that strong women need not invoke feminism to stand up for themselves.

Many of these reflexes were significantly shaped by the mainstream knowledge production systems (school, university, and media) at her disposal at that time: Belgium, and Flanders especially, serves its public a particularly monocultural, monochrome, and Eurocentric version of reality. As such, both in her education and, eventually, professionally as a researcher, it was only later on – well into her PhD – that she was first exposed to post-structural, post-development, and postcolonial critiques. More often than not, this happened through random self-study rather than in the sustained, supportive, or legitimizing setting of the classroom. Similarly, it was pop culture, traveling, moving abroad, and the inescapability of racist and sexist experiences in the everyday, rather than any of the (really good!) schools and universities she frequented, that exposed her to African-American thought, which brought her to include in a more sustained way issues of race and racism in her academic work. Eventually, toward the end of her PhD, she was exposed to the work of Meera Sabaratnam (e.g. 2011, 2017), and her engagement in International Relations with decoloniality. In addition to the insights into the workings of power from the other critical approaches, it is by embracing decoloniality as a research framework and political project that the necessity, inescapability, as well as the added value of feminist approaches and concerns, fully revealed themselves, and with them – not in the least because the exposure went through Black feminisms (e.g. bell hooks) – to a richer understanding of the coloniality of power through queer theories (e.g., Rahul Rao, 2014, 2018; also Audre Lorde).

This delayed encounter with the critical approaches that have informed her current research and activism is all the more significant, as from the onset as an IR student/scholar, her focus has been on ethical foreign policy; on how the Western-led international system tries to contribute to the "Other's" well-being. In her chapter in this volume, she elaborates how, in the absence of an engagement with decoloniality and feminisms, a full understanding of where we go wrong when it comes to global ethical engagement and solidarity is impossible, but also how, once we do, International Development Studies as it exists today is untenable.

Encountering (each) other: decolonizing learning across the Global North/South divide

During the work as editors on this book, we have each grown in our capacity to listen to various less familiar feminisms and de- and postcolonial theories. We consciously use "feminisms" in the plural to acknowledge different strands of thought and praxis, and acknowledge that the chapters and manifestos – some departing from a woman-centered standpoint, others explicitly from a queer perspective – never fully represent the breadth of queer, womanist, and feminist interventions. Echoing Ramamurthy and Tambe's perspective, we are attentive to "how [postcolonial and decolonial perspectives speak about each other], and how they can speak to each other" (2017, p. 503) and recognize that they are at time pitched against each other rather than examined for their potentially complementary contributions. Belonging to different geo-genealogies – including Amerindian cosmologies, African Diaspora thinking and Africana philosophy, anti-colonial thought, Chicana feminisms – and grounded in the differences and particularities of local colonial histories and lessons of anti-colonial pursuits – this book is continuing a path for understanding how colonization and coloniality play out in multiple academic and other spaces today.

It is striking how many "different political projects and understandings" are associated with decolonization (Mendoza, 2017, p. 637), some of which converge with one another, while others are "incommensurate" (Carrillo Rowe, 2017, p. 525). Decolonization has meant different things for different people across times and places. For instance, it has been a powerful concept to capture "psychological, spiritual and the physical decentering of whiteness" and the need to undo internalized racism (Leyva, this volume; Xaba, this volume; cf. hooks, 1994), as well as land-based political demands by indigenous colonized nations in the so-called global South. It has been a term that unites different struggles, but also "still alienates a lot of people" (Wekker, in Icaza, 2018, p. 256). In contemporary North America, Tuck and Yang (2012) warn about the dangers of using "decolonization" as an ambiguous metaphor signifying everything that needs to be improved in societies and schools. Across Abya Yala (Americas), interestingly, calls for the decolonization of disciplinary canons, academic perspectives, research methodologies, and pedagogies are connecting the restitution of indigenous and Afro-descendants' lands to curricular interventions in order to avoid ambiguous or metaphoric uses of the term "decolonization" (Leyva Solano, this volume, Motta, this volume).

Privatization of higher education mushroomed parallel to popular universities, indigenous universities, and social movements universities. In the context of current calls for the decolonization of the university, a plurality of localized projects of 'University' coexist in spite of dominant global designs pushing for internationally ranked universities. To account for this plurality, Santos (2016) views universities as a particular, but not exclusive, site of knowledge production involved in highly diverse complex politics. For example, in Western Europe as in Brazil, we are witnessing local calls to defend the publicly funded and inclusive university that has national and local state politics as a horizon (Fernández & Gill, this volume).

This edited volume should also be read as a response to students who mobilized worldwide to challenge the structures of the university and disciplinary canons, demanding changes in their education. In recent years various local calls for a decolonization of education, the curriculum, and the university system connected voices and struggles in cities such as Cape Town to other voices in the margins of academic institutions in both the Global South and the Global North. As the Rhodes Must Fall University of Cape Town mission statement recognizes, "experiences of oppression on . . . campus are intersectional".

Black, Chicana, 'First Nations'/indigenous/communitarian, and decolonial feminisms are central to struggles to decolonize the university and the knowledge structures that remain complicit with intersectional forms of domination (see Leyva Solano, this volume; Leyva et al., 2015; Simpson, 2011; Smith, 1999). Movements in the Global South are at the forefront of calls to radically rethink and restructure university institutions, curricula and modes of learning. Protesters at universities in South Africa mobilized around the campaigns #RhodesMustFall (RMF) and #FeesMustFall (FMF) to end institutionalized racism, and to promote the democratization of access in universities and their decolonization (Suransky, Pitstra & Toyana, 2017). In 2016, poor Black students occupied universities across Brazil demanding from the national government to say no to the implementation of austerity measures in education (Fernández & Gill, this volume). In Mauritius, the African Leadership University recently decided to make decoloniality central to their work, pledging, for instance, to include languages other than English in the curriculum and to assign students publications that are open source only (Auerbach, this volume). In the UK and the US, university students have been asking: "Why is my curriculum white? Why isn't my professor black?" In 2013, in the Netherlands, students proclaimed during protests that there was no democratization of the university without decolonization (de Jong, Icaza, Vázquez, Withaeckx, 2017; de Ploeg & de Ploeg, 2017).

Roots and praxis

To root this book in the political struggles that inspire it, and to maintain the close connection between political action and reflection in praxis, chapters in this book are interspersed with manifestos formulated by activists and activist/artists – some of whom are also students or scholars – from across the world. Each of the four parts is introduced by a manifesto, and each also ends on a manifesto. Part I – "Knowledge" – is opened by "CarteArte: below and on the left in purple", a feminist manifesto written by a collective of Mexican female hip-hop artists, Batallones Femeninos (Feminine Battalions). CarteArte constitutes an invitation to engage with women struggles to decolonize and depatriarchalize their activism for social justice in the context of rampant sexism, feminicides, and racism. This part closes with the manifesto "About the Transnational Network Other Knowledges: La Red Trasnacional Otros Saberes (RETOS) between crises and other possible worlds", written by the network RETOS, which comprises activists, artists, and academics across different locations in the Abya Yala/Americas and Europe. It delineates a decolonial politics of knowledge within and outside academia inspired by practices of Zapatista autonomy.

The following part, "Voice", opens with "The decolonization manifesto", by Wanelisa Xaba, a Black Radical activist, decolonial writer, and thinker from South Africa. She calls for the intimate unlearning of the internalized domination of whiteness and the disruption of the colonial imagination, and encourages us to recognize and be inspired by new ways of reimaging Blackness – for instance, by Black *trans, non-binary, intersex youth. Part II closes with "ATELIER IV Manifesto", which was collectively written in the context of a workshop organized by Françoise Vergès. The manifesto calls for a renewed utopian imagination and action in light of the imperial violence that has not only created dystopian condition of lives in the Global South, but also framed these as inevitable and irredeemable.

Part III, "Institutions", opens with Jess Auerbach's "What a new university in Africa is doing to decolonize social sciences", which articulates a set of commitments collectively developed at the new African Leadership University in Mauritius. These commitments present a practical translation of calls to decolonize institutions: from the explicit inclusion of non-textual sources as learning material, to students' role in co-production of alternative discourses about Africa, and the decentering of the English language. The part ends with Roselyn Masamha's "Post-it notes to my lecturers", which are similarly concrete tools to help create more inclusive classrooms. Some of the Post-it notes are reminders or warnings to prevent the reinforcement of the university as modern/colonial site, while others offer strategies and encouragement for any lecturer who is willing to unlearn their knowledge frames and expectations.

Part IV, "Disciplines", considers decolonization in relation to specific academic fields and disciplines (each with their own histories and particularities; cf. Bala, 2017) and is introduced by "Intervention", a text collectively written by sixteen participants of the "Crossing Borders" Conference in Lesbos, Greece, in July 2016. The intervention was staged to challenge the coloniality of knowledge/power/ being reproduced at academic conferences organized to address the so-called refugee crisis in Europe, elevating international experts, marginalizing migrants and refugees, and silencing locally affected people. As the reading of "Intervention" was censored by the organizing committee, its reproduction here constitutes one way of overcoming systematic silencing of critical voices within academia struggling for its decolonization. We close Part IV, and the book, with "Notes on Europe and Europeans for the discerning traveller", by Robbie Shilliam. Mimicking the genre of colonial travel guides, through poetry and irony, he lays bare Europe's contradictions and exposes its fraught knowledge projects.

These manifestos, interventions, and poetry capture the combination of anger, creativity, and commitment underpinning decolonial feminist pedagogies. As sources they remind us of the movement origins of critical pedagogy and, at the same time, they are resources for future teaching and learning outside their original contexts. The manifestos and reflection pieces, presented here alongside more conventional research chapters, allow a richer presentation of the connections between movements and struggles in and outside of the academy.

Resonances and bridges

Reading the manifestos and the chapters in this book alongside each other reveals expected and unexpected resonances, which bridge geographical distance, despite each of the chapters being rooted in their respective locations. While Sereana Naepi in her chapter "Pacific peoples, higher education and feminisms" was understandably committed to referencing Pacific feminists in her quest to work against their invisibility and erasure, reading her reflections reminded us, as editors, of struggles centered around indigenous ontologies and epistemologies as a key step towards the decolonization of research in the Americas (e.g. Escobar, 2015; Leyva, this volume; Smith, 1999; Suarez-Krabbe, 2016). Sereana Naepi tells us about the practices within higher education and feminisms that actively silence Pacific peoples in both higher education and feminisms, foreclosing the possibility of Pacific ontologies to exist within feminisms. Her observations find echoes in ongoing struggles for epistemic justice led by indigenous women's "*feminismo comunitario*" in South and Central America, which is grounded on communal ontologies, in the sense of communal selves struggling for liberations that are not individual but communal (Cabnal, 2012; Guzman & Paredes, 2014; Méndez Torres, López Intzín, Marcos & Osorio Hernández, 2013; Millan, 2014). Precisely, decolonial feminism is attentive to the complex and unintended effects that "gender" as a central category in many feminisms has in the erasure of plural experiences of being "women" often disregarded as "backward" or as "reproducing heteronormativity" (Icaza & Vazquez, 2016).

Naepi's chapter on the Pacific region also resonates with Françoise Vergès' discussion of the erasure of the Creole language and the orchestrated colonial amnesia concerning the history, geography, and culture of Reunion Island in her chapter "Decolonial feminist teaching and learning: what is the space of decolonial feminist teaching?" This alienating and disconnecting experience was only counterbalanced by the resistance of activist parents, who provided an alternative politicizing education. Vergès' contribution, in which she takes us both to Reunion Island and France, also reminds us of the relation between the colonial periphery and metropole, sustained through migration. In another chapter in this volume, Roselyn Masamha's account of her own experience as an African migrant nursing student in the UK, alongside her analysis of the educational journey of other Zimbabwean nursing students, demonstrates the continuities of colonizing education. She insists on the rights of so-called "foreign" students in Europe to challenge the Eurocentrism of the education they receive, refusing to be a silent "guest". The postcolonial link between the metropole and the periphery so well captured by Ambalavaner Sivanandan in the aphorism "We are here, because you were there" (quoted in Younge, 2018), has been given a new twist in the context of the so-called refugee crisis, reminding us of the link between conflict, Western arms transport, and military intervention. Decolonizing education within migrant-receiving countries with historical and contemporary links to the roots of displacement necessarily includes interrogating how border practices intersect with modern/colonial educational structures. For instance, the lucrative fee-paying student quickly becomes an undesirable migrant when they have finished their studies, while highly skilled asylum seekers are barred from education during the endless asylum procedure – yet they do feature as objects of research, being the subjects of academic expertise.

In "Feminizing and decolonizing higher education: pedagogies of dignity in Colombia and Australia", Sara Motta takes the differences between two sites – one a colonized nation, the other a settler nation – as the starting point for her discussion of feminist decolonial pedagogical interventions. While in both locations her approach is inspired by a pedagogy of dignity, in Colombia this means co-creating a community of trust and mutual recognition with other activist scholars, and in Australia it requires guiding students to recognize their relationality with those they deem "Other" and open their minds to alternative ways of knowing and being. However, Sara Motta also notes the increasing convergence between Colombia and Australia as the neoliberal "Enlightened" university model encroaches upon both locations. Marta Fernández and Andréa Gill also address the growing neoliberalization of learning and teaching worldwide in their chapter "Coloniality of power, knowledge and modes of (des)authorization: occupation practices in Brazilian schools and universities". They view the occupation as having offered a significant contribution towards decolonizing modern/colonial structures and argue that the experimental, affective, and responsive occupation practices introduced a new way of doing politics and producing knowledge.

All the chapters elaborate personal reflections of their authors, some of them deeply painful experience of racialization and discrimination, which are interwoven in their research and teaching praxis. Roselyn Masamha puts it poignantly in her chapter "The liability of foreignness: decolonial struggles of migrants negotiating African identity within UK nurse education": "I am constantly reminded of the additional challenges faced by migrant students and recognize in them, 'that could be me – *that was me*'." For us, this points to an emergent political positionality, a feminist decolonial one, with the potential of challenging dominant academia's body-less, emotion-less, un-rooted, abstract pedagogies. As Françoise Vergès (this volume) observes, it is only through learning through our senses that we can (re-) establish the connection between the topics discussed in class and the outside world, and that dominant modes of learning can be denaturalized.

Writing about pedagogy as an embodied practice, sharing personal experiences that are deeply political, and communicating how alternative engagements in the classroom can generate joy, pain, care, and passion, requires a different register of expression. It is no coincidence that several chapters in this book cite poems to express decolonial feminist pedagogical encounters (e.g. Leyva Solano, Motta, and Naepi). Others combine personal testimony with research findings, or vignettes with so-called "high" theory, as these mixed forms appeal to both our bodies and minds (Masamha, Varadharajan, and Vergès). Indeed, as Mohan Dutta has observed, auto-ethnography might be a form particularly suited to decolonial knowledge production, opening up the "contours of the personal, the political, and the professional", and inspiring the imagination through storytelling (2018, p. 95; cf. Adriany et al., 2017). While for some authors and readers this constitutes a liberation from the narrow frameworks of academic expression, venturing outside of circumscribed vocabulary and style can also be challenging. What to hold onto in this experiment, who to speak to, who to please?

Also, in what language to write? Language is highly political, and some languages have been conduits of the colonizing civilizing mission, with the ridicule and erasure of indigenous languages being common practice. For example, English is also a language of exclusion, as the authors of the intervention at the "Crossing Borders" conference in Lesbos pointed out, creating yet another border between migrants and 'natives'. At the same time, as bell hooks writes,

> translation into standard English may be needed if one wishes to reach a more inclusive audience. In the classroom setting, I encourage students to use their first language and translate it so they do not feel that seeking higher education will necessarily estrange them from that language and culture they know most intimately.
>
> *(1994, p. 172)*

In some chapters in this volume, we similarly use this double mode, offering some words or poems in other languages accompanied by translation. However, English remains the problematic dominant language that we succumb to because it is paradoxically simultaneously accessible and exclusive, mediating conversations across different regions while at the same time foreclosing certain exchanges. This led to ambivalent editorial decisions – perhaps, as one author suggested to us, the sound of a Spanish poem could have spoken to readers across language barriers, or maybe the encounter with an indigenous Pacific or Amerindian word should prompt the reader to broaden their horizon by looking for its meaning, rather than being presented with a fraught English mis/translation. In Chapter 16, "'Straight from the heart': a pedagogy for the vanquished of history", Asha Varadharajan addresses the dilemma of intercultural translation in powerful yet beautiful form when speaking about herself reading works in English growing up in India:

> Being lured *out* of my self was precisely the point, as was comprehending the virtues of both proximity and distance in the pleasures of reading. The struggle against stereotypical notions, for example, is futile if reading and writing are always a matter of recognition rather than of defamiliarization.

This book features different generations and positions within and in relation to research and teaching. Within its pages, experienced and well-known feminist academics and intellectuals met those in the early steps of the academic hierarchy – postgraduate researchers – whose thinking and experiences are often ignored and neglected. Moreover, we also featured everyday critical praxis of people involved in academia in contributions that focus on their alternative and innovative pedagogical practice, both inside and outside of the academy. In "Learning from prisons: decolonial feminism and teaching approaches from prison to university", Elena Vasiliou draws on her experience of teaching in a Cypriot prison to develop her thinking about decolonial pedagogies in the academy. She demonstrates not only that the disciplinary and punishing function of the prison is not that dissimilar to that of the university, but also that important lessons can be learned from the margins of the prison space.

In "Undoing colonial patriarchies: life and struggle pathways", Xochilt Leyva Solano draws on her decades of experience to decolonize and depatriarchalize knowledges and learnings in a context of war against Zapatista autonomous communities in Chiapas, Mexico, to offer us powerful experiences of her collective doings. She tells us about *Sjalel kibeltik* as a creative process of learning what is not already known as an "act of working together, in the dialogue as equals". She also shares her encounter with a *wix* (older sister) in the form of the book *This Bridge Called My Back: Writings by Radical Women of Color*, which inspired the foundation of epistemic-political communities. In sharing this, Xochilt Leyva Solano offers us the margins as a site of enunciation from where an embodied re-theorization of power as potency emerges from collective walkings and doings "in her body and her mind" and "after seeing how the Zapatistas build their autonomy step by step, as their right and without asking permission to anybody".

Situating us

As editors of this book, we have reflected on our own positionalities and the role they played in the conception and implementation of this project. We are all based in European universities and teach or have taught in departments or faculties of international development studies. As highly educated women, but also as teachers and researchers of international development and politics, we have learned to be critical of the contentious and even violence of education as "a will to improve" the "other" (Li, 2017) common in the modern/colonial development civilizational enterprises (de Jong, 2017; Motta, this volume; Rutazibwa, this volume). Leyva Solano's contribution (this volume) helps us name what could be our role as feminist and decolonial teachers. She narrates one scene of the movie *Chocó*, directed by Afro-Colombian filmmaker Jhonny Hendrix Hinestroza, where, according to her, the viewers are "surprised by the way that Chocó [the protagonist] is beaten and the rest of the town is left unmoved, seeing her but without supporting her. *It is the complicit silence that hurts more than the blows*" (Leyva Solano, this volume; our italics). As teachers, we see this project as a contribution in the direction to break complicit silences that sustain and reproduce epistemic racism and violence in academia, and, as Rutazibwa indicates (this volume), can take the form of "over-representation, hyper-visibilizing . . . , neglect or literal silencing . . . oversimplification . . . vilification, criminalization . . . or victimization".

The disciplining function of disciplines has long been exposed. Moreover, disciplines from international development, anthropology to English literature bear the historical and contemporary traces of colonialism. Some of the contributors to this volume reflect on the disciplining effects of their own colonial education, including their learned investment in speaking "proper English" and their interpellation in colonial canonical traditions (Masamha, this volume; Vergès, this volume). For each of us, to engage in decolonial teaching again inevitably requires a (re- and un-) learning of the ways we have been taught and the disciplines we have been trained in. Or, as Elena Vasiliou put it in this book, we might need to recognize "the necessity to exercise a disobedience against [our] discipline[s]", while Xochitl Leyva Solano already offers us a "collective process of creation [that] allowed us to continue cracking the walls of the disciplinary prisons where we felt imprisoned".

In her chapter "On babies and bathwater: decolonizing International Development Studies", Olivia Rutazibwa practices this disobedience in her provocation about her own discipline, International Development Studies, with its long colonial heritage. She argues for a radical rethink that goes beyond deconstructing International Development Studies, advocating instead for the necessity of throwing out some of the bathwater that is irredeemably polluted. Her provocation resonates with Leyva Solano and Motta's contributions in this volume on concrete experiences of epistemic (and political) disobedience within and outside classrooms as a de-linking from "the magic of the Western idea of modernity, ideals of humanity and promises of economic growth and financial prosperity" (Mignolo, 2009, p. 3).

In preparing this book, and this introduction in particular, we have all shared with enthusiasm our teaching experiences and our passion and dedication to teaching and students. We are critically aware of the dominant trends in corporate academia pushing us to build up hierarchies between teaching and research, and to separate and compartmentalize what we do/are: teachers-educators-researchers-activists within learning communities. At the moment of writing, one of us is participating in the trade union struggles against pension reforms in British universities. She is also receiving phone calls from a young woman from a Commonwealth country facing deportation, whose UK education was disrupted when she was taken into detention. Meanwhile, one of us currently participates in networks and collectives resisting the backlash against anti-racist feminism in the context of the right wing and neo-fascism within universities and larger societies, both in Europe and Latin America and the Caribbean. Hence in our lives this compartmentalization and separation is both undesirable and untenable as we are intimately connected and confronted with the violent structures of academia and beyond.

The structures of the neoliberal academy have increased the risks that the decolonial feminist teacher and students need to take. The focus on peer-reviewed publications as a measure of success has come at the detriment of the validation of contributions to students' learning and engagement with society at large (Withaeckx & Essed, 2017). Also, as some of the contributions to this book show, critical pedagogical spaces are not always comfortable and can be challenging for the students (see also hooks, 1994). If these same students are considered valuable consumers of education in the context of high-fee regimes, pedagogical approaches that might produce uneven teaching evaluations could be penalized. To interweave teaching and research, to us means transgressing dominant parameters in contemporary academia, but it is also an affirmation of the possibilities of decolonizing teaching and research grounded on an ethics of care and relationality. Despite the pertinent critiques articulated by the contributions to this edited volume, hope and commitment runs as a common thread through the chapters (cf. Heinemann & do Mar Castro Varela, 2017; Wekker, in Icaza, 2018). The encounter of feminism and decolonial thinking with (critical) pedagogy seems to us full of (liberatory) possibilities for our feminist struggles within and outside university classrooms.

Our perspective on the transformations of teaching and learning in universities and of universities as modern/colonial institutions has tried to shed light on the struggles of many others that preceded us, and that contribute to our contemporary decolonizing thinking and doings. Sadly, emerging linear readings of decolonial feminism as a "fashion" that has rendered passé postcolonial critique, as indicated by Ramamurty and Tambe (2017) and by Leyva in this volume, forecloses the possibility of understanding the temporal relationality (Vazquez, 2017, p. 88) connecting both of these rich geo-genealogies of anti-racist and anti-colonial pursuits. The new fashionability of decolonial approaches also carries the risk that it is embraced as an image booster or a quick-fix solution to upgrade universities and other institutions. This precludes engagement with the rich and long history of decolonial thought as well as with the radicality of its demands. We hope this book is a (modest) opening to the possibilities of listening to our feminist foremothers, who grounded our feminist endeavors as teachers in today's contemporary academia, to reconfigure our experiences of gender and teaching.

Note

1 This chapter is the result of a collaborative writing process to which both authors contributed equally.

References

Adriany, V., Pirmasari, D. A. & Satiti, N. L. U. (2017). Being an Indonesian feminist in the north: an autoethnography. *Tijdschrift voor Genderstudies, 20*(3), 287–297.

Andreotti, V. (2007). An ethical engagement with the other: Spivak's ideas on education. *Critical Literacy: Theories and Practices, 1*(1), 69–79.

Arashiro, Z. & Barahona, M. (2015). (Eds.) *Women in Academia Crossing North–South Borders: Gender, Race, and Displacement.* Lanham, MD: Rowman and Littlefield/Lexington Books.

Autar, L. (2017). Decolonising the classroom: credibility-based strategies for inclusive classrooms. *Tijdschrift voor Genderstudies, 20*(3), 305–320.

Bala, S. (2017). Decolonising theatre and performance studies. *Tijdschrift voor Genderstudies, 20*(3): 333–345.

Bhambra, G. K. (2014). Postcolonial and ecolonial dialogues. *Postcolonial Studies, 17*(2), 115–121.

Bhambra, G. K., Nisanciouglu, K. & Gebrial, D. (Eds.). (2018). *Decolonizing the University.* London: Pluto Press.

Cabnal, L. (2012). Acercamiento a la construcción del pensamiento epistémico de las mujeres indígenas feministas comunitarias de Abya Yala. In L. Cabnal & ACSUR-Segovia (Eds.), *Feminismos Diversos. El Feminismo Comunitario* (pp. 11–25), retrieved from https://poruna vidavivible.files.wordpress.com/2012/09/feminismos-comunitario-lorena-cabnal.pdf

Carrillo Rowe, A. (2017). Settler Xicana: postcolonial and decolonial reflections on incommensurability. *Feminist Studies, 43*(3), 525–536.

Castro-Gómez, S. (2007). Descolonizar la universidad: la hybris del punto cero y el diálogo de saberes. In S. Castro-Gómez & R. Grosfoguel (Eds.), *El giro decolonial* (pp. 79–91). Bogotá, Colombia: Siglo del Hombre Editores.

de Jong, S. (2017). *Complicit Sisters: Gender and Women's Issues Across North–South Divides.* Oxford: Oxford University Press.

de Jong, S. (2009). Constructive complicity enacted? The reflections of women NGO and IGO workers on their practices. *Journal for Intercultural Studies, 30*(4), 387–402.

de Jong, S., Icaza, R., Vázquez, R. & Withaeckx, S. (2017). Editorial: decolonising the university. *Tijdschrift voor Genderstudies, 20*(3): 227–231.

De Ploeg, M. & De Ploeg, C. (2017). No democratisation without decolonisation. *Tijdschrift voor Genderstudies, 20*(3), 321–332.

Dutta, M. J. (2018). Autoethnography as decolonization, decolonizing autoethnography: resisting to build our homes. *Cultural Studies ↔ Critical Methodologies, 18*(1), 94–96.

Escobar, A. (2015). Thinking-feeling with the earth: territorial struggles and the ontological dimension of the epistemologies of the south. *Revista de Antropologia Iberoamericana, 11*(1), 11–31.

Grande, S. (2003) Whitestream feminism and the colonialist project: a review of contemporary feminist pedagogy and praxis. *Educational Theory, 53*(3), 329–346.

Grosfoguel, R., Hernandez, R. & Rosen, E. (2016) (Eds.). *Decolonizing the Westernized University Interventions in Philosophy of Education from Within and Without.* Lexington, MD: Rowman and Littlefield.

Guzman, A. & Paredes, J. (2014). *Que es el Feminismo Comunitario?* La Paz, Bolivia: Mujeres Creando Comunidad, retrieved from www.academia.edu/24294734/

Julieta_Paredes_Adriana_Guzman_-_El_tejido_de_la_Rebeldia._Qu%C3%A9_es_el_feminismo_comunitario

Hall, R. & Winn, J. (2017). *Mass Intellectuality and Democratic Leadership in Higher Education.* London: Bloomsbury.

Harcourt, W., Icaza, R. & Varas, V. (2016). Exploring embodiment and intersectionality transnational feminist activist research. In K. Biekart, W. Harcourt & P. Knorringa (Eds.), *Exploring Civic Innovation for Social and Economic Transformation* (pp. 148–167). London: Routledge.

Heinemann, A. & do Mar Castro Varela, M. (2017). Contesting the imperial agenda: respelling hopelessness: some thoughts on the dereliction of the university. *Tijdschrift voor Genderstudies, 20*(3), 259–274.

hooks, b. (1994). *Teaching to Transgress: Education as the Practice of Freedom.* New York: Routledge.

Icaza, R. (2015). Testimony of a pilgrimage: (un)learning and re-learning with the south. In Z. Arashiro & M. Barahona (Eds.), *Women in Academia Crossing North–South Borders: Gender, Race and Displacement* (pp. 1–27). Lanham, MD: Rowman and Littlefield/ Lexington Books.

Icaza, R. (2017). "I am still hopeful": an interview with Gloria Wekker on diversity, anti-racism, and decolonising the academy. *Tijdschrift voor Genderstudies, 20*(3), 249–258.

Icaza, R. (2018). Social struggles and the coloniality of gender. In Robbie Shilliam & Olivia Rutazibwa (eds.), *Routledge Handbook on Postcolonial Politics* (pp. 58–71). London: Routledge.

Icaza, R. & Vazquez, R. (2016). The coloniality of gender as a radical critique of developmentalism. In W. Harcourt (Ed.), *The Palgrave Handbook on Gender and Development: Critical Engagements in Feminist Theory and Practice* (pp. 62–76). London: Palgrave Macmillan.

Icaza, R. & Vazquez, R. (2018). Diversity or decolonization? Researching diversity at the University of Amsterdam. In G. K. Bhambra, K. Nisanciouglu & D. Gebrial (Eds.), *Decolonizing the University* (pp. 108–128). London: Pluto Press.

Lander, E. (Ed.) (1993). *La colonialidad del saber: eurocentrismo y ciencias sociales. Perspectivas latinoamericanas.* Buenos Aires, Argentina: CLACSO.

Leyva Solano, X. et. al. (2015). *Practicas otras de conocimiento(s).* San Cristobal de las Casas, Chiapas, Mexico: Cooperativa Editorial Retos.

Li, T. (2017). *The Will to Improve. Governmentality, Development, and the Practice of Politics.* Durham, NC: Duke University Press.

Lugones, M. (2008). The coloniality of gender. *Worlds & Knowledges Otherwise, 2* (Spring), 1–17.

Lugones, M. (2010). Toward a decolonial feminism. *Hypathia, 4*, 742–759.

Méndez Torres, G., López Intzín, J., Marcos, S. & Osorio Hernández, C. (2013). *Sentipensar el Genero. Perspectivas desde los pueblos originarios.* Guadalajara, Jalisco, Mexico: Red Interdisciplinaria de los Pueblos Indios de Mexico/Red de Feminismos Descoloniales/ La Casa del Mago, retrieved from https://sylviamarcos.files.wordpress.com/2015/12/ senti-pensar-el-genero-2.pdf

Mendoza, B. (2016). Coloniality of gender and power: from postcoloniality to decoloniality. In L. Disch & M. Hawkesworth (Eds.), *The Oxford Handbook of Feminist Theory* (pp. 100–121). Oxford: Oxford University Press.

Mendoza, B. (2017). Colonial connections. *Feminist Studies, 43*(3), 637–645.

Mignolo, W. (2009). Epistemic disobedience, independent thought and de-colonial freedom. *Theory, Culture & Society, 26*(7–8), 1–23.

Mignolo, W. (2010). Delinking: the rhetoric of modernity, the logic of coloniality and the grammar of decoloniality. In W. Mignolo & A. Escobar (Eds.), *Globalization and the Decolonial Option* (pp. 303–368). London: Routledge.

Millan, M. (2014). (Ed.) *Mas alla del Feminismo. Caminos para andar.* Mexico City: Red de Feminismos Descoloniales, retrieved from www.rosalvaaidahernandez.com/wp-content/uploads/2016/08/mas-alla-del-feminismo.pdf

Minh-ha, T. T. (1991). *When the Moon Waxes Red: Representation, Gender and Cultural Politics.* New York: Routledge.

Minh-ha, T. T. (1992). *Framer Framed.* New York: Routledge.

Mohanty, C. (1984). Under Western eyes: feminist scholarship and colonial discourses. *Boundary 2*(12–13), 333–358.

Motta, S. (2017). Mass intellectuality from the margins. In J. Winn & R. Hall (Eds.), *Mass Intellectuality and Democratic Leadership in Higher Education* (pp. 185–195). London: Bloomsbury.

Muñoz, V. & Garrison, E. K. (2008). Transpedagogies: a roundtable dialogue. *Women's Studies Quarterly, 36*(3–4), 288–308.

Parker, P. S., Smith S. H. & Dennison, J. (2017). Decolonising the classroom: creating and sustaining revolutionary spaces inside the academy. *Tijdschrift voor Genderstudies, 20*(3), 233–247.

Ramamurthy, P. & Tambe, A. (2017). Preface: decolonial and postcolonial approaches: a dialogue. *Feminist Studies, 43*(3), 503–511.

Rao, R. (2014). Queer questions. *International Feminist Journal of Politics, 16*(2), 199–217.

Rao, R. (2018). The state of "queer IR". *GLQ: A Journal of Lesbian and Gay Studies, 24*(1), 139–149.

Sabaratnam, M. (2011). IR in dialogue . . . but can we change the subjects? A typology of decolonising strategies for the study of world politics. *Millennium, 39*(3), 781–803.

Sabaratnam, M. (2017). *Decolonising Intervention: International Statebuilding in Mozambique.* London: Rowman & Littlefield International.

Santos, B. d. S. (2016). The university at a crossroads. In R. Grosfoguel, R. Hernandez & E. Rosen (Eds.), *Decolonizing the Westernized University Interventions in Philosophy of Education from Within and Without* (pp. 3–14). Lexington, MD: Rowman and Littlefield.

Santos, B. d. S. (2017). *Decolonizing the University. The Challenge of Deep Cognitive Justice.* Newcastle upon Tyne, UK: Cambridge Scholars Publishing.

Simpson, L. B. (2011). *Dancing on our Turtle's Back: Stories of Nishnaabeg Re-creation, Resurgence, and a New Emergence.* Winnipeg, Manitoba: ARP Books.

Smith, L. T. (1999). *Decolonizing Methodologies. Research and Indigenous People.* London: Zed Books.

Spivak, G. C. (1990). *The Postcolonial Critic: Interviews, Strategies, Dialogues* (S. Harasym, Ed.). London: Routledge.

Spivak, G. C. (1999). *A Critique of Postcolonial Reason: Toward a History of the Vanishing Present.* Cambridge, MA: Harvard University Press.

Spivak, G. C. (2011). The engaged feminist intellectual. In M. Kress & K. Ryan (Eds.), *I Am Not a Good Enough Feminist* (pp. 117–126). New York: Concrete Utopia.

Spivak, G. C. (2004). Righting wrongs. *South Atlantic Quarterly, 103*(2–3), 523–581.

Suarez-Krabbe, J. (2016). *Race, Rights and Rebels. Alternatives to Human Rights and Development from the Global South.* London: Rowman and Littlefield.

Suransky, C., Pitstra, S. & Toyana, L. (2017). Decolonising universities: learning in tension. *Tijdschrift voor Genderstudies, 20*(3), 299–304.

Tlostanova, M. & Mignolo, W. (2012). *Learning to Unlearn: Decolonial Reflections from Eurasia and the Americas.* Columbus, OH: Ohio State University Press.

Trinidad Galván, R. (2016). Collective memory of the female brown body: a decolonial feminist public pedagogy engagement with the feminicides. *Pedagogy, Culture and Society*, *24*(3), 343–357.

Tuck, E. & Yang, K. W. (2012). Decolonization is not a Metaphor. *Decolonization: Indigeneity, Education & Society*, *1*(1), 1–40.

Vazquez, R. (2015). Decolonial practices of learning. In J. Friedman, V. Haverkate, B. Oomen, E. Park & M. Sklad (Eds.), *Going Glocal in Higher Education: The Theory, Teaching and Measurement of Global Citizenship* (pp. 92–100). Middelburg, The Netherlands: University College Roosevelt.

Vazquez, R. (2017). Precedence, earth and the anthropocene: decolonizing design. *Design Philosophy Papers*, *15*, 77–91.

Walsh, C. (Ed.). (2013). *Pedagogias Decoloniales: Practicas insurgentes de resistir, (re)existir and (re)vivir.* Quito, Ecuador: Editorial Abya Yala.

Walsh, C. (2015). Decolonial pedagogies walking and asking: notes on Paulo Freire from Abya Yala. *International Journal of Lifelong Education*, *34*(1), 9–21.

Withaeckx, S. & Essed, P. (2017). Two steps forwards, one step back: a conversation with Philomena Essed on difference and decolonisation in the academy and beyond. *Tijdschrift voor Genderstudies*, *20*(3), 275–285.

Younge, G. (2018). Ambalavaner Sivanandan obituary. *Guardian*, February 7, 2018, retrieved from www.theguardian.com/world/2018/feb/07/ambalavaner-sivanandan

PART I
Knowledge

1

CARTEARTE[1]

Below and on the left in purple[2]

Batallones Femeninos[3]

Commander Sisters of the Zapatista Army of National Liberation

Insurgent Sisters of the Zapatista Army of National Liberation

Militant Sisters in the Zapatista communities

Support–grassroots sisters of the Zapatista Army of National Liberation

Sisters of 'the Sixth'[4]

Feminist Sisters from below and on the left

Sisters of indigenous peoples

Sisters in the basements of the world, where we all of us live and be.

Many are the sufferings, many the rages we share, and which are the base of our struggles with our male comrades in our communities, collectives and other organizations. We all fight against the repression, exploitation, contempt and dispossession from those above. To these struggles, we want to add our own struggle against violence from governments, media and political parties enacting violence from above and attacking us because we are women. Because we as poor women do not fulfill their standards of success, education, beauty (weight, seize, height, skin color, features, age). Because we do not live a heterosexual family life that serves the system. Because we are in their way to produce more capital.

We welcome, honor and respect all those struggles below and on the left aiming to destruct the conditions that make possible the war against those who live in the basements of the world and the indigenous people. We are constructing spaces with no room for such war and for weapons fulfilling their task.

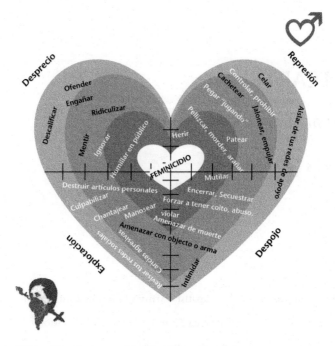

FIGURE 1.1 'Vivas Nos Queremos' by Batallones Femeninos

Today, however, as an act of female rebellion, I return the gaze to us, the recipients of this letter, which I claim is an art for the sake of life and that I call 'CarteArte.' By doing so, many faces come to my mind, with and without balaclavas, with and without scarves covering parts of them, with and without make-up. Serious faces, faces in pain, in tears, with anger, with smiles. I hear memories of female voices in every tone and volume. I recall naked, covered, tattooed, pierced, painted bodies; light, dark, burned, pale, healthy, damaged, wounded skins; children, girls, adults, elder women of all sizes and heights. I see us shouting and talking, crying and laughing, working and organizing and always doing.

This act of addressing many of us reminds me of a conviction that there shall be no protagonist, no usurpers. With this conviction in mind, and with the fear – or because of the fear – to be misinterpreted and sanctioned, I transform my action into an artistic practice of writing, to dare to collectively speak to many of us who are called in to explain how they resisted and experienced the third and fourth workday of struggle – struggles inside the first struggle mentioned above. Inner struggles, which occupy our time and energies, and are absolutely necessary to us.

To clarify: in my view, the third struggle inside the other struggles is the resistance we build to face each and every attempt by men in our collectives, groups and communities to dominate us through leadership, defeating us, to supplant us and impose themselves upon us. It is the struggle against them being the only protagonists, silencing our voices and proposals. It is the struggle against their assumption that our resistance has to be shaped in the same ways as our households – just another place where they suppress us – and our jobs, where they exploit our workforce, that is to say, to serve them.

We fight against the smug looks and condescending attitudes when talking about our feelings, when expressing ideas that have been constructed-deconstructed-reconstructed based on different criteria than the one imposed on us by a system that prioritizes what men assume as their own, just because they have been programmed for that. Thought and speech are but a few elements of what is supposed to be human, which men – even those from below and on the left – have claimed as their own.

We fight against each and every harassment, such as unwanted touching, sexual attack, misogynist expression and violation and threat, that our comrades perform in all spaces, assuming that they are entitled to do so, or that we are flattered by it, or both things at once, or else. We fight to unmask the outrageous violations carried out by comrades from below and on the left, which is a space where we recognize anger, but also suffer harassment and abuse. Friendly fire? Collateral damage?

We have to fight against what I call first domination, prior to that of humans over nature or of men over other men (slavery). Primary domination is the one sustaining the current system, committed and also sustained by male over female individuals. It was created when sexual intercourse was symbolized and signified as an act of domination, and then it became naturalized. What is natural is the mating between male and female animals to reproduce something that is alive. All the rest – romantic love, heterosexuality as a way to give men a permanent and unrestricted access to our bodies – is not natural, but a social construction like the idea of complementarity between men and women based on the subordination of the latter by the former.

Male and female genitals perform the same role and functioning during the reproductive intercourse, but to force on us the coitus in the name of 'romantic love' and to have children in the name of 'family' is not natural: it is a social construction which ends up negatively affecting our lives. Men's sexual arousal is not irrepressible, nor is their lascivious gaze natural; these are all social constructs.

Sisters, how do we fight against all this? I raise the voice in my collective and get the microphone when I think it's the right moment to talk. I express my opinions, I make proposals, I discuss (without male comrades hearing me, of course). Above all, I look for my sister comrades. I insist to restart all over again together with them and all the other women who, like me, are committed to all struggles – not just the primary one. I try to create alternative spaces and times that make no room for the war waged by our comrades to dominate us.

How does media from below report our struggles, our complaints? Do they name us? When it comes to women, do they have a different approach or do they just do the same as all media? How can men below and on the left join our struggles? I understand that the fight against capitalism involves everyone, men and women from below, because we all suffer from it – but we suffer more than they do. Therefore, I wonder: what are the struggles of the men below and on the left? Are these the same as those of the people above who are committed to maintain their privilege?

How do we share the experience of resistance of our third form of struggle with everyone taking place in other and much needed struggles? As much as capitalism encompasses, conditions, bounds and subjugates all men and women living in the basements of the world, so does the relation of domination of men over women – even spaces of resistance and struggle are shaped by it. In capitalism we as women experience a double or triple workload, with or without salary, in order to maintain the system. We also experience triple and quadruple workload to sustain and not undermine other struggles. But, up to what point? Up to what degree of contempt? Up to what extent of repression, dispossession, and exploitation? These are all manifestations of the war of men from above and below to dominate women from below.

I confess that, from my basement, I find myself comparing more and more often men with the government and the system. Just like the Zapatistas have pointed out that those above do not see and do not listen to those who are below, I think-feel the same: that men down below and on the left behave with us in the same way as those above. They tolerate us from time to time because we are useful, even necessary to them, like are those below to those who are above, they need us. Yet our sufferings do not affect them; they do not recognize their domination over us women is socially constructed nor that it has to be destroyed. It seems as if they wouldn't want to lose any of their privileges.

To clarify: I am writing about what I experience, see, think, and feel. I would like to know how you, sisters, endure this struggle inside the struggle. I cannot avoid to say that this struggle has been acknowledged within the Zapatista communities. I know this because in their statements they have been mentioning this to us for years; because they are committed to build up a world where girls are born and raised without fears; because of the work carried out by the Zapatistas in the Freedom Schools;[5] because of what has been developed in the permanent seedbeds[6] because of the Zapatista Revolutionary Law of Women.[7] The male comrades have discovered our struggle, and one of them recognizes his machismo and reluctance to get rid of it. He recognizes the war against women when men dominate us. But this is a side note, and now I would like to go back to my thoughts on the fourth form of struggle – yes, there's a fourth and it is an unpaid struggle within the other struggles, one that we often fight on our own against the whole system.

I am talking about recognizing inside myself the social construction I was taught, which made me feel incomplete without a man by my side and respected only when given my husband's surname. This construction had made me believe that my sexuality was only possible together with a man who would love me and for whom I could always be available; that my voice and words were worth less than those of other men, and much less than those of cultivated men, and even much less than those of cultivated European men. It taught me that I had to get rid of my instinct, mistrust it, and always seek guidance/advise/confirmation from a man: brother, father, priest, teacher, comrade, and friend. I learned I had to like men and even be thankful of their gazed on me – even when their gaze would awaken my faltering and suppressed instinct. I assumed then that other women were potential enemies, yes, fighting for male attention. I accepted uncritically that things can change and 'improve' without undermining the basic assumptions. That is, without putting into question the relation of domination which gives shape to the struggle we live in this war: the relation of domination of men over women. This domination includes: the appropriation of our bodies for their sexual gratification and of our capacity to think, make proposals and organize for the sake of their privilege; the exploitation of our unpaid domestic labor and fighting force that maintain the system; the repression of our emotions, claims, needs and pains; repression in the form of physical, verbal and psychological abuse. They discriminate against us when they do not question, but even demand their privileges, and as each of their privileges is maintained, our qualities are belittled and while more responsibilities are imposed on us.

I learned that my body ought to be fragile and even my muscles, which could protect me, are to be given up. Now I am in the process to unlearn this, step by step. I am unlearning that I do not depend on the gaze or validation of any man: if I need a gaze, it's only that of women. Always.

I was taught, and I erroneously learned as an adult, that the comrades below and on the left were able to feel our sufferings and understand the violence committed against us just for being women. I absurdly believed that all women, including those from above or aspiring to that position, would be able understand our sufferings from down below.

I am learning that the 'us' we have in common is a political and ethical construction based not so much on our sex or gender role, as on our social class.

I have believed and experienced and suffered all this, which for me represents the fourth form of our struggle, inside the struggle. It requires time, effort, pain, questioning of all my social constructs, thinking and acting differently, unlearning and continuously learning anew and coming up with new principles to avoid any form of domination, including the first fundamental domination.

The fourth form of struggle compels me not to be frightened by men or to doubt my thoughts of my way of being that has been constructed in submission. At the same time, I try not to reproduce what men have constructed and legitimized as the 'right' way of being. I look at myself, destroy myself and protect myself from the permanent attempts to dominate and reconstruct myself, starting from ways that do not yet exist. I find my own way, to learn from my sisters, my mother, my comrades, my daughter.

Sisters, if you want, you can come to know how to steal some time from so many other struggles. Let's share between each other the ways we face this fourth form of struggle. I am asking for your experiences to learn from each other at how to build 'us'.

How can we live down below and on the left in purple? How can we build up other worlds without the domination of men over women? How can we bring together these struggles into a direction that constructs other territories where our struggles don't exist insofar as the warring parties themselves stop to exist?

I devoted much thought to the seven ethical-political principles[8] of the Zapatista autonomies as a way to conduct my life and relations. I proposed to use them as a guide to make decisions about our sexual and affective practices, and more recently to fight against the violence committed against us. I enclose the poster with this proposal, and hopefully this CarteArte will be looked at and find its way through feelings and thoughts (*sentipensares*), and will eventually fly back and be transformed by each one of this 'us' that makes a 'we'.

If there is enough time to exchange correspondence, I suggest to make the answers/proposals/stakes among us neither 'private' nor 'public', but collective with multiple recipients, with many of us writing and reading. I speak to us because that's the site where we can start building worlds wherein life can flourish without fear, where our vulnerability and persistence is acknowledged. In my view, we still need the purple of feminism, intertwined with what's below and on the left – feminisms that seek the roots of domination and unmask them, recognize them and fight against them; feminisms that walk side by side with what's down and on the left, coloring the walk itself with purple.

In this CarteArte, which I take responsibility for, I read the voices of many of us whom I have been reading, or talking and living with or whose videos I have seen. To all of us: thank you. From a small and marginal corner in the basements of the world; without the possibility to share this CarteArte in the Zapatista Arts Festival "COMPARTE" on July 30, 2016.[9]

Below on the left in purple!

A sister of the Rebellious Law for Ourselves in Abya Yala.[10]

WE WANT US ALIVE

NEVER AGAIN, A WORLD WITHOUT US

LONG LIVE TO THE ZAPATISTA REVOLUTION

LONG LIVE TO FEMINISM, down below and on the left

WE WANT THEM ALIVE! 43 Ayotzinapa Students[11] are missing together with thousands more worthy women and men

BUILD UP A WORLD IN WHICH MANY WORLDS FIT

This text was originally written in Spanish as "CarteArte: Abajo y a la Izquierda en Morado" by the women's collective Batallones Femeninos/Feminine Battalions, to be presented at the Zapatista Arts Festival "COMPARTE" on July 30, 2016. The text can be found here: www.facebook.com/Ley-Rebelde-de-NosotrAs-en-Abya-Yala-Ixach%C3%ADtlan-660855124056529/

Notes

1 This manifesto is the collaborative product of conversations among women in Mexico that seeks to delineate feminist political and epistemic principles for liberation. Participants are supporters of 'la Sexta', which is the short name in Spanish for 'Sixth Declaration of the Lacandona Jungle' of the Ejercito Zapatistas de Liberacion Nacional (EZLN)/Zapatista National Liberation Army. The Sixth Declaration can be accessed here: http://enlacezapatista.ezln.org.mx/sdsl-en/. Last access February 27, 2018. The more recent collective discussion of CarteArte can be followed at www.facebook.com/ Ley-Rebelde-de-NosotrAs-en-Abya-Yala-Ixach%C3%ADtlan-660855124056529/. Last access February 27, 2018.

2 CarteArte has two meanings in Spanish: the act of sending letters that implies a dialogue and the activity of writing letters as an art. Meanwhile, *abajo y a la izquierda* (at the bottom and to the left) is the Zapatistas' way of referring to a position that is critical towards institutionalization and elitisms of 'official' leftist organizations and political parties in Mexico. Finally, purple has been the color associated to feminism in Latin America.

3 Batallones Femeninos' Facebook page describes them as: "a project of Hip Hop and Artivism by women in movement in Mexico. [They] work with rap, design, urban art, free media, and education, as writers, singers and fighters of life. [They] give testimony of the situation of women in Ciudad Juarez and Mexico, our lyric and visual work denounces the sociocultural conditions that, in our view, encourage gender violence. Batallones Femeninos seek to empowerment of women in their emotional, economic and work relationships. Vivas nos Queremos! Alive we want each other! Source: www.facebook. com/pg/BatallonesFem/about/?ref=page_internal. Last access February 27, 2018.

4 See note 1.

5 *Escuelita de la Libertad segun los Zapatistas* (Freedom Little School According to the Zapatistas) was organized in August 2013 by the Zapatistas. 1,500 attended it and two subsequent schools were organized in December 2013 and January 2014. A good source of information on the schools is the website of the organization "Schools for Chiapas" which can be accessed here: www.schoolsforchiapas.org/advances/schools/la-escuelita/. Last access February 27, 2018.

6 The seedbeds in English are what the Zapatistas call 'seminarios', in the sense of making a seedbed of ideas, of analysis and of critical thinking about how the capitalist system currently works. An excellent resource to understand the role of seedbeds is the Enlaze Zapatista website and the text "The storm, the sentinel and the night watch syndrome", available at: http://enlacezapatista.ezln.org.mx/2015/04/04/the-storm-the-sentinel-and-night-watch-syndrome/. Last access February 27, 2018.

7 The Zapatista Women's Revolutionary Laws were made public in the first week of January 1994, shortly after the armed uprising. The full law can be accessed here: www.schoolsforchiapas.org/library/zapatista-womens-revolutionary-laws-2/. Last access February 27, 2018.

8 The Zapatistas' principles are: 1. Obedecer y no mandar (To obey and not to command); 2. Representar y no suplantar (To represent and not to supplant); 3. Servir y no servirse (To serve, not to serve yourself); 4. Convencer y no vencer (To convince and not to win); 5. Bajar y no subir (To go down and not to go up), 6. Proponer y no imponer (To propose and not to impose), 7. Construir y no destruir (To construct and not to destroy).

9 CompArte por la Humanidad Festival/CompARTE for Humanity FESTIVAL was organized by the Zapatistas on July 17–30, 2016 for "all those who practice ART . . . For

Zapatismo, an artist is anyone who considers their activity as art, independent of canons, art critics, museums, wikipedias, and any other 'specialist' schemas that classify (that is, exclude) human activities". Source: http://radiozapatista.org/?p=16252&lang=en. Last access February 27, 2018. A digital archive of the festival can be accessed at: http://comparte. digital/. Last access February 27, 2018.

10 The full text of "Ley Rebelde de NosotrAs en el Abya Yala" can be accessed here: www.facebook.com/Ley-Rebelde-de-NosotrAs-en-Abya-Yala-Ixach%C3%ADt lan-660855124056529/ Last access February 27, 2018.

11 On September 26, 2014, the town of Ayotzinapa in the State of Guerrero, Mexico made it to world news. Headlines when 42 male students at the Raúl Isidro Burgos Rural School, some of them minors and indigenous, were kidnapped by local police, according to the Interdisciplinary Group of Independent Experts (GIEI) of the Inter-American Commission of Human Rights, handed to members of the drug cartel "Guerreros Unidos". More information can be accessed here: www.oas.org/en/iachr/activities/giei. asp. Last access February 27, 2018.

2

PACIFIC PEOPLES, HIGHER EDUCATION AND FEMINISMS

Sereana Naepi

Introduction

Despite Pacific peoples living across a space that covers 15 percent of the entire world, our voices have been marginalized in both higher education and feminisms (U.S. Pacific Command, 2017). It is because of this history within both higher education and feminisms that teaching Pacific feminisms can be seen as a decolonizing act for both the higher education classroom and feminist theory. To understand this potential, it is important to take some time to reflect on Pacific peoples and their relationships with feminisms. In order to give some context as to why Pacific voices can be understood as silent in both higher education and feminisms, this chapter will first discuss Indigenous critiques of higher education and Indigenous feminist critiques of higher education. From there, it offers a look into the tensions between Pacific peoples and feminisms moving into where Pacific feminisms are today. Once this basic understanding has been established, the chapter will open up a discussion on the potential of Pacific feminisms to disrupt higher education norms through teaching.

Given the size of the Pacific and its immense diversity, it is important to locate myself and the space from which I write. I write from a Fijian perspective and, beyond that, a Fijian perspective that was filtered through my upbringing in Aotearoa, New Zealand. Within Aotearoa, when we speak of the Pacific, we differentiate between the Pacific region (the Pacific outside of Aotearoa, New Zealand) and Pasifika (people with Pacific ancestry who live in Aotearoa, New Zealand). I write from a Pasifika perspective, as I am a first-generation New Zealand-born Pacific person. Pacific peoples have had four waves of migration, beginning some 1,200 years ago. The first wave was that of settlement. Eastern Pacific people explored and settled in Aotearoa and became *tangata whenua* (people of the land/Māori). Then, 150 years ago, during

European colonization of the Pacific, Pacific peoples arrived in Aotearoa as trainee teachers, missionaries, sailors and whalers in a second wave of migration. The third wave of migration, 80 years ago, was driven by those who had served the colonial government as civil servants within the Pacific 'territories' or in the colonial armed forces, and as such were able to move to Aotearoa. The final and fourth wave of migration occurred 50 years ago and is the migration story that most people are familiar with today. This migration was driven by economic needs and many people found jobs in the manufacturing and service sectors of postwar Aotearoa, and is the migration that my family participated in and that led to me becoming a member of the Pasifika community (Fleras & Spoonley, 1999). This means that my mother's teaching of *nai tavi ni na marama ena matavuvale* (the woman holds the family) was learned not on the banks of the Wainimala River, like her, but rather on the streets of Mount Wellington in Aotearoa, New Zealand.

Decolonization and indigenization

Higher education has played, and continues to play, a role in the subjugation of Indigenous peoples, not only through research and teaching, but also in its very nature through decisions made in the formal and informal structures of higher education institutions. In response to this, Indigenous and allied academics and activists have called for the decolonization and/or indigenization of higher education. Before continuing, it is important to have some understanding of what I refer to when I use the terms "decolonization" and "indigenization". "Indigenization" suggests that there is something redeemable in the current higher education institution and that the integration of Indigenous worldviews and people will address the inequity and marginalization within the current system (Durie, 2009). "Decolonization" in higher education refers to the belief that there is no redeeming of the current colonial system, nor is there a desire for inclusion. Instead, the end goal for decolonization is a structure change so complete that Indigenous land and life are taken back in a way that is irreversible and unrecognizable to the current system (Battiste, 2017). This becomes clear when we look at Frantz Fanon's description of decolonization as, "the substitution of one 'species' of mankind by another. The substitution is unconditional, absolute, total and seamless" (Fanon, 1963).

Decolonization and indigenization are also often used together within higher education texts. This can be explained by reflecting on what Rauna Kuokkanen (2007) and Michelle Pidgeon (2008, 2016) have argued about the process of indigenization: that it opens up the pathway for the academy to become decolonized. This is an important aspect to keep in mind about the two theories and how they operate in higher education; many people work hard at indigenizing the academy with the expectation that their work will lead to decolonization, yet, as Angela Wilson reminds us, indigenization is a "means to an end, but not the end itself" (Wilson, 2004, p. 54). This chapter therefore understands indigenization as a belief that the academy is redeemable and integration of Indigenous worldviews and people will address the inequity and marginalisation within the current system. Furthermore, this chapter understands decolonization as a rejection of the current system that advocates for an entirely new system built from Indigenous ontologies. However, it also notes that decolonization and indigenization operate together, and in many ways the process of indigenization is a step towards decolonization. Indigenous academics have written on how higher education can be indigenized and/or decolonized through research, teaching and structural reform.

Higher education research has consistently framed Indigenous peoples in problematic ways, through misunderstanding and misrepresenting Indigenous knowledges and peoples in a colonial effort to represent the "other". As a result of this misunderstanding and misrepresentation, researchers have helped to inform harmful policies for, and social perceptions of, Indigenous communities (Alfred, 2004). Therefore, reframing research to center Indigenous ontologies and epistemologies is a key step towards the overall decolonization and/or indigenization project in higher education. This reframing focuses on "the restoration and legitimation of Indigenous knowledge systems and methods of conducting research" (Stewart-Harawira, 2013, p. 43), and highlights "that there are other epistemologies and other standpoints from which Indigenous people come to know the world and from which we understand and analyze our more recent encirclement by Western knowledge over the last few centuries and its legacies" (Nakata, Nakata, Keech & Bolt, 2012, p. 124). Education is a space where society teaches norms, values and beliefs through a hidden (and sometimes overt) curriculum that is key to "maintaining social and cultural divisions within society" by reinforcing the notion that Indigenous knowledge is not legitimate (Pidgeon, 2016, p. 341). Rather, it rewards students who subscribe to mainstream value sets. As a result of education's power to teach societal norms, some Indigenous academics believe the indigenization or decolonization of teaching can deconstruct these social and cultural divisions (Alfred, 2004).

Organizational structures have been recognized as a key part of the decolonization and/or indigenization project (Ahenakew & Naepi, 2015). Tongan academic Epeli Hau'ofa, was one of the first to write about decolonizing the academy's ideas and imagination about the Pacific. When introducing Hau'ofa's series of essays on Oceania, Eric Waddell notes that Hau'ofa is asking questions that are poignant to consider when critiquing the university:

> Who is at the helm? Who sets the course? Who reads the sky and searches the horizons for signs? Is it us? Or is it someone else? Who are we? Are we satisfied, even conscious of the way we are going?
>
> *(Waddell, 1993)*

These are questions that decolonizing and/or indigenizing organizational structures are attempting to address and explore. In asking these questions academics have begun to critique who holds power within seemingly unbiased structural systems. Keith James shows how informal and invisible rules, social groupings and identitiessupersede formal university ideals, goals and policies (James, 2004). It is these invisible rules that show that universities continue to inform their actions based on the same colonial ideals that their institutions are built on. University gatekeepers enforce these rules by deciding, "who is amiable enough to be hired, neutral enough in their writing to be published and Euroamerican enough in their outlook to earn rewards or qualify for grants and fellowships." (Mihesuah, 2004, p. 31) In other words, in order to be acceptable to gate-keepers, Indigenous scholars and their work must be non-threatening to those in powerful positions (Mihesuah, 2004, p. 31). Indigenous staff who are given access to the institutions are only given a limited amount of access. As James observes, Indigenous staff, "often seem to find themselves excluded from access to important information, excluded from important decisions and excluded from important resources" (James, 2004, p. 48). As such, an important part of indi-genizing and/or decolonizing higher education is considering the structures that dictate higher education and how they need to be changed.

Given these critiques of higher education, it is unsurprising that teaching or engaging in Indigenous feminist theory within higher education is seen as an indi-genizing and/or decolonizing act. The indigenizing and/or decolonizing act of centering Indigenous feminist theory in the higher education classroom can be understood as a step towards the restoration and legitimation of Indigenous knowl-edge systems. Cannella and Manuelito argue for a reimagining of social sciences where "native epistemologies and marginalized feminisms can actually serve as foundational for the construction of an anti-colonial, egalitarian social science" (Cannella & Manuelito, 2008, p. 45). More work is needed at this intersection of gender, sovereignty and decolonization in higher education so that higher educa-tion can begin to address the assumptions of patriarchy and colonialism that higher education is built upon.

Pacific silences

Higher education and feminisms generally lack Pacific voices, and although this is slowly changing, there are still a number of practices within higher education and feminisms that actively silence Pacific peoples in both higher education and feminisms. This active silencing includes the omission of Pacific thought in both feminisms and Indigenous feminist texts, the incorporation of the Pacific into the Asia-Pacific and, as shown in the following section, building a definition of feminism in a certain way that forecloses the possibility of Pacific ontologies existing within feminisms.

As I have pointed out in my earlier work, there is a long history of Pacific voices being silenced within feminisms (Naepi, 2016). I recounted my search for Pacific feminisms within feminist literature and found that, similar to other disci-plines within higher education, Pacific peoples' voices are missing or ignored. My frustration at the willingness for these same academic spaces to consume Pacific literature, resources and culture is expressed in the following poem:

As I run my fingers along the sisterhood bookshelves
Do you see us
Do you hear us
Do you know we are here;

As I listen in your symposia
Do you see us
Do you hear us
Do you know we are here;

As I read your journals
Do you see us
Do you hear us
Do you know we are here;

As you drink our water, add our coconut milk to your lattes, savor our sweet
pineapple, grill our tuna, sunbath on our beaches, swim through our ocean,
and walk on our land
Do you see us
Do you hear us
Do you know we are here?

Do you see us, do you hear us, do you know we are here?

(Naepi, 2016, p. 1)

The Asia-Pacific region is a geopolitical area that encompasses 50 percent of the
world's population, 3,000 different languages, and 36 nations. The United States'
military (and thereby other global powers) understands the Asia-Pacific as a

> vital driver of the global economy and includes the world's busiest inter-
> national sea lanes and nine of the ten largest ports. The Asia-Pacific is also
> a heavily militarized region, with seven of the world's ten largest standing
> militaries and five of the world's declared nuclear nations.
>
> (U.S. Pacific Command, 2017)

It is still commonplace for the Pacific to be subsumed into the Asia–Pacific. Hall
referred to this common practice as active erasure of Pacific peoples (Hall, 2009).
Within the feminist field this looks like

> Asian American feminist theories that insist on retaining an "API" nomen-
> clature while having no Pacific Islander-related analyses or constituencies;
> indigenous feminist theories that presume a North American indigenous
> land-base; and postcolonial feminist theories that ignore the colonial posses-
> sions of the United States and their ongoing struggles.
>
> (Hall, 2009, p. 16)

This non-critical acceptance of the Pacific and Asia being lumped together, despite cultural, linguistic, geographical, political and economic differences, is at the very least problematic and could further be interpreted as willful ignorance on behalf of the academy.

This active silencing is being fought; there have been calls for Pacific academics to stand up and take back the narrative of the Pacific. A turning point for how Pacific peoples interacted in the academy was Hau'ofa's 1993 essay "Our Sea of Islands". The text critiqued the academy for its role in ensuring that the Pacific was understood as islands in the far sea with "primitive" people; and for its ignoring of the history of Pacific people navigating the largest ocean in the world in order to maintain a complex economic, political and relational world (Hau'ofa, 1994). Hau'ofa reminds Pacific academics that when writing about the Pacific they should actively resist their disciplines' Western habits of defining the Pacific as islands in the far sea, and instead reminds them that:

> We are the sea, we are the ocean, we must wake up to this ancient truth and together use it to overturn all hegemonic views that aim ultimately to confine us again, physically and psychologically, in tiny spaces that we have resisted accepting as our sole appointed places and from which we have recently liberated ourselves. We must not allow anyone to belittle us again and take away our freedom.
>
> *(Hau'ofa, 1994, p. 16)*

This chapter is part of that process, as it enables the Pacific story of feminisms not only to be included within the higher education and feminisms narrative, but also to ensure that this narrative is told from a Pacific perspective. This perspective is intentional about taking Hau'ofa's call to action to heart and implores feminisms to recognize what Pacific peoples have to offer and to make space for Pacific peoples and communities.

Indigenous feminisms

Indigenous feminist theory is a powerful theoretical tool for decolonization. Indigenous feminist theory practices a form of feminism that centers on decolonization and sovereignty for Indigenous peoples. In practice, this means that feminism is called to account for the role that colonization played in introducing patriarchy, and therefore any discussion on patriarchy needs also to include a discussion on the impact of colonization (Guerrero, 2003). There are also Indigenous academics who argue that feminism itself is a colonial force, as it fights for a single narrative about what it means to be a woman and as a result silences the different positionalities and identity intersections of women (St. Denis, 2013). As a result, Indigenous academics like Sandy Grande reject the feminist label and instead identify as *Indigena* as a way to show that, although Indigenous women have shared positionality as part of a marginalized gender, they still have more in common with Indigenous men than any other subcategory of women (Grande, 2003). Indigenous feminist theory gives us another lens through which to understand our current social and political systems and provides a stable base from which to understand Pacific feminist theory.

Pacific peoples have been engaging with feminism despite the silences found within feminisms. This engagement has been, and continues to be, complicated. Many Pacific peoples refuse to identify as a "feminist" and reject the concept completely, while others have organized symposia dedicated to gender and Pacific peoples. However, as Teaiwa noted, "globally, feminism has laid extensive claims to discourses on gender and the body, but in Pacific scholarship it seems slow to gather momentum" (Teaiwa, 1999, p. 257). This slow momentum can be attributed to a clash in core ontologies between feminisms and Pacific peoples, an unwillingness to "dive deep" into Pacific theory by inviting Pacific peoples into the feminist discourse and stereotypical understandings of what feminism is by Pacific peoples. In spite of this, some Pacific peoples still identify as feminist and use feminist theory, as they argue that a feminist lens will contribute to the wider Pacific decolonization project.

It is clear that there has always been tension between Pacific peoples and feminisms. In 1978, during the First National Conference of Vanuaaku Women of Efate,[1] Ni Vanuatu poet Grace Mera addressed the crowd with: "Women's Liberation or Women's Lib is a European disease to be cured by Europeans. What we are aiming for is not just women's liberation but a total liberation. A social, political and economic liberation" (Jolly, 1991, p. 56). What Grace Mera is referring to here is the collective ontology that is found throughout the Pacific. For us it is not just about liberating an individual woman; instead, liberation must be sought for the whole community. Communal liberation is seen in how Pacific families pool resources to advance the whole community, not just individual members of the community, and until feminisms can understand this it will not be able to address Pacific community concerns.

Using feminist theory has also worked against Pacific scholars when trying to write with their own people on their community's desires. Hawaiian scholar Haunani-Kay Trask reflected on how feminist political teachings worked against her when she was trying to organize communities for national sovereignty movements (Trask, 1996). Trask noted that working with her people made her realize that feminisms had limited theory and praxis, as feminist "language revolved around First World 'rights' talk, that Enlightenment individualism that takes for granted 'individual' primacy" (Trask, 1996, p. 909). Around the same time in the South Pacific, Samoan scholar Selina Tusitala Marsh also found "that many theories simply did not apply to me or my family" (Marsh, 1998, p. 667) due to the foundational incompatibility of the individual or communal ontologies. This clash in ontologies caused me to reflect that: "I value what feminist theory has to offer, but I also wish to see feminist theory value what my community offers" (Naepi, 2016, p. 4). It is this clash in ontologies that causes tension between feminism and Pacific peoples and it will continue to exist unless feminist theory shifts yet again, not just to include marginalized voices, but also to include communal ontologies that are significantly different to the individualistic ontology that feminist theory was built upon.

Pacific peoples are rarely invited to contribute to feminist theory discussions. In 1984, Vanessa Griffen was included in the global anthology of feminisms *Sisterhood is Global*. This anthology has faced earlier critique, as it is "predicated on a definition of the *experience of oppression* where difference can only be understood as male/female", and women can only be understood as victims; it is this shared victimhood that creates the sisterhood (Mohanty, 1995, p. 74). Griffen's section was the "Pacific Islands", and although the preface to the chapter notes that the Pacific is diverse and complex, it does not directly state that it is problematic to have one voice speak for the many countries within the Pacific. This same anthology did not have "Europe" and "Asia", but rather countries within Europe and Asia were given separate chapters to address their concerns with feminism. So, in many ways, the book does a disservice to Pacific feminisms by not naming the specific space from which Griffen[2] writes. When writing on Pacific feminisms, I try to be clear that I am writing from a Fijian perspective and, beyond that, a Fijian perspective that was filtered through my upbringing in Aotearoa, New Zealand. This clarification on my worldview enables the reader to understand that I offer a very specific view on Pacific feminisms and perhaps encourage them to 'dive deeper' into Pacific theory. Pacific feminist Teresia Teaiwa commented on this issue as late as 2013, asking, "how can feminists still be reproducing such hierarchies of knowledge and authority in the twenty-first century?" (Teaiwa & Slater, 2013, p. 447). This lack of acknowledgment of the diversity within the Pacific deems Pacific knowledge as less important, as people do not see the worth in digging beyond a surface appreciation of Pacific thought, instead believing that an acknowledgment of diversity is sufficient and does not require that the field seeks to uncover and engage in the diversity of thought from the Pacific.

Finally, working against a relationship between feminisms and Pacific peoples is a widely stereotypical understanding of what feminisms are. Selina Tusitala Marsh notes that feminism is still widely unaccepted within Pacific communities, and points to stereotypical notions of feminism that still exist as a possible explanation to why Pacific communities continue to reject feminisms (Tusitala, 1998). Related to this understanding is the troubling notion that if identifying as "feminist" can cause individuals within Pacific communities to question their ability to "comfortably fit within the boundaries of the Pacific social imaginary" and therefore their ability to be "Pacific" (Mila-Schaaf, 2009, p. 3). This questioning is tied to understandings of feminism as individually driven. Understanding feminisms as a strictly individualistic pursuit for equality, results in the idea that you cannot be a Pacific person whose ontology is driven by collective wellbeing when you identify with a political movement that is driven by an individualistic ontology. However, Pacific peoples are starting to reconcile these differences and recognize what feminisms do have to offer. Interestingly, when Pacific peoples engage with feminisms, it is becoming clear that their entry point is through feminist-of-color understandings of feminisms. Recently Diva for Equality, a Pacific social activist group, printed T-shirts with this quote from Alice Walker: "Activism is the rent I pay for living on this planet". In my own experience of searching feminists' literature beyond the Pacific, I began with bell hooks, Leanne Simpson and Sara Ahmed.

In more recent years, Pacific peoples located within the academy have begun to view feminism as having something to offer wider Pacific theory and political movements. In 2006, Noelene Nabulivou noted that after speaking on feminism's relevance in the Pacific, she had been challenged by other Pacific women (Nabulivou, 2006). Despite this challenge, Nabulivou continues to identify as a feminist and uses the term *feminist* because it enables her to "honor feminism as concept and practice because in my life, most of the women who inspired me called themselves feminist" (Nabulivou, 2006). In 2009, Lisa Hall argued that

> Feminist theory remains integral to the process of decolonization for Hawaiian and other indigenous women because colonialism takes place through gendered and sexualized forms that reconstitute both individual and communal indigenous identities in stigmatized and disempowering ways.
>
> *(Hall, 2009)*

Both Hall and Nabulivou show it is possible to identify as both Pacific and feminist; however, due to the current frayed relationships between feminisms and Pacific peoples, it becomes necessary to 'take a stand' on this identification and justify why you would choose to do so.

Rebuilding of relationships between Pacific peoples and feminisms

In spite of the history of tensions between Pacific peoples and feminisms, there is a current resurgence of Pacific peoples identifying as feminist. In 2016, Fiji hosted the first Pacific feminists' forum. This gathering bought over 100 Pacific feminists from 13 Pacific countries and culminated in the launch of the Pacific Feminists Charter for Change (Fiji Women's Rights Movement, 2016). This forum showed the potential for a feminist resurgence in the Pacific with one youth participant reflecting: "we're only going to move forward, it's great to have a strong feminist movement that supports and encourages young women in the Pacific who are still trying to find their journey" (Fiji Women's Rights Movement, 2016). The development of the Pacific Feminists Charter for Change also indicates that Pacific feminists are defining their own agenda, a process in which Fijian human rights activist Nabulivou noted, "women across the Pacific are really interested in universal human rights, social economic and ecological justice. It's not just about women and girls but about equity and fairness for everyone" (Fiji Women's Rights Movement, 2016). This Pacific-defined and Pacific-driven brand of feminism is already reverberating around the Pacific. On October 3, 2017, a *talanoa* (a relational-based conversation or discussion) entitled "Fearless on the Frontlines:

Pacific Young Feminists" was held at the 13th Triannual Conference of Pacific Women and the 6th meeting of Pacific Ministers for Women.

Beyond the academy, Pacific feminisms are finding a foothold in digital spaces, such as on social media. Social media in general have changed how people in the Pacific communicate, with more and more online Pacific communities being established that enable Pacific peoples from across the Pacific Ocean and beyond to communicate with each other and share our concerns and political movements. Social media have also become an education space in the Pacific, enabling us to share resources for understanding the world through a feminist lens across the Pacific within moments. Within the Pacific feminist space, the Twitter handle @diva4equality was established in 2015. It now has 728 followers and a partner Facebook page with 2,204 likes, which therefore shows that there is space in the Pacific for feminisms and that people are actively fighting for space. This may be considered a small number by some social media standards, but when you consider that only 10 years ago Mila-Schaaf identified that to call yourself a feminist was to call into question your very ability to be Pacific, this Twitter account could be the beginning of a larger revolution in the relationships between Pacific peoples and feminisms (Mila-Schaaf, 2009).

Much like other Indigenous feminisms, Pacific feminisms are and must be tied to the land and the ocean (Kermoal and Altamirano-Jimenéz, 2016). @diva4equality serves as an example of how Pacific feminists link gender justice to climate justice. In the 23rd session of the Conference of the Parties (COP23) discussions, @diva4equality provided a way for Pacific feminists to engage in COP23 from afar with tweets such as: "The struggle is long, AND WE ARE STRONG. We will never give up on this beautiful planet #WomenDefendCommons #WomenClimateJustice #COP23" (Diva for Equality, 2017). This effort was acknowledged by others, with tweets such as "Thank you @diva4equality for a great panel focusing on Pacific women's voices from the frontlines of climate change. #COP23 🐚 (350 Pacific, 2017)." It is possible that, given the current impact of climate change on the Pacific, there is room for Pacific feminisms to grow as Pacific people who are interested in climate justice begin to understand how it is also linked to gender justice.

Pacific feminisms and teaching

As outlined above, Pacific peoples' relationship with feminisms and higher education is one filled with tension and exclusion. As Pacific peoples develop the voices they wish to use when discussing their own brand of feminisms, others need to provide a space for those voices to be heard. Pacific peoples have something to offer feminisms and the simple act of teaching one Pacific feminist paper in a course can have far-reaching implications.

During graduate school, in an effort to unpack Pacific feminisms, I enrolled in an Indigenous feminisms class to try and understand more about how other Indigenous feminists navigated the pull between one's family and feminisms. The course instructor went to the effort of locating a Pacific feminist text to include within the main course readings and discussion. There were two significant outcomes to this. One was a personal outcome for me. I began to understand how Pacific feminisms linked to other forms of Indigenous feminisms; I started to grasp how to locate Pacific thought globally; and I also found my Pacific feminist voice. Second, for my peers, the inclusion of a Pacific feminist text within the main course readings and discussions legitimated Pacific worldviews, as many of them were unaware of the Pacific beyond Fiji water and tropical holidays. Due to the underrepresentation of Pacific peoples within the academy and in wider global discourses, the first step in Pacific feminist pedagogies is simple inclusion. This inclusion not only enables Pacific feminists to find their voice but also widens allies' understandings of the world around them.

Pacific feminisms past and present give us the ability not only to imagine feminism's future, but also to consider how we might shape the future through teaching. The inclusion of Pacific feminisms within the feminist narrative would enable a shift towards including a communal understanding of gender, sex, equity and equality. The link between gender justice and climate justice found within Pacific feminisms also provides an opportunity to push for more radical changes in people's patterns of consumption.

For those of us from the Pacific, teaching Pacific feminisms enables us to see that it is possible for us to define our own brand of feminism. I attempted to do this with Fijian feminism, arguing that any form of Fijian feminism would need to be built from a collective and communal space in order to be meaningful to Pacific peoples (Naepi, 2016). This means taking the traditional argument of pay equity and thinking about what this means from a collective space. For Fijian families, any individual income contributes to the wider family and community income. How does this understanding of wealth and wellness impact how we understand feminist arguments for equity? Questions such as these may shake the individualistic foundations of feminist theory; however, feminisms have been open to critique and change in the past. Thus, Pacific feminists may provide another teaching and learning moment for us all.

Pacific feminisms linked to climate justice enable us to widen the scope of feminisms to consider how our everyday consumption actions impact the world around us. The challenge of teaching non-Pacific peoples about Pacific feminism lies in helping people realize that, beyond tropical holidays, romantic backdrops for literature and film, and the occasional global political contestation, there are people who live their everyday lives in the Pacific. These are people who rely on the Pacific Ocean to survive, whose livelihoods are threatened by a warming ocean, rising sea levels, and extreme weather patterns. However, once this challenge is addressed, it becomes possible to encourage people not only to understand the Pacific as a region in and of itself, a region that is populated with diverse cultures, languages and peoples, but perhaps also to change their current consumption patterns as they begin to understand how their actions impact the lives of other peoples.

Like other Indigenous feminisms, Pacific feminisms are tied to critiques of colonization. Teaching Pacific feminist theory in the classroom strengthens the call to decolonization and adds to people's understanding of what decolonization can look like. For Pacific peoples, it is not possible to talk about decolonization without also considering the ocean. The ocean has and always will be part of Pacific people's lives. Pacific feminist Teresia Teawia once noted that "We sweat and cry salt water, so we know that the ocean is really in our blood" (in Hau'ofa, 2000, p. 32). This visceral connection to the ocean is something that needs to be discussed in decolonization movements. The Pacific has been, and continues to be, a site of colonization, from early "discovery" to nuclear testing (Bikini Atoll), to the very recent threat to Guam. Colonization is also inevitably tied to our current rates of consumption – consumption that is choking our ocean with plastic and warming it to irreversible levels. Perhaps if Pacific feminisms became part of the core curricula of decolonization texts, it would be possible to have conversations about the global impact of consumption and colonialism.

Conclusion

Although Pacific people and feminisms have not always agreed on everything and are unlikely to in the future, the current political climate (the United States Pacific pivot, North Korea's threats to the Pacific, climate change and the denial of climate change by powerful countries, etc.) has resulted in Pacific peoples beginning to embrace feminisms. This embrace is tentative, and engaging in teaching feminist theory should include a careful recognition of Pacific feminist theory. This diversification of feminist thought serves all people as we begin to critique the individualistic foundation of feminisms and consider how we might shift our thinking to be inclusive of communities whose foundational beliefs lie in communal understandings of the world. Pacific feminisms also call to decolonize feminist theory and to consider the role of colonization within feminisms by considering communal ontologies, the role of the ocean in Indigenous ontologies, and how gender justice is tied to climate justice. The inclusion of Pacific feminist theory is one small teaching step that we can take to further indigenize and/or decolonize higher education through the integration of Pacific worldviews and people. This step will further destabilize the academy by teaching students it is possible to reject the status quo and push for an alternative higher education system.

Notes

1 A gathering of Indigenous peoples of Vanuatu.
2 Griffen is a well-known Pacific feminist who was involved in many of the feminist movements within the Pacific. It is not her voice I trouble here, but the acceptance that one voice was able to speak for many.

References

350 Pacific. (2017). 350 Pacific, *Twitter*, November 13, 2017, retrieved from https://twitter.com/350Pacific/status/930017189628989440

Ahenakew, C. & Naepi, S. (2015). The difficult task of turning walls into tables. In M. Webber, S. Macfarlane & A. Macfarlane (Eds.), *Sociocultural Theory: Implications for Curricula across the Sector* (pp. 181–194). Christchurch, New Zealand: University of Canterbury Press.

Alfred, T. (2004). Warrior scholarship: seeing the university as a ground of contention. In D. A. Mihesuah & A. C. Wilson (Eds.), *Indigenizing the academy: Transforming scholarship and empowering communities* (pp. 88–99). Lincoln, NE: University of Nebraska Press.

Battiste, M. (2017). *Decolonizing Education: Nourishing the Learning Spirit.* Sakatoon, Canada: Purich Publishing Limited.

Cannella, G. S. & Manuelito, K. D. (2008). Feminisms from unthought locations: Indigenous worldviews, marginalized feminisms, and revisioning an anticolonial social science. In N. K. Denzin, Y. S. Lincoln & L. T. Smith, *Handbook of Critical and Indigenous Methodologies* (pp. 45–59). Thousand Oaks, CA: Sage.

Diva for Equality. (2017). Diva for equality. *Twitter*, November 13, 2017, retrieved from https://twitter.com/diva4equality

Durie, M. (2009). Towards social cohesion: the indigenisation of higher education in New Zealand. *Vice-Chancellors' Forum* (pp. 1–20). Kuala Lumpur, Malaysia: Massey University.

Fanon, F. (1963). *The Wretched of the Earth.* (R. Philcox, trans.) New York: Grove Press.

Fiji Women's Rights Movement. (2016). *Partners of the Inaugural Pacific Feminist Forum,* November 28, 2016, retrieved November 13, 2017, from www.fwrm.org.fj/events/pac-feminist-forum-2016

Fleras, A. & Spoonley, P. (1999). *Recalling Aotearoa: Indigenous Politics and Ethnic Relations in New Zealand.* Oxford: Oxford University Press.

Grande, S. (2003). Whitestream feminism and the colonialist project: a review of contemporary feminist pedagogy and praxis. *Educational Theory, 53*(3), 329–346.

Griffen, V. (1984). The Pacific Islands: all it requires is ourselves. In R. Morgan & R. Morgan (Eds.), *Sisterhood is Global: The International Women's Movement Anthology* (pp. 517–524). New York: Anchor Books.

Guerrero, M. J. (2003). Patriarchal colonialism and indigenism: implications for native feminist spirituality and native womanism. *Hypatia, 18*(2), 58–69.

Hall, L. K. (2009). Navigating our own sea of islands: remapping a theoretical space for Hawaiian women and indigenous feminism. *Wicazo Sa Review, 24*(2), 15–38.

Hau'ofa, E. (1993). Our Sea of Islands. *Contemporary Pacific, 6*(1), 147–161.

Hau'ofa, E. (2000). *The ocean in us, 33*, 1032. Canberra: Asia Pacific Press.

James, K. (2004). Corrupt state university: the organizational psychology of native experience in higher education. In D. A. Mihesuah, A. C. Wilson, D. Mihesuah & A. Wilson (Eds.), *Indigenizing the Academy: Transforming Scholarship and Empowering Communities* (pp. 48–68). Lincoln: University of Nebraska Press.

Jolly, M. (1991). The politics of difference: feminism, colonialism and decolonisation in Vanuatu. *Intersexions: Gender/Class/Culture/Ethnicity,* 52–74.

Kermoal, N., & Altamirano-Jiménez, I. (Eds.). (2016). *Living on the Land: Indigenous Women's Understanding of Place.* Edmonton, Alberta: Athabasca University Press.

Kuokkanen, R. (2007). *Reshaping the University: Responsibility, Indigenous Epistemes, and the Logic of the Gift.* Vancouver: University of British Columbia Press.

Mihesuah, D. A. (2004). Academic gatekeepers. In *Indigenizing the Academy: Transforming Scholarship and Empowering Communities* (pp. 31–47). Lincoln: University of Nebraska Press.

Mila-Schaaf, K. (2009). The magical metaphor man. *An Oceanic Imagination: A Tribute to the Life and Mind of Epeli Hau'ofa* (pp. 1–14). Dunedin, New Zealand: University of the South Pacific.

Mohanty, C. T. (1995). Feminist encounters: locating the politics of experience. In L. Nicholson & S. Seidman (Eds.), *Social Postmodernism: Beyond Identity Politics* (pp. 68–86). Cambridge: Cambridge University Press.

Nabulivou, N. (2006). Feminisms, identities, sexualities: a personal journey. *Development*, *49*(1), 30–34.

Naepi, S. (2016). Indigenous feminisms: a South Pacific perspective. *Canadian Graduate Journal for Social Justice*, *1*(1), 1–10.

Nakata, M. N., Nakata, V., Keech, S. & Bolt, R. (2012). Decolonial goals and pedagogies for Indigenous studies. *Decolonization: Indigeneity, Education & Society*, *1*(1), 120–140.

Pidgeon, M. (2008). Pushing against the margins: Indigenous theorizing of "success" and retention in higher education. *Journal of College Student Retention*, *10*(3), 339–360.

Pidgeon, M. (2016). More than a checklist: meaningful Indigenous inclusion in higher education. *Social Inclusion*, *4*(1), 77–91.

St. Denis, V. (2013). Feminism is for everybody: Aboriginal women, feminism, and diversity. In M. Hobbs & C. Rice (Eds.), *Gender and Women's Studies in Canada: Critical Terrain* (pp. 12–16). Toronto, Ontario: Women's Press.

Stewart-Harawira, M. (2013). Challenging knowledge capitalism: indigenous research in the 21st century. *Socialist Studies*, *9*(1), 39–51.

Teaiwa, T. (1999). Reading Paul Gauguin's Noa Noa with Epeli Hau'ofa's Kisses in the Nederends: militourism, feminism, and the "Polynesian" body. In V. Hereniko & R. Wilson (Eds.), *Inside Out: Literature, Cultural Politics, and Identity in the New Pacific* (pp. 249–263). Lanham, MD: Rowman and Littlefield.

Teaiwa, T. & Slatter, C. (2013). *Samting Nating*: Pacific waves at the margins of feminist security studies. *International Studies Perspectives*, *14*(4), 447–450.

Trask, H.-K. (1996). Feminism and indigenous Hawaiian nationalism. *Signs*, *21*(4), 906–916.

Tusitala Marsha, S. (1998). Migrating feminisms: maligned overstayer or model citizen? *Women's Studies International Forum*, *21*(6), 665–680.

U.S. Pacific Command. (2017). *USPACOM Area of Responsibility*, retrieved December 29, 2017, from www.pacom.mil/About-USPACOM/USPACOM-Area-of-Responsibility/

Waddell, E. (1993). Introduction. In E. Hau'ofa, E. Waddell, V. Naidu & E. Hau'ofa (Eds.), *A New Oceania: Rediscovering Our Sea of Islands* (pp. 1–3). Suva, Fiji: University of the South Pacific in association with Beake House.

Wilson, A. C. (2004). Reclaiming our humanity: decolonization and the recovery of indigenous knowledge. In D. A. Mihesuah & A. C. Wilson (Eds.), *Indigenizing the Academy: Transforming Scholarship and Empowering Communities* (pp. 49–69). Lincoln: University of Nebraska Press.

3

FEMINIZING AND DECOLONIZING HIGHER EDUCATION

Pedagogies of dignity in Colombia and Australia

Sara C. Motta

Embodying a feminizing, decolonizing praxis as a critical educator in a deeply neoliberalized higher educational space, which intensifies the logics and rationalities of coloniality that shape the very emergence of the "Lettered City", is an inherently contradictory and ambiguous endeavor (Rama, 1996). The epistemological politics and resultant knowing-subjectivities that are constitutive of the Enlightenment project – of which the University is the jewel in the crown – have been premised upon a violent monologue which has consistently denied, violated and elided the knowing-be-ing of raced and feminized Others. A feminizing, decolonizing praxis is an (im)possibility within this space. Our praxis must therefore work knowingly within and beyond such (im)possibility, breaching the borders and transgressing the separations between theory and practice, mind and body, university and community, education and life at the heart of the modern University project.

In this contribution, I explore some of the complexities of such a feminizing, decolonizing praxis working within and beyond its very (im)possibility. In particular, I reflect critically upon my attempts to develop a feminist decolonial pedagogy within the settler colonial context of Australia, at undergraduate level in a regional university, and within the post-colonial context of Colombia at postgraduate level at a regional university. I situate my reflections within the broad framework of decolonial feminism and in dialogue with Freirean and feminist critical pedagogy that focuses on the role of pedagogies of discomfort in transformatory educational praxis. However, I develop the conceptual framing of this praxis, by tentatively thinking through a pedagogy of dignity as a means of capturing the deeply onto-epistemological embodied dynamics of such work. These dynamics involve embracing our other decolonizing knowing-subjectivities able to enflesh multiple forms of knowledge and multiple collaborative ways of creating knowledge for transformation.

Living under, surviving and resisting a state of siege

Indigenous people, people of color and other marginalized peoples live under a constant, cruel state of siege (Dillard, 2016). The police on our streets kill our young people every year, humiliate far more through searches, raids and arrests and continue deeply racialized and classed practices of child removal which negate Black and Indigenous motherhood (Motta, 2016). At school, our children are more likely to be labelled problematic, be violently excluded and often be subjected to everyday forms of abusive intervention. At the welfare office and in all interactions with "officialdom", we are met with the gaze of suspicion already marked as undeserving and deviant.

Through these daily practices, we are urged to see ourselves as less than human. As Frantz Fanon describes, such systemic negation "forces the people it dominates to ask themselves the question 'in reality' who am I?" (1961, p. 200). We are treated as incapable of reason and self-government, and therefore of political freedom, represented as the feminized and racialized non-subjects of savage, irrational and dangerous territories.

We are treated as lives which matter less.

Our bodies are made visible to those in power as raced and feminized Others to be tamed, developed, (mis)named and shamed. Our own forms of knowledge and social life are made invisible – often even to ourselves. Such practices turn vast swathes of the global population – mostly Indigenous peoples and communities of color into objects to be acted upon, rather than subjects with reason, wisdom and agency. Such strategies of bio-political dehumanization are increasingly being enacted upon white working-class communities and other marginalized groups, such as refugees, queer subjects and radicalized subjects who contest the liberal consensus such as the black bloc in the United States.

Black, Indigenous, Migrant, Mestiza/Chicana and other excluded communities struggle against such destructive and traumatizing logics of dehumanization. Rich traditions of praxis rooted in the wisdom of our foremothers are emerging through the increasing presence of a marked feminization of resistance (Motta, 2013; Motta & Seppälä, 2016). Yet it is often these voices, predominantly those of Black, Indigenous, Queer and other feminized and marginalized communities and movements, that are drowned out by institutions of knowledge creation and political power.

This is not a coincidence.

These traditions and subjects unsettle the subordination of marginalized people as objects. They disrupt systems of thought and being which attempt to render us as uni-dimensional, dangerous and unworthy. They thus help us to break out of our containment in subordinate positions and nurture our emergence as subjects of rationality and political actors with our own wisdoms and knowledges.

These traditions foreground how the violence of living under siege and containment create "soul wounds", as we are rendered the objects of intervention, to be known about, labeled, named and contained (Duran, Firehammer & Gonzalez,

2008, p. 289). This experience of subjectification as non-beings affects our relationship to knowledge and reality, including internalization of the oppressor's logic, impacting how we talk, feel and think about ourselves, as well as how we relate to other people. We can come to believe in parts of our being – as Frantz Fanon (1961) and bell hooks (1990) so forcefully demonstrated – that we have nothing to offer, that our lives and experiences lack value and that we are unlovable.

It becomes essential for our very survival not only to resist the palimpsest of power as an external force, but also to decolonize our internal territories of knowledge and social life. Furthermore, it is important to create other decolonized ways of knowing-being, such as collective forms of the organization of land and wellbeing based on "other" cosmovisions, or the re-occupation of the city and the development of democratic forms of social reproduction (Alexander, 2006; Anzaldúa, 1987 hooks, 1990; Lugones, 2010; Motta, 2014, 2015). Such decolonizing politics centers trauma as a systemic consequence of the everyday and repeated realities of violence we experience. Healing thus becomes essential to, and theorized as part of, our enfleshed yearnings for emancipation (Morales, 1998; Motta, 2017).

It would be amiss to elide how the "Knowing-Subject" is himself[1] wounded in this relation of dehumanization with the Other. His knowing-subjectivity is premised upon containment and control over those subjugated as feminized and racialized Others, but also upon his internal affective territories. This results in a disembodied monological rationality marked by an incapacity to listen (epistemologically) to, and receive from, the other within and without (Motta, 2017). This loss is a form of dehumanization in which the capacity to speak and know is actually a form of muteness. As Fanon suggests, "Superiority? Inferiority? Why not the quite simple attempt to touch the other, to feel the other, to explain the other to myself? Was my freedom not given to me then in order to build the world of the You?" (1961, pp. 231–232).

Our new maps and territories of healing decolonization cannot, thus, be drawn and created as Audre Lorde (1983) reminds us "with the master's tools". Rather, we have been and will continue to breathe life into new literacies of politics, such as art, spirit, body, song and ritual (Motta, 2017). These processes are inherently epistemological, as they involve a deep healing dive into the feminized and racialized inner and outer territories that have been rendered abject, empty or irrational.

This epistemological task involves a return to our embodied wisdoms and recognition that our experiences, when collectively worked with, can be kneaded into the metaphorical and material bread with which to nurture our existence, survival and flourishing. Such a return involves remembering our stories of survival, dignity and resistance (Morales, 1998). It makes visible how our stories have always defied and belied the racialized categories which render us abject and attempt to separate us from one another.

Such a return involves a politics of *ancestralidad* and rooting into the "herstories" of our foremothers and grandmothers, reconnecting with their wisdoms. It is worth quoting Patricia Hill Collins at length here, as she describes:

[We] cannot afford to be fools of any type, for our objectification as the Other denies us . . . protection. This distinction between knowledge and wisdom and the use of experience as the cutting edge dividing them, has been key to [our] survival. In the context of race, gender and class oppression, the distinction is essential. Knowledge without wisdom is adequate for the powerful, but wisdom is essential to the survival of the subordinate.

(2000, p. 208)

By re-rooting these kinds of pedagogical practices into our lived and ancestral wisdoms, we become subjects through which a politics of wholeness and integrity might be visioned. Here, we begin to enflesh a coming to knowing-being-power that is "neither white nor surface; [but] dark . . . ancient . . . deep" (Lorde, 1984, p. 37).

Such a politics of knowing-be-ing-becoming is deeply pedagogical, as it involves unlearning/unrooting the processes of subjectification that have separated us from ourselves and each other, and the collective nurturing of our wisdoms to foreground our becoming otherwise in theory and practice. As bell hooks describes, this can be realized through creating "[a] meeting place where new and radical happenings can occur" (1990, p. 31). Below, I outline the (im)possibilities of such decolonizing and feminizing encounters within two formal educational space-times.

Decolonizing critical pedagogy

In my own pedagogical practice in higher education I have attempted to embody such a politics of knowledge by combining Freirean and feminist traditions of critical pedagogy with decolonizing and feminizing pedagogical innovations and experimentations.[2] Here, in particular, I will focus on two of the various pedagogical axes of this praxis: the pedagogy of discomfort and the pedagogy of dignity.

Freire's work theorizes a pedagogical philosophy that is committed to empowerment of oppressed and marginalized communities. It aims to democratize access to powerful knowledges whilst nurturing the development of knowledges of the oppressed (Freire, 2012, 2014). Central to such pedagogical commitments is an ethics of careful recognition of the realities, experiences, histories and knowledges of oppressed communities. This contests their/our misrepresentation in the knowing-subjectivity and politics of knowledge of coloniality as empty and lacking subjects, in need of the teacher's expert knowledge.

Such attentiveness to holistic work with communities and learners also extends to the teacher/facilitator, who is theorized as an intellectual co-creator of knowledges for democratization and transformation (Darder, 2015; Freire, 2012, 2014). This is in contradistinction to the framing of the teacher-subject of coloniality who is a transmitter of particular skills to students, has an instrumental and competitive motivation as a scholar, separates their lives, experiences and histories, and controls their unruly and unsettling emotions from the realm of professional academic labor (Motta, 2013). In contrast, a Freirean attentiveness to collaboration, collectivity and critical reflexivity between educators, and between students and educators, is centered. This is viewed as essential in co-creating the conditions of possibility for the emergence and nurturance of democratizing educational praxis and emancipated subjects. The pedagogical space thus extends outside of the class-room, and into the creation of the infrastructure of democratizing and caring multi-dimensional work (Darder, 2012).

Such democratizing pedagogical work and active subjectivities are nurtured and nurture attentiveness to creating deeply relational time-spaces. These foster dia-logical and collaborative co-creations of understanding and knowledges. Much work has focused on the role of comfort and discomfort in this process. Feminist theorists have focused on the need to create safe spaces, which enable exploration of unchartered and unknown territories of thought and analysis. For example, they challenge taken-for-granted hegemonic narratives of self, other and society (Boler & Zembylas, 2003). This work foregrounds how working with discomfort and moments of disruption to create moments of pedagogical possibility can result in re-narrativizations of self, other and society, as well as foster new and unim-aginable relationalities and possibilities (Boler & Zembylas, 2003; Pereira, 2012). Importantly, this foregrounds a holistic sense of the pedagogical as a relational practice. Furthermore, it brings attention to the experience of joy, vulnerability, empowerment and powerlessness, and their role in pedagogical processes of liber-ating transformation. Such pedagogical work requires immense and complex forms of affective awareness and practice. They are premised on the integral presence of the educator in the learning space in which shame/shaming practices and competi-tion are eschewed in favor of vulnerability and openness to alterity, difference and the unknown (Motta & Bennett, 2018).

Freirean critical pedagogy (CP) enables recognition of the potential liberatory role of education and foregrounds the recognition of experiential knowledges as sites from which to collectively forge knowledges by and of the oppressed. Dialogical relationality between all subjects is the underlying ethical principal struc-turing learning/unlearning. This relationality is neither confined to the classroom nor the formal curriculum. However, this work has been critiqued for its focus on the cognitive conceptualization of learning, knowledge and knowing. It has also been argued that it presumes an already-existing White "humanistic" subject able to embrace and work with such knowledges.[3] Feminist-inspired CP that turns to a pedagogy of discomfort foregrounds the role of the affective in our learning and unlearning. It centers disruption and discomfort as key to this process of question-ing and un/relearning. However, whilst often written by other subjects within formal education, this perspective often involves thinking through a pedagogical process in which the hegemonic student-subject is confronted by the Other, and thus their privileged certainties are shaken and potentially unlearned.

What is missing, therefore, is a decolonization of these two framings which: (1) begins from and centers the perspective of the other, recognizing their non-subjectivity as the onto-epistemological terrain of possibility, such that their/our embodied realities and experiences form the epistemological grounds of possibility for emancipatory learning and unlearning; (2) embraces multiple forms of knowledge, knowing and knowing-subjectivity; (3) centers all that has been negated, denied and alienated, which is referred to as endarkened wisdoms. I propose that a way we might conceptualize such a pedagogy is as a pedagogy of dignity. Here liberation becomes linked to healing and homecoming of the raced and feminized Other. This involves descent into our endarkened wisdoms to embrace embodied, ancestral and spiritual knowledges and ways of knowing and pedagogical processes of inter-relational recognition. This enables us to move from surviving to flourishing subjects and communities as our dignity is epistemologically recognized, pedagogically foregrounded and carefully nurtured.

Within this pedagogy of dignity, all are recognized as wounded, including those subjects that embody the Knowing/Privileged Subject. These processes involve recognition of complicity, being open to listening and receiving, and unlearning the subjectivity of the oppressor as it crisscrosses their knowing-being. The objective of such a pedagogy is not to re-reify closed and one-dimensional identities and subjectivities, such as raced and feminized Others and Knowing/Privileged Subjects. It is rather to expose these dualisms as fantasies and foreground the divisions and wounds they have fostered and inflicted without denying the differential (epistemological and ontological) positioning of different subjects within these processes of subjectification. As Gloria Anzaldúa describes:

> From this vantage point of greater conocimiento we recognise otro consejos del fuego – the rhetoric of racial categories imposed on us is partial and flawed and only serves to cage us in "race" and class-bound spaces . . . These categories do not reflect the realities we live in, and are not true to our multicultural roots. Liminality, the in-between space of Nepantla is the space most of us occupy. We do not inhabit un mundo but many, and we need to allow these other worlds and peoples to join in the feminist-of-colour dialogue. We must be wary of assimilation but not fear cultural Mestizaje. Instead we must become nepantleras and build bridges between all these worlds as we traffic, back and forth between them, detribalizing and retribalizing in different and various communities. The firing has bequeathed us el conocimiento (insight) that humans and the universe are in a symbiotic relationship; . . . we live in a state of deep interconnectedness en un mundo zurdo (a left-handed world). We are not alone in our struggles, and never have been. Somos almas afines and this interconnectedness is an unvoiced category of identity.
>
> *(2015, p. 264)*

Australia: unlearning the knowing-subjectivity of coloniality

"The Global Politics of Indigenous People", a class that I designed and developed at a regional Australian university, is an elective undergraduate upper-level course that students from across the social sciences can take. It develops a politics of knowledge and pedagogy embedded in decolonial, feminizing and indigenous philosophies of education. The course is realized through and in reference to multiple knowledges, ways of knowing and knowing-subjects, thus foregrounding the struggles and knowledges of Indigenous peoples across the globe. The pedagogical practices of the course revolve around experiential and participatory learning experiences. These include the embodied, spiritual and cultural, such as music, poetry, storytelling, mapping and visual representation, as well as cognitive, oral and written reflection and dialogue. This aims to prefigure and mirror the practices of indigenizing and decolonizing knowledge and politics introduced throughout the course.

The assessments include reflexive journals, which have students link the readings to their own experiences and lives. It does this to overcome binaries that re-impose the idea that Indigenous politics is an identity politics calling for inclusion within the terms of political possibility of the present which can subsequently reinforce the (mis)representation that decoloniality is only for Indigenous peoples and not relevant for non-Indigenous peoples. It also fosters students' autonomous thinking through supporting them to design and write an independent case study that develops key themes and issues from the course. In it, they are also free to experiment with different forms of writing and representation as the embodiment of the multiple epistemologies they learn about during their studies.

During the latter part of the course, I nurture a pedagogical moment of encounter that prefigures and embodies the different cosmologies underlying much Indigenous political practice and political visions.[4] I take the group (usually half self-select not to participate) to a sacred site of a lake where our campus is situated. It is a place that many don't know exists and most don't enter. On our journey there, I sense-smell the different emotions floating in the air: expectation, uncertainty, nervousness. There are uncomfortable silences and muffled giggles, but also moments of flow as the group begins to walk at a similar pace. As we come to the uneven terrain and walk down a slope to get to the lake, talking tends to lessen as the relative silence and newness of the space welcomes us. Sometimes, even before we get to the place of encounter, a student might decide to leave. The discomfort is too great and I sense the fear of a vulnerability that might be too painful/unsettling. This I accept and honor with grace.

In this place, we experiment with deep listening to the body of the land and our own bodies, share sacred stories and/or songs, and co-create a musical or poetic expression of our experiences. This involves the pedagogical embrace of silence and a turning away from the idea that speech is *the* sign of knowing and wisdom. The sacred, in this sense, involves (re)connection to the energy of life, which is deeply relational not only between us as human subjects, but also with non-human subjects of the land, the ecology and the cosmos (Alexander, 2006; Motta, 2018). I actively hold the space and guide the students into a descent to the darkened territories of their own bodies, minds and the land around them. We represent what we hear through the silence, our heartbeat, our fear, the voice in our head, the flies buzzing, some beautiful birds landing on the lake, the breeze moving the leaves and caressing our cheeks. There is a softening of the energy between us as the word as embodied enters to (re)connect us to ourselves and each other. There is an opening of the body to another listening and knowing. As we sit *in circle* to read a sacred story or sing a sacred song, there remain whispers of uncertainty and nervousness at the vulnerability that is present and palpable. As holder of that space, I welcome all these emotions openly, explicitly and tenderly. Tense shoulders begin to relax, heartbeats slow, breathing deepens, the flies that bothered now become part of the tapestry of sacred time-space we are weaving. As we come to the co-creation of music or story, there is a deepened flow of (re)connection between us; the sacred energy of life and the cosmos is here. Whatever emerges is "right", and has synchronicities that students positively remark about afterwards. This moment embodies other rhythms and enables us to enflesh both individual and collective sacred text.

Reflections

To make sense of this experience we turn to the pedagogy of discomfort, as it is a more obvious moment of disruption to the "normalized" time-spaces and affectivities that structure hegemonic learning. Rethinking (political) learning and the affective as collaboratively constructed, rather than repressed, is about revaluing the role of emotion and the embodied as generative epistemological dynamics and resources. It contests a politics of knowledge that renders these as only about the private or personal, and thus results in their epistemological and pedagogical devaluing (Boler, 1999; Darder, 2012). Learning in my practice is thus returned to the embodied, the time-space of the land and our bodies. Multiple emotions are fostered and explicitly embraced as meaningful to our learning experience, including discomfort, fear, relaxation, joy and connection. To enable such a moment of discomfort to become a pedagogical moment of opening involves the invisible tender nurturing of trust and the slow unraveling of hegemonic performances of passive student-consumer, which is overwhelming in the current university context (Motta, 2013).

These invisible labors gradually include introducing other rhythms into the formal classroom space. For example, embedding experiential learning in which we prefigure the kinds of Indigenous political practices we dialogue with in the course, such as participatory mapping of territories and fostering individual reflections on their relationship to the themes discussed, through the relative safety and protection of individual reflexive journals. Importantly, through the relatively short time of four years that I have coordinated the course and dwelled in Australia, I have learned that the settler colonial present is negated and repressed in everyday White consciousness, culture and subjectivity (Nakata, Nakata, Keech, & Bolt, 2012). As most of our students are white Australian, this means that the attempt to approach and broach the realities of this violent continuing present of settler colonialism often results in closure to engagement, which is expressed in the small numbers that take the course. A way to create this opening to engage with Indigenous struggles, politics and epistemology is to externalize this engagement through a focus on Indigenous peoples outside of Australia. This seems to sidestep the shame, silence and defensiveness that comes with stepping into internal terrains of coloniality/settler colonialism. Thus, the first part of the course explores struggles of Indigenous peoples in the Americas and connects this to a slow self-questioning about their perceptions of Australia's internal Others, its First Peoples.

There are other layers to be explored here, layers that can be grasped with the pedagogy of dignity. There is the pedagogical attempt to breach the very boundaries that separate this "imagined" Other from themselves. Indeed, the course materials attempt to show the inter-relationality of White knowing-subjectivity upon the negation and violence towards the feminized and racialized Other. The aim is not only to bring to light this ongoing reality to foster reflections on complicity. Rather, it is to open possibilities for un/relearning themselves through exploration of their darkened wisdoms. Such possibilities are embodied in encounters such as those at the sacred lake, in which they (re)turn to their body and that of the land in which they dwell.[5] My aim is to foster individual and collective consciousness that, as settler colonial subjects, we are all implicated in decolonization "because we are all products of a shared colonial history [and present], we are all [also] subjects of the enquiry" (Mackinlay & Barney, 2014, p. 56).

This opening has two intentions. The first is to foster recognition of the ways in which coloniality and settler colonialism wound them and their communities, as loss opposed to guilt or blame, and is thus a moment of deconstructive un-learning. The second is the opening of horizons to other political/epistemological possibilities. This is done through deep engagement with Indigenous cosmopolitics and knowledges to feel-think alternative possibilities for society, politics, self/other and wellbeing. Ultimately, these alternatives transgress the dualistic boundaries of the confines of coloniality that shape our knowing-being in and outside of the university.

This practice is an (im)possibility in the Western university. It is made ever more distant through neoliberal logics, rationalities and time-spaces. Situated within this (im)possibility results in distinct limits to this practice. Institutionally, audit culture values output, quantity and quantifiable measures of success. A small course that focuses on process as much as output, and develops multiple lenses through which to value meaning, can easily fall through the cracks of these measures, and become read as a failure and a drain on resources (Lynch, 2014). A one-semester course in a sea of relative unquestioned coloniality can also lead to the course being experienced by students, and recuperated institutionally, in a multicultural narrative. This leads to Indigenous issues being seen as side-issues, rather than as a challenge to the very logics and rationalities of what it means to know, who knows and how we know, as reproduced in the university and broader society.[6]

My intention is to expose the mystifications of the categories used to subjugate, separate and divide us into Knowing-Subjects and those that are known, as feminized and racialized Others. However, and those that are known, or feminized and racialized Others, it is understandable that in the time and resource precariousness that our students live with, their engagement will often be instrumental and partial. This reality, both as process of subjectification and experience of precarity, means that the kinds of intimacies, fragilities and vulnerabilities that I would like to foster can be experienced as alienating, unimportant and without value. Indeed, the process of unraveling of self and recognition of complicity and loss that the pedagogy foregrounds is a tall order expectation for a ten-week course! For my students, there is often a lack of ontological urgency to be recognized in the world, for many feel and have been represented as 'successful' subjects. Many students are 'first in family' to attend university. Their desire to succeed can be understood as 'success' within the terms of the political economy of the present (Bennett et al., 2017). The unsettlement and uprooting that is suggested through the pedagogical encounters of the course, without a broader decolonizing politics of knowledge in and outside of the University, remains an (im)possibility.

These reflections are not to suggest that the course is not transformative. Many students have shared how it has transformed the way they view the university, other courses, their society and selves. Such transformations should never be downplayed or devalued. They are the embodied moments of (im)possibility that maintain my desire, hope and dignity alive in this context. Furthermore, they suggest other pathways out of and beyond the West's onto-epistemological crisis. However, for these seeds of decolonizing and feminizing possibility to grow, they need the emergence and flourishing of decolonizing movements across borders in Australia and beyond.

Colombia: becoming wo(man)

In January 2016, The Centre for Gender, Women and Development, located in Univalle, Cali, Colombia, launched a master's in Gender, Popular Education and Development. Its uniqueness lies in its pedagogical foundations which combine popular, feminist and decolonial pedagogical philosophies, and thus embed contestation and transgression of the mind/body, university/community, education/life and personal/political violent dualisms of patriarchal capitalist coloniality. It is the only master's program of its kind in Colombia. The course lasts for two years. At the time of writing this chapter, the program drew a cohort of twenty-five students, educators, community organizers and activists – twenty-three women and two men. It was designed and coordinated by an academic-activist collective, all contract workers at the university, who are deeply linked to feminist struggles, experiences and movements in the region. This collective drew on their pedagogical expertise and experience to shape the course structure and content.

I was invited as a visiting professor on two occasions to participate in the first-run (2016–2018) of this master's program – the first time, to be the opening speaker with Professor Gaby Castellanos, the (then) head of the Centre, at the inauguration of the new program in January 2016; the second time, at the closing of the course in October 2017. At both, I gave a keynote address and then conducted a series of two-day workshops. The keynote addresses were not 'ordinary' keynote addresses, in that I intentionally spoke in multiple tongues, including opening with a ritual to our ancestors and the elements, and weaving poetry, analysis, narrative and myth into my shared words. The intention was to prefigure the enfleshing of sacred word, which would touch not only through the mind but deep into the heart and the soul. On the first occasion, I enfleshed my be-ing in word and into the world in a way I had not done previously in public. It was the taking of a liberating risk, one that I had prepared for through years of collective healing-emancipatory practices to rebuild my voice and believe in my right to be here and to speak. When I reflect on it now, it was very much as Gloria Anzaldúa describes in relation to the written word, in which she speaks of "chiselling herself into being" (1987, p. 22).

To become visible like this, to stand naked as a subject in her tender process of healing as emancipation, and to speak through traumas as fonts of my wisdom, I enacted the affectivities of a pedagogy of dignity. I embraced and opened to vulnerability, the complexities of my/our embodied life/lives and wisdom/s and enfleshed a process of becoming and epistemological recognition. This attempt to bridge to the other in compassionate and kind ways "models a process of self-disclosure that invites (and sometimes compels) us to take new risks as we reflect on our own experiences, penetrate the privacy of our own lives" (Anzaldúa, 2000, p. 2). This act of bridging was of an onto-epistemological kind, as much to myself as to the others present. It enfleshed our right to tenderness. The connections forged across the time-space of that encounter were thus less those of discomfort and more those of recognition. I felt a sigh of relief pass across the audience like a wave, as experiences were spoken, validated and resignified. Tears came, from me and from many in the audience. It was a time-space of radical decolonizing and sacred connection, which transgressed the traumatic encounters of hegemonic education and pedagogy in which we continue to be misnamed, misrecognized, vilified and denied.

The workshop spaces on both occasions prefigured the decolonizing and feminizing politics of knowledge and pedagogical practices outlined previously. Thus, they embraced multiple subjects of knowing, ways to know and knowledges, as well as nurtured my/our multiple tongues. It prefigured emancipatory pedagogy as onto-epistemological healing, and thus the days were woven around exploring and speaking from our darkened wisdoms, or those territories that have been rendered abject, absent and dangerous.

Here I will focus on elements of the second sets of workshops at the closing weekend of the master's program. We worked with the role of affect in our practices of knowledge construction and, more specifically, in relation to the action and participatory research thesis projects that each would finalize in the following six months. The workshops followed the following rhythm and the key steps outlined below, with many smaller steps of sacred encounter in between. These included practices of active listening, a shamanic meditation to meet a core emotion and receive its medicine and the writing of a collective poem to reflect on their experience of the two days.

Participants were invited to create a visual representation, or cartography of their emotions, in relation to thematic questions asked, such as: which emotions they had experienced in their practices of research, how these emotions had acted as a barrier to their desires and hopes and how they had facilitated their desires and hopes. They were then invited to write an autobiographical narrative of their cartography, putting their visual representation into textual form. Finally, participants worked in small groups and were invited to: (1) share their narratives and cartographies; (2) choose one narrative to work with; (3) reflect on this narrative in relation to the thematic questions and the theories and experiences they had journeyed with throughout the program; (4) rewrite the narrative with the new knowledge gained. Once these steps were taken, each group shared this new narrative, their reflections on this process of collaborative knowledge-creation and any other significant new knowledge they had created.

As the water system had broken down in the university for the first day, we moved to hold the workshop in the "house" of the feminist organization MAVI, which stands for "Fundación Mujer, Arte y Vida" (Foundation of Women, Art and Life).[7] This building has a history of over two decades working with cultures of feminist resistance and creation and feminist forms of social communication. It was as if were we literally being held in the arms of our foremothers, their struggles, their joys and creations.

By the time participants had created their individual cartographies of emotions on that first day, night had arrived. There was a slight breeze and the night sky was clear. We chose to end the day with a sharing circle in MAVI's outside courtyard. Participants were asked to share the most significant element of their cartography. They shared the poetics of their journeys of becoming, of recognition and of resignification of themselves and their possibilities. They also reflected on the new ways they were thinking-feeling about their practices, and how they were learning to recognize the key role of affect, in the creation of knowledge that is (self-)liberatory.

Cartography of emotions

I closed the circle with a shamanic journey of descent into our creative gardens of the womb-space to meet the emotion that wanted to speak with them and to share its medicine. A sacred silence of time-space connection, which had been nurtured throughout the day, deepened as we descended further into the territories of our darkened wisdoms. I embodied the priestess of the *encrucijadas*, in which our cultural work of writing, teaching or facilitating brings into be-ing the healing of which it speaks (Motta, 2013). Building on Gloria Anzaldúa's work, Ana Louise Keating describes this as a poet-shaman[ka] aesthetics in which:

> Words have causal force; words embody the world; words are matter; words become matter . . . in which words, images and things are intimately interwoven and the intentional ritualised performance of specific, carefully selected words shifts reality- poet-shaman[ka] aesthetics enables us to enact and concretise transformation.
>
> *(2012, p. 51)*

The moment we shared was a decolonizing encounter of shared healing and onto-epistemological possibility. It was a moment of becoming whole against and beyond the black hole of absence I/we had/have been shaped to be.

Reflections

This work was a labor of love, a poetic pedagogics of dignity. It nurtured our 'walking to our borders' and the co-creation of onto-epistemological possibilities, as well as our enfleshed becomings through exploration of our darkened wisdoms. Expressed through these words, without prior planning or conscious thought, is my enchantment with, and deep participation in, this process. In my writing-being experience, I do not stand outside even as I hold the space with tenderness, wisdom and feminine strength. In this sacred space-time there is a flow, there is mutual recognition, there is ease. I do not have to struggle to convince or to bring urgency to this space-time and these subjects. This is the reality and the onto-epistemological urgency that these students face every day. The rhythms and textures of the space are deep, satisfying and playfully rebellious. The terrain nurtures these pedagogical practices so that they grow, flourish and open into the unthought, the unseen, the unplanned. Trust comes to the heart of this pedagogical relationality, and trust and surrender into the process itself.

This ease is deepened by the reality that the students are activist scholars in movements and their communities. Most are educator-subjects researching the struggles they participate in and the processes of knowledge creation that they co-facilitate. Furthermore, this process of nurtured by the institutional terrain in which the master's sits; a feminist activist scholar collective, with decades of experience in developing multi-dimensional pedagogical practices of liberation, decolonization and emancipatory healing (Bermudez, 2013; Bermudez & Gutiérrez, 2016). These flows of decolonizing and feminizing pedagogies and politics of knowledge are already/always breaching the violent boundaries and borders of the Enlightenment University project. They are already/always subverting in body, mind and spirit those divisions. They involve the co-production of philosophy and social theory as existential be-ing/becoming.

Such a space-time of decolonizing and feminizing pedagogical possibility sits precariously in the contemporary neoliberal university. It has been pushed forward and struggled for by precarious workers. This means that it dwells on the edge between existence and eradication (at least within that space), with uncertainties about its continuation. The practices of mutual recognition and resignification, fostered through such a pedagogy of dignity and decolonizing and feminizing encounter, also runs the risk of reinforcing dualisms between us as 'others' and them as Subjects of/as Coloniality/Patriarchy. This potentially masks the ways in which we are co-constitutive of each other, and are all deeply mixed and internally multiple. It thus potentially evades encounter with, and recognition of, those elements of our being that occupy the space of privileged subjectivity and are complicit in the reproduction of these violent and hierarcichal binary relationships and ways of being-knowing. Yet such exploration of our complicities and internal-relational complexities can only really come after we have come into be-ing as knowing subjects, after we have rediscovered our voices and serpents' tongues. It is an ongoing process, one that flows beyond the formal university space, and will continue with or without institutional recognition.

Conclusion: decolonizing and feminizing pedagogies of dignity

I hope that these reflections on my/our decolonizing and feminizing pedagogical practices within the university across borders can contribute to our collective reflections as to how much, when and if "we" should remain within the confines of the Enlightenment University project as the West's crisis deepens.

The Australian experience foregrounds the centrality of engaging with Whiteness and hegemonic-subjectivities, and urges recognition that this is an essential element in our struggles for decolonization and emancipation otherwise. It suggests the (im)possibilities for co-creating encounters within the time-space of the classroom, which disrupt and unsettle coloniality as an everyday practice of being and knowing, which are able to nurture connections across the borders that separate us and fostering the embrace other cosmologies with which to face the (coming) crisis. The fragmentation of broader practices, communities and struggles of decolonization render such attempts as "cracks" in a broader landscape of increasing authoritarian neoliberalism. The lifeblood of such pedagogies comes when the political is pedagogized and the pedagogical politicized (Motta & Cole, 2014) in broader movements of decolonizing and feminizing liberation (Motta, 2018).

The Colombian experience demonstrates the kinds of deepening and nurturing decolonizing encounters that can be co-created when the fault lines of patriarchal heteronormative capitalist-coloniality are politicized. This creates a fertile terrain of enfleshed philosophies and decolonizing praxis into which decolonizing and feminizing pedagogies within the higher education space might contribute. However, the precarity and (im)possibility of such encounters with the university are also foregrounded as the monological violence of the neoliberal version of the enlightenment university (Motta, 2012) increasingly colonizes the geopolitics of knowledge and knowing-subjectivity from Australia to Colombia.

There is no ending to this pedagogical labor of decolonizing and feminizing liberatory love, for it supports our survival and opens pathways to our flourishing. We, as racialized and feminized others, are always/already shapeshifters who have had to contort ourselves to the hegemonic rhythms of thought and being to avoid social annihilation and epistemological death. Now, however, instead of shapeshifting to survive and acquiesce, we are shapeshifting to heal and open other possibilities of onto-epistemological becoming. We have realized the necessity to co-create our own ways of seeing-feeling and dialogical practices of epistemological recognition. We have learned through the pain of consistent misrecognition to let go of the desire to be seen by formal Institutionality and Power. We embrace the (im)possibility of a decolonizing and feminizing university and exist often undercover, as we choose to remain invisible and silent to Power. This does not mean that we are absent, or that we will cease to exist. Our lifeblood is other, and it is through the embrace of decolonizing and feminizing pedagogies that we can surrender into the darkened terrain which our ancestors gift us and the spiritual arms which hold us. Such a politics of knowledge nurtures our everyday tender determination and devotional dignity with which we "walk our talk" in the margins of the university time-space.

Un torrente de alegria fluye en el espacio
sanación
No somos maquinas, tenemos Corazón ...
Depender la alegria, organizar la Rabia
Gracias negra de mi vida por el ombigo que me diste
al nacer. Gracias por mi ombigo que no me deja caer.
REINVENCION
guía amorosa y libertaria para creer
Desnudar el espíritu y escuchar, amar, perder
renovar, aprender ...
con fragilidad e inocencia reencuentro
con mi derecho al amor
Me corté las alas y aprendí
                a nadar
buscamos nuevos caminos
Alegria, Respuestas, Sanación, Avances, entre lanzamientos
Gracias a la vida por este espacio
Más allá de la historia ...
Conspiramos para reencontrarnos con
lo que nos hace Feliz[8]

[A torrent of water flows in the space
healing
We are not machines, we have a Heart ...
Depend on joy; organize our Rage
Thank you, Negra of my life, for the ombligo that you gifted me
at my birth. Thank you for my ombligo that doesn't let me fall.
REINVENTION
loving and liberatory guide of creation
Strip down to the spirit, and listen, love, lose
renovate, learn ...
with fragility and innocence, I reconnect
with my right to love
I cut off my wings and learn
*   to swim*
we search for new paths

Joy, Answers, Healing, Advances, between attempts
Thank you to life for this space
Beyond the horizon of history
We conspire to reconnect
with what makes us Happy]

Notes

1 "Him" is used here to indicate reference to the Knowing-Subject who embodies/performs Whiteness and Hegemonic Masculinity. It does not indicate a biological or phenotypical reading of race or gender but is rather phenomenological. See Ahmed (2007) for further explication in relation to raced subjects.
2 See Mackinlay and Barney (2014) for reflections on the tensions in such work of combination and crossing.
3 See for example, Allen (1997, 2004), Leonardo (2002) and Motta (2012).
4 See de la Cadena (2012) for an introduction to Indigenous cosmopolitics, with reference to the Andes.
5 For sister embodied decolonizing pedagogies in the Australian context, see Mackinlay (2008).
6 See Nakata et al. (2012) for a similar critique of assimilation of decolonizing and indigenizing desires/practices/knowledges.
7 See www.fundacionmavi.org
8 This is a collective poem co-created during the master's workshop in Cali, Colombia, in October 2017.

References

Ahmed, S. (2007). The phenomenology of whitness. *Feminist Theory, 8*(2), 149–168.
Alexander, J. M. (2006). *Pedagogies of Crossing: Meditations on Feminism, Sexual Politics, Memory, and the Sacred.* Durham, NC: Duke University Press.
Allen, R. L. (2004). Whiteness and critical pedagogy. *Journal of Educational Philosophy and Theory, 36*(2), 121–136.
Anzaldúa, G. (1987). *Borderlands/La Frontera: The New Mestiza.* San Francisco, CA: Aunt Lute Books.
Anzaldúa, G. (2000). *Interviews/Entrevistas* (A. Keating, Ed.). New York: Routledge.
Bennett, A., Motta, S. C., Hamilton, E., Burgess, C., Relf, B., Gray, K. & Leroy-Dyer, S. (2017). *Conceptualising the Pedagogical Practices of Enabling at the University of Newcastle Australia,* University of Newcastle, Centre of Excellence for Equity in Higher Education. Callaghan, NSW: CEEHE.
Bermúdez, N. L. (2013). Cali's women in collective crossing for three worlds: popular education, feminisms and nonviolence for the expansion of the present, memory and for nurturing life. *Education and Social Change in Latin America,* 239–259.
Bermúdez, N. L., & Gutiérrez, J. T. (2016). *Liderazgos Sutiles: Historias de Re-Evoluciones Cotidianas de Mujeres Populares en la Comuna 18 de Cali, Colombia.* Cali, Colombia: Casa Cultural Tejiendo Sororidades.
Boler, M. (1999). *Feeling Power: Emotions and Education.* New York: Routledge.
Boler, M., & Zembylas, M. (2003). Discomforting truths: the emotional terrain of understanding difference. In P. P. Trifonas (Ed.), *Pedagogies of Difference: Rethinking Education for Social Change* (pp. 107–130). New York: Routledge.

Byrd, R. P., Cole, J. B. & Guy-Sheftall, B. (Eds.). (2009). *I am Your Sister: Collected and Unpublished Writings of Audre Lorde*. Oxford: Oxford University Press.

Cadena, de la, M. (2010). Indigenous cosmopolitics in the Andes: conceptual reflections beyond politics. *Cultural Anthropology, 25*(2), 334–370.

Darder, A. (2012). Schooling bodies: critical pedagogy and urban youth. *Fine Print: A Journal of Adult English Language and Literacy Education, 35*(2), 3–10.

Darder, A. (2015). *Freire and Education*. New York: Routledge.

Dillard, C. B. (2016). We are still here: declarations of love and sovereignty in black life under siege. *Journal of Educational Studies, 52*(3), 201–215.

Duran, E., Firehammer, J. & Gonzalez, J. (2008). Liberation psychology as the path toward healing cultural soul wounds. *Journal of Counseling & Development, 86*, 288–295.

Fanon, F. (1961). *The Wretched of the Earth* (C. Farrington, Trans.). London: Penguin Books.

Freire, P. (2012). *Pedagogy of the Oppressed*. (M. B. Ramos, Trans.). New York: Penguin Bloomsbury.

Freire, P. (2014). *Pedagogy of Hope: Reliving Pedagogy of the Oppressed*. (R. R. Barr, Trans.) London: Bloomsbury Academic.

Hill Collins, P. (2000). *Black Feminist Thought: Knowledge, Consciousness, and the Politics of Empowerment*, 2nd ed. New York: Routledge.

hooks, b. (1990). *Yearning: Race, Gender, and Cultural Politics*. Boston, MA: South End Press.

Keating, A. (2012). Speculative realism, visionary pragmatism, and poet-shamanic aesthetics in Gloria Anzaldúa—and beyond. *WSQ: Women's Studies Quarterly, 40*(3–4), 51–69.

Leonardo, Z. (2002). The souls of white folk: critical pedagogy, whiteness studies, and globalization discourse. *Journal of Race, Ethnicity, and Education, 5*(1), 29–50.

Lorde, A. (1983). The master's tools will ever dismantle the master's house. In C. Moraga & G. Anzaldúa (Eds.), *This Bridge Called My Back: Writings by Radical Women of Color* (pp. 94–101). New York: Kitchen Table Press.

Lorde, A. (1984). *Sister Outsider: Speeches and Essays*. Berkeley, CA: Crossing Press.

Lugones, M. (2010). Toward a decolonial feminism. *Hypatia: A Journal of Feminist Philosophy, 25*(4), 742–759.

Lynch, K. (2014). Control by numbers: new managerialism and ranking in higher education. *Critical Studies in Education, 56*(2), 190–207.

Mackinlay, E. (2008). Making space as white music educators for Indigenous Australian holders of song, dance and performance knowledge: the centrality of relationship as pedagogy. *Australian Journal of Music Education, 1*, 2–6.

Mackinlay, E. & Barney, K. (2014). Unknown and unknowing possibilities: transformative learning, social justice, and decolonising pedagogy in Indigenous Australian Studies. *Journal of Transformative Education, 12*(1), 54–73.

Morales, A. L. (1998). *Medicine Stories: History, Culture and the Politics of Integrity*. Boston, MA: South End Press.

Motta, S. C. (2012). Teaching global and social justice as transgressive spaces of possibility. *Antipode: A Radical Journal of Geography, 45*(1), 80–100.

Motta, S. C. (2013). Pedagogies of possibility: in, against and beyond the Imperial patriarchal subjectives of higher education. In S. Cowden & G. Singh (Eds.), *Acts of Knowing: Critical Pedagogy in, Against and Beyond the University* (pp. 85–124). London: Bloomsbury Academic.

Motta, S. C. (2016). Decolonizing Australia's body politics: contesting the coloniality of violence of child removal. *Journal of Resistance, 2*(2), 100–133.

Motta, S. C. (2017). Latin America as political science's other. *Social Identities: Journal for the Study of Race, Nation and Culture, 23*(6), 701–717.

Motta, S. C. (2018). *Liminal Subjects: Weaving (Our) Liberation*. Lanham, MD: Rowman and Littlefield.

Motta, S. C. & Bennett, A. (2018). Challenging toxic masculinities: pedagogies of care in nabling education. *Teaching in Higher Education*.

Motta, S. C. & Cole, M. (2014). *Constructing 21st Century Socialism in Latin America: The Role of Radical Education*. London & New York: Palgrave Macmillan.

Motta, S. C. & Seppälä, T. (2016). Feminized resistance. *Journal of Resistance Studies*, *2*(2), 1–28.

Motta, S. C. & Todorova, T. (2013). *Priestesses of the Encrucijada/Crossroads*, August 20, 2013, retrieved 16 December 16, 2017, from www.newleftproject.org/index.php/site/article_comments/priestesses_of_the_encrucijada_crossroads

Nakata, M. N., Nakata, V., Keech, S. & Bolt, R. (2012). Decolonial goals and pedagogies for Indigenous Studies. *Decolonization: Indigeneity, Education & Society*, *1*(1), 120–140.

Pereira, M. (2012). Uncomfortable classrooms: rethinking the role of student discomfort in feminist teaching. *European Journal of Women's Studies*, *19*(1), 128–135.

Rama, A. (1996). *The Lettered City* (J. C. Chasteen, Trans.) Durham, NC: Duke University Press.

Zembylas, M. (2015). "Pedagogy of discomfort" and its ethical implications: the tensions of ethical violence in social justice education. *Journal of Ethics and Education*, *10*(2), 163–174.

4

UNDOING COLONIAL PATRIARCHIES

Life and struggle pathways[1]

Xochitl Leyva Solano

Introduction

This chapter deals with our *sentipensar* – sensingthinking – doings that I have called in academic grammar "other knowledges practices."[2] They have allowed us many things, but for the purposes of this chapter and this book I will say that they have allowed us to continue cracking the dualist structuring opposition inherent in Western philosophy that opposes pure theory to the passive state of matter or corporeity.

With these doings, we have sought to decolonize and depatriarchalize our bodies, minds, hearts and 'lived lives' – forgive this redundancy – and not only academia and the social sciences. These are doings/practices carried out in political-epistemic communities created *ex profeso* by ourselves[3] under contexts of war. Sensingthinking doings are one form of defending life. I stress this in a time when humanity is facing multiple violences: strife and epistemic war take new forms. Even in many spaces of formal education "the ecology of knowledges", "decolonial feminism", "the epistemologies of the South", "co-laborative research", "decolonial pedagogies", "the modernity/coloniality turn", "the coloniality of gender" and other insurgent epistemologies and methodologies are gaining visibility and legitimacy – but at the cost of becoming, for many, a fashion, in slogans, in consumer objects, which recreates comfort zones and politically correct discourses that do not disturb, in any depth or significant form, systemic ways of being and been in the world. Paradoxically, at the same time, these analytical perspectives are contributing to decolonize the university, academia and social sciences.

In my experience, one way in which I have tried to avoid falling into this has been through embodying a political, practical and ethical dimension of my/our theoretical and systemic approaches. As the coordinator of the University of the

Earth in Chiapas, Mexico, Raymundo Sánchez Barraza, affirms: "we are what we do". This is why I would like to frame this text with a fragment of a Colombian *vallenato*,[4] as an expression of popular knowledge that emphasizes how difficult the pathways of life are for ordinary people; 'Los caminos de la vida / no son lo que yo pensaba . . . Los caminos de la vida / son muy difícil de andarlos'. This translates as 'The ways of life, they are not what I thought . . . The ways of life, they are very difficult to walk'.[5] It is not by chance that we are common people, myself and many of the women I am going to refer in this text and with whom I have woven political-academic-activist networks. How difficult, I would add, it is to walk both, decolonization and depatriarchalization, as a way of life!

This chapter is about what I/we have done to (un)learn, share, enjoy, but also suffered to build other possible worlds with women and men *from below and to the left*,[6] with community communicators, Mayan artists, young alter and anti-globalization activists and postcolonial[7] and decolonial[8] feminists from different parts of planet Earth who arrived in Chiapas (Mexico) between 1994 and 2017, attracted by the Zapatistas and with whom I/we worked both, politically and in academia. Many outputs resulted from our meetings, disagreements, dialogues, tensions, which are printed as documents, produced as DVDs and/or can be accessed in cyberspace.[9] What I am trying to do in this text is to weave together some bits of these experiences in order to rethink them out loud and against the light of the present, hoping that this chapter and the book of which it is part will become an input for our collective (un)learning spaces where we are seeking some ways out from violence, domination and oppression.

Audiovisual languages, multiple oppressions, decolonial and depatriarchalized doings

> Imagine this scene: two women are sitting on a bus bound for Quibdó. One of them begins to tell the other that years ago she was raped. Maintaining a quite disturbing tranquility (as if it were a simple gossip), she tells her that the man in question is now her husband and the father of her three children. Two seats back, unable to believe what he hears, is Jhonny Hendrix.
>
> Just when he thought the conversation could not be more disturbing, one of the women tells the other that the man she describes is also *her* husband. Very quiet, Jhonny waits for them to insult each other or at least stop talking. To his surprise, the two women continue in their chat as if nothing. "Am I the only one who thinks it's amazing what just happened?" he asked as he watched the rest of the passengers remain silent looking out the windows.
>
> It was at that moment that he understood: these two women are not the only ones sharing this story and that was a reason enough to . . . make a movie . . . This is how *Chocó* was born, the first Afro film made in Colombia . . . The film tells the story of Chocó, a 20-year-old *mazamorrera*, a displaced

woman, who has to support her two children and her husband, who only knows how to play marimba, play dominoes and drink biche. Her *via crucis* begins when her eldest daughter asks for a birthday cake and she has to do the unthinkable to achieve it.[10]

I came to know about this film released in 2012, thanks to the videography I was provided with as a trainee on one of the virtual graduate courses taught by colleagues and compañeras[11] of the grupo latinoamericano de Estudio, Formación y Acción Feminista (GLEFAS; the Latin American Study, Training and Feminist Action Group).[12] *Chocó* was directed by Afro-Colombian film-maker Jhonny Hendrix Hinestroza and was performed by women and men from the community of Chocó region, Colombia. The first thing that caught our attention, in a positive way, was the time of the cinematographic composition: the history does justice to the times of the black, indigenous and rural communities. From the beginning, this introduces us to another world – a world that goes beyond "magical realism" à la García Márquez and that we could call the "tragic-magical realism" of daily struggle and resistance of black, indigenous, "poor" women of the countryside or the city. In one scene, we were surprised by the way that Chocó is beaten and the rest of the town is left unmoved, seeing her but without supporting her. It is the complicit silence that hurts more than the blows. It is as if one would like to hear Chocó saying "Ain't I a woman?" like the nineteenth-century black abolitionist Sojourner Truth (1851) by demanding their rights, permanently denied.

Throughout different cinematographic scenes, the multiple oppressions that hit Chocó are present, but the agency and the power of women also occupies an important place in the screen. They understood and inhabited their bodies as weapons of struggle that they possess. Even in the most adverse conditions, they get up, and in their own way they rebel and say, "*¡Ya Basta!*" ("Enough!") to the multiple oppressions to which they are subjected. The scene with which the film closes moves in that direction and is as shocking as it is powerful.

Chocó, who is reduced by the violence of the husband to a vagina that contains him, cuts with her teeth the genitals of the violent husband and sets fire to the hut with him inside. Someone could argue that the scene is a call to a Fanonian-type violence, but at the same time it is a possible way for the protagonist to be freed from the multiple and simultaneous oppressions that are shown in detail in her everyday life: the exploitation due to the open-pit mine; the persistent violence of the shopkeeper (who prostitutes her), of the drunken and violent husband and of the protective-controller-caretaker son. Chocó also has to face the violence generated by other women, who use gossip and troublemaking to access a shared object: the genitals of local men. Men – who, together with women, children, elders are the impoverished communities, displaced by the Colombian narco-war – are reduced to supplying gold to mining companies that destroy the life of Mother Earth, human, animate and inanimate beings that inhabit her.

The parallelism drawn by the film director between the Chocó region and the protagonist, whom he also names 'Chocó', is not accidental. Chocó-beautiful Mother Earth, grandiose land assaulted by mining that contaminates, destroys and mistreats her. Chocó-women in the middle of that exuberance are assaulted, raped, beaten again and again. But neither one nor the other give up. Mother Earth can burp at any moment, shake, expand her veins and overflow her rivers. Chocó-*mujer* (woman) was able to use her body as a liberation weapon. That scene reminded me of what the black feminist bell hooks has told us again and again:

> They do not understand, they cannot even imagine, that black women, as well as other groups of women who live every day in oppressive conditions, often become aware of patriarchal politics from their lived experience, as they develop strategies of resistance – even if it does not occur in a sustained or organized way.
>
> *(2004, p. 45)*

I also remembered the words of Maya Kaqchikel feminist Aura Cumes (2015), who affirms that through everyday practices of resistance – and not only through mobilizations, collective rebellions or revolts – Mayan women, since the early years of what the conquerors called the General Captaincy of Guatemala, endured or faced violence, exploitation and expropriation caused by colonial and patriarchal life.

There was one scene in the film that particularly caught my attention, perhaps due to the lineage of strong Oaxacan, Mixtec, black and mestizo women I come from – the power of Chocó-*mujer*. "Power" understood as potency, as capacity of doing things. Power that allowed her to escape a reduced understanding of "power" as "control" and absolute "dominion". This subtle epistemic difference between one and another power did not come from any famous and renowned author legitimized by the academy. Instead, it came to my body and my mind as part of the reflections that we have built up within the *neozapatista* network[13] and after seeing how the Zapatistas build their autonomy step by step, as their right and without asking permission to anybody.

This idea of power came to me when, in the middle of building the Zapatista "Other Campaign"[14] at the University of the Earth in Chiapas, we collectively read the dialogues between scholar/activists Majid Rahnema (Iran) and Jean Robert (Belgium). It was at that moment and in that context of collective unlearning that I realized how engulfed we are by Western definitions of power. It was through the two referred authors talking as equals with Illich, Spinoza, Gandhi, Foucault and Deleuze, the Zapatistas, Sem Terra Movement and Janadesh Indian movement, and many more, that I returned to the Latin verbal root of *power:* to be able, to be possible.[15]

Rahnema and Robert had invited us to think about what they call "the power of the poor". "Poor" understood not as the World Bank understand them, but as a simple and convivial way of life of relative dignity. "Poor" denigrated and fought by the modern economy. "Power" understood as that indestructible force that every human being has and that has nothing to do with money or social position. Rahnema and Robert tell us that what everyone – as a society – loses each time a human being is diminished in its potential strength is the possibility of "bringing more happiness and beauty to the world that is common to us" (2011 [2008], p. 16).

From a different angle, but in a similar vein, *Chocó* made me think about what the German feminist Claudia von Werlhof shared with us in the seminar "Weaving Voices for the Common House", held in Mexico Ciy in November 2015, when she mentioned that women and nature have in common that they are creators of life, while pointing out that patriarchy not only attacks women but Mother Earth – that is, the planet as such. In that sense patriarchy is "a system, a culture, a way of life, which is defined by a hatred of life. It is the hatred of life. Each patriarchy, patriarchal man or patriarchal woman, hates life",[16] and in doing so "it harms us all, enemies and friends" (Werlhof, 2015 [2010], p. 31).

Let us now get to know and reflect on some aspects of the collective doings that I/we have embarked when walking under the Zapatista lighthouse, thanks to the construction of two transnational networks: the Other Knowledges Trasnational Network (RETOS)[17] and the Network of Mayan Artists, Community Communicators and Anthropologists of Chiapas (RACCACH).[18] For the purposes of this chapter, I will only refer to specific aspects of some particular activities of each network. In RACCACH I will refer to our creative process of the book and interactive website called *Sjalel kibeltik. Sts'isjel ja kechtiki', Tejiendo nuestras raices, Weaving Our Roots* (Köhler et al., 2010). I will connect this with the work and the book of the North American lesbo-feminist women's movement, published 22 years before, called *This Bridge Called My Back: Voices of Third World Women in the United States* (Moraga & Castillo, 1988).

Weaving Our Roots/*Tejiendo nuestras raíces* (Sjalel kibletik): walking our descolonization under the Zapatista lighthouse

Between 2007 and 2008, the communiqués of the Zapatista Good Government Juntas affirmed that in Chiapas there was once again an escalation of violence, characterized by dispossession and eviction from the lands previously recovered by the Zapatistas, in the form of poisoning springs as well as burning cornfields, coffee plantations, houses and Zapatista educational centers. These violent actions were conducted by non-Zapatista settlers and instigated by local commissioners, municipal presidents, representatives of political parties, caciques, members of former peasant organizations and indigenous brothers accused of being "paramilitaries" in collusion with elements of the state police, the Mexican Army and the Federal Investigation Agency (AFI). These four forces also violently raided houses belonging to Zapatista support grassroots, threatened women and children with death, stole their belongings, arbitrarily detained them, beat them or kidnaped them.

At the same time, due to our work with young people from the highlands of Chiapas, we knew about the increase in suicides among young Mayas. In 2013, the

National Institute of Psychiatry statistics showed a 74 percent increase in suicides of 15- to 24-year-olds in Mexico between 1990 and 2011 (Jiménez & Cardiel, 2013, p. 217). From a detailed study by Imberton (2014), it is known that, from 1985 to 2005, suicides among the indigenous in Chiapas reached unimaginable rates in certain rural locations (Imberton, 2014). In 2008, in San Cristóbal de Las Casas it was common to hear that this was due to the use and abuse of alcohol and drugs. Drugs are more and more present in the indigenous and rural localities, as well as in the cities. The exception is the Zapatista territories, where the consumption of both alcohol and drugs is forbidden by decree.

Within this context, we met in the (then) most important cultural center, which had been created as a form of political convergence with the Zapatista communities in resistance. This cultural center was located in the heart of the colonial city now called San Cristóbal de Las Casas. This city was founded in 1528 as Villa Real by the Spanish conquistador Diego de Mazariegos. As a colonial city, free transit of the Indians was forbidden for centuries. At the dawn of the twenty-first century, with dignified Zapatista rage, that colonial space was occupied by young Mayan indigenous women and men, as well as neo-Zapatista network members.

In that center/heart, we celebrated our first meeting. It was not an academic meeting, but a political-cultural meeting of seven young Mayas, a Mexican mestiza (myself), a Japanese woman and a German man. Of the ten, eight were men, and two were women. We set ourselves up as an autonomous creative work space, and we named it RACCACH, which operated through plenary sessions, assemblies, agreements and consensus. It was through this way of work that we agreed the following:

> 1) to contribute to transmit the seeds of respect and appreciation for all knowledges, arts and forms of communication, as well as creating a positive awareness of diversity. . . 4) to promote a struggle for our art, our organizations and communities . . . 6) to promote unity to fight discrimination against indigenous people . . . 10) to contribute to raise the councisouess of children and young indigenous people in communities against of taking "easy" paths (for example, alcohol and drugs abuse, suicide).
> *(RACCACH Minutes 09/02/2008, cited in Köhler et al., 2010, p. 266)*

Among the members of RACCACH, one is a peasant, three shared writing as their daily work, while others produce visual images (painting, videos, photography) or create music. Our sharing was not about each one doing what he/she already knew. Instead, our challenge was to share with one another our own knowledges, so that someone else could create something that she/he normally does not do. Thus, for example, the painter wrote lyrics and produced audios, the musician and the videographer wrote, the anthropologist post-produced audios and armed his messages with music and with photos, not just with lyrics. In the act of working together, in the dialogue as equals, questions were raised for each other, and dialogues emerged – questions and dialogues that many times allowed us to unlock not only writings (for example, by the artist-communicator), but life issues. Our harvest was a creation of a network that worked for three years and that connected us in a human level, beyond time and work. At the same time, we gave birth to an audiobook that included radio programs, paintings and photos, as well as texts written by each one of us, in three Mayan languages and in Spanish. All this became available in an interactive website.[19]

Our enormous undertaking required 21 months of work in which the ten people involved conducted an intrapersonal reflection in dialogues of "creative couples" and in assemblies. It was a self-sustained work whose driving force was our own human energy and that of the political struggle that encouraged us. Without any funding, we work as political movements do: everyone contributes his/her time, knowledge and creativity to advance the shared cause. The mere existence of this way of working challenged the logic of the academic projects in which I had previously participated – I have been a teacher and researcher since 1991 in the Research Center of Higher Studies of Social Anthropology (CIESAS).[20] Projects usually only exist if they have an initial *ex profeso* funding and one person thinks up and writes them. That person (called the "responsible" for the project) normally defines a priori the steps that each and every one has to follow, as well as the times and results to be obtained. Many of these projects are bounded to disciplinary fields and expressed in academic jargon and are to be consumed by a group of people already knowledgeable in those fields.

Although *Sjalel kibeltik* was not born in the academic field, academia has had an effect on it: as several of us have attended the university, while others are professors or active students. *Sjalel kibeltik* openly challenged the academic grammar that continues to speak of "producing knowledge". This grammar structures the jargon of "academic capitalism" that continues to see knowledge as part of a chain of production where "knowledges" are produced, distributed and consumed first and foremost for the reproduction of the academic machinery and then for profit of various industries. In this mode of production, the motor is knowledge understood as a commodity that is bought and sold (with salaries, scholarships, etc.), while, in the Zapatista mode, in the *Sjalel kibeltik* mode and in that of many other people, collectives, organizations and movements anti and alter globalization that I don't have a chance to mention here, the engine is human creativity. This is in direct opposition to the productivity evaluated with the global market of knowledge indicators such as quality, excellence, efficiency and productivity indexes.

All that I have narrated so far cannot be fully understood if I do not mention that, in June 2005 before starting *Sjalel kibeltik* work, the Clandestine Revolutionary Indigenous Committee-General Command of the EZLN in the Sixth Declaration of Lacandona Jungle, had made a call for unity in each of the places where people were living and fighting. All this happened at the time of presidential elections in Mexico. In this context the Sixth Declaration was an invitation to build up other kind of politics beyond the state and representative democracy. Zapatista told us:

what we think is that, with these people and leftist organizations, we make a plan to go to all parts of Mexico where there are humble and simple people like us.

And it's not that we're going to tell or order you or them what to do.

Neither are we going to ask them to vote for a candidate, as we already know that there are neoliberal ones.

Nor is it that we are going to tell them to do the same we do, or to rise up in arms.

What we are going to do is to ask you and them what their life is like. Your struggle, your thoughts of how is our country and how we can do it for not been defeated.

What we are going to do is to take the thinking of simple and humble people and maybe we will find the same love that we feel for our country.

And maybe we will find an agreement between those of us who are simple and humble and, together, we organize ourselves throughout the country and we agree on our struggles that are now isolated, separated from each other, and we find something like a program that has the same that we all want, and a plan of how we are going to get this program, which is called "national program of struggle", to be fulfilled.

(CCRIC-CG of the EZLN, 2005, p. 16; author's italics)

The truth is that I do not know how humble and simple we were, we the ten that work in the RACCACH, but now, seen from a distance, what we were doing was far from the conventional or dominant academy but also far from the conventional canons of doing politics. At the same time, it was highly political, insofar as it was decolonizing. In fact, our work could also be seen as a way of walking "the other politics" that emerges from the meeting of the diverse who rebel against the established norm and create their own rules in autonomy (*auto*: self; *nomos*: rules). We were *de facto* promoting what the Zapatistas today call "the anti-capitalist seedbeds", where the exchange currencies are reciprocity, solidarity and autonomy.

Walking my/our depatriarchalization at the lighthouse of a wix *(big sister in Tseltal):* **This Bridge Called My Back . . .**

Four years later, I came across with our *wix* (older sister), *This Bridge Called My Back: Writings by Radical Women of Color in the United States.* To understand why I call this work our *wix*, I recall their collaborative work and the letter that was written in 1980, by Chicana lesbian feminist Gloria Anzaldúa.[21] In her letter, Gloria addresses women of color, feminists from the United States and the world, and wonders why it is so unnatural to write, why her voice, her languages and cultures are invisible to white men and white feminists of her country. Anzaldúa wonders who she is and where she comes from. She answers herself with irony, "Am I a poor country girl?" And she adds that she has mastered written English and dared to write to disperse impotence, to confront her own demons, to keep her spirit of rebellion alive even against herself. Anzaldúa acknowledges that, in the late 1970s, the writings and makings of lesbian feminist women of color were perceived as dangerous, but affirmed that in this very act she found "her survival because a woman who writes has power" and – she added – "a woman of power is feared".[22] The meaning of this was nothing less than confronting the "Patriarchal White America".[23] Gloria closes her letter with an invitation to join her in her struggle and she tells her pen partners the following:

> *Busca la musa dentro de ti misma.*
> *La voz que se encuentra enterrada debajo de ti, desentiérrala.*
> *No seas falsa con ella. Ni trates de venderla por un aplauso,*
> *ni para que se publique tu nombre.*

> [Find the muse within yourself.
> The voice that is buried under you, *desentiérrala*.
> Do not be false with her. Do not try to sell it for applause,
> nor for your name to be published.]
> *(Anzaldúa, 1988a, p. 227)*

In 2012, I was inspired by Gloria and the feminist self-named "women of color", by their political and epistemic struggle. In fact, I wrote a text to the members of another epistemic-political community that I had promoted and of which I was a part: the International Virtual Seminar "Creating Practices of Knowledge from the Gender, Movements and Networks". This was a virtual space, that lasted for three years, in which 13 activists and feminist researchers from the Americas and Europe, met monthly and shared our activist experiences and academic knowledge in order to build up political alliances, emotional support and common academic debates.[24] I transcribe below part of my reflections written at that time and in that context, as a way to contribute to the visibility and the weaving of our de(colonizing)depatriarchalization struggles that have occurred in different times and spaces. This text acquires a new dimension as it interweaves with the ideas and practices of this book's editors and collaborators.

May 3, 2012: on this Holy Cross day . . .

. . . I see from my window El Huitepec, the sacred hill of the Mayan inhabitants of the Jobel Valley (Chiapas, Mexico). I take my pen and as a starting point *This Bridge called my Back* . . . There are several reasons for this, which now I share with you:

First, I had a basic realization, literally felt on the surface of my skin, as both authors of that book and myself, we all fit in the category of "women of color" and in the "mestiza" for some of them and me.

Second, like the authors of that pioneering work, we the authors of the book *Sjalel kibeltik* trusted in returning to our roots as a radical political act from where we could build change, transformation of the world, starting with ourselves.

We started by recognizing ourselves as who we are "with all our integrity, as beautiful and full as we see ourselves naked in our bedrooms", as pointed out by lesbian feminist-socialist writer Merle Woo in the 1980s. Or, as the Zinacanteco rock pioneer Damián Guadalupe Martínez Martínez[25] said in 2008, "undressing us" to approach the world with our own flavors, pains and colors.

Third, I share with those women of color the same social class: we are women from below who ascended socially via the university to a status that allowed us to acquire our own voice, a command of writing and its concomitant power.

Fourth, these women of color (Latinas, Chicanas, blacks and Asian-American feminists, mostly lesbians), like us in the RACCACH, wrote and struggled taking as point of departure the crossroad formed by their art, politics, culture and roots.

Fifth, *Sjalel kibeltik* as a collective process of creation allowed us to continue cracking the walls of the disciplinary prisons where we felt imprisoned. And I do not mean only those of the social sciences; this same feeling was shared by musicians and painters of the RACCACH after they attended the painting academy and the university of sciences and arts. In my case, this sense of disciplinary prison persisted even if I practiced inter- and transdisciplinarity. I was not able to even imagine that one can live beyond disciplines. This I learned when I became an active participant of the University of the Earth in Chiapas.

May 5, 2012: oppressed by ourselves and others

The path walked by the authors of *This Bridge Called My Back* . . . invites us to "untie the knot" of the forces that have formed us, just like the Puerto Rican-Californian feminist writer Aurora Levins Morales[26] says. She invites us to reconsider the way we have been "placed within psychological imprisonment camps" by "unnatural disasters", as the feminist Asian-American writer Mitsuye Yamada[27] calls them. They invite us to visualize, recognize and affirm ourselves as women of a certain color, rising in particular times and spaces. *Encampadas* in the streets, in the fields of agricultural crops (the field), in the plains, in the neighborhoods, in the Indian reservations. Imprisoned us, where? They invite us to review how we have internalized our own oppression, how we have oppressed, how we have internalized classism, racism and (hetero)sexism and how we have become oppressed by ourselves and others.[28] They invite us to touch our wounds, to see the nightmare within ourselves but also to recognize that we need one another to have joy in our lives and to overcome our fears.[29] They invite us to take responsibility for our own racism, (hetero)sexisms and classisms. To leave our "limited views" and awaken among us the "atrophied potentialities". Once again, power as potency was before my eyes.

As a way to close

I have taken a Vallenato song, the first Afro-Colombian fiction film and lesbian women of color Gloria Anzaldúa's letter as my starting points because, as my own and collective experiences have shown me, these are fundamental to delineate the paths that we walk in life, in academia, in politics, etc. The starting points that we select have a strong imprint that is not only symbolic but also concrete and practical in what we do, think and feel and, above all, in how we do it, think and feel it. The starting points intersect with the place of enunciation, but cannot be reduced to it.

I started this chapter with making use of languages used in the arts because, as it can be seen in the body of this text and in the materials cited in the end-notes, they have allowed me/us to free ourselves from the tyranny of academic writing, so common in the temples of knowledge of university students, activists, feminism and other "isms". What I am saying here took me/us more than two decades to actually live it and through it to (un)learn it. It was neither theoretical nor academic readings that led me to this conclusion – they certainly helped – but the creative and political work alongside Zapatista fighters, anti-capitalist glocal activated[30] people, indigenous video-makers, community communicators, Mayan artists and feminists who work in the margins.

With all of this I do not mean that all writing is despicable and that we should stop writing. It would be arrogant to declare this as an absolute thought, and contradic-tory to say it and at the same time to be writing this text. What I want to say is that the audiovisual, arts and creative languages that we and the feminist sisters of color cited here have explored, have allowed us to go beyond the normative, of what is allowed and legitimated, all central elements of colonialities and colonizations. These languages and authors have helped us to expand our political imaginary and practices and have allowed us to see beyond wars and the civilizatory crisis in which we find ourselves trapped with all the inhabitants of planet Earth. In this 'networked society and information age' – as the Catalan Manuel Castells called it in which we live, these languages have allowed many to undertake de(colonizing)patriarchalizing tasks (note the active and procedural tone of this long word). As I have shared, we are trying not only to (un)learn, but also to better connect or reconnect with the people we come from, and with whom we politically converge, to build ourselves here and now the other possible worlds beyond capitalism, the State, representative democracy and what at the end of the 1990s North Atlantic colleagues called academic capitalism.[31]

Early on, the 1977 Combahee River Collective Declaration by black lesbian feminists affirmed that the most profound and radical policy comes from our own identity. As black lesbian feminist poet Audre Lorde said: "From the knowledge of the genuine conditions of our life we have to draw the strength to live and the reason to act." [32] And this is what I consider the authors of *This Bridge Called My Back* were doing, each of the 30 authors of that collaborative piece of work, who in a clear, simple but profound and creative way introduced to us their roots, wounds and concrete forms in which the oppressions due to our race, class and gender-sex-sexuality are experienced.

Sjalel kibeltik and *This Bridge Called My Back* opposed the universal, rigid and cold theory of conventional or dominant social sciences, which we might call in an antagonistic tone "without flesh" – that is, the ones that claim to be "neutral" and "objective" and that have no "emotional cover that is felt in the heart",[33] those which do not merge our personal experience and our perspective of the world with the social reality in which we live, those which prevent us touching the enemy that we all carry inside ourselves because, by doing this, we would touch our own privileges, as the Chicana feminist, poet, editor and dramatist Cherríe Moraga pointed out.[34]

The authors of *This Bridge Called My Back* and *Sjalel kibeltik* have showed us with their/our practice and writing outside the academy, and beyond the conventional academic grammar, that we also created theory and not just a collection of texts and images ready to be swallowed by the book industry or by academic capitalism. From these collective doings emanated what the authors of *This Bridge Called My Back* early on called "embodied theory", which tacitly opposes conventional ideas on theory as what "illuminates" practice.

Since the end of the 1970s and until today, the dawn of the 21st century, rivers of ink have run and embodied doings have been incorporated into movements, feminisms and academia. Many of these have questioned the dominant notion of disembodied theory, which is reduced to an essentially human activity of thinking as rational, universal and masculine. In other words, a reduced thinking subject has been questioned, his "abstract masculinity" versus the too corporeal and feminized other: women, ethnic others, children, non-humans, matter itself.[35] Critique has also come strongly from theorists of new feminist materialism, post-structuralist and feminist materialists as well as feminist thinkers and poetesses, theorists of sexual difference and nomadism,[36] subaltern studies, post and decolonial feminists as well as from us, barefoot feminists. But above all these critiques have come in non-academic grammars, from the members of the alter and anti-globalization resistance.[37] But today, the questions 'What is theory?' and 'What does it mean to think?' – which are as old as Western rationality dualisms, the notion of polis and science and academia – have shifted in certain academic spaces in which the terms of the dialogue have changed and the questions are rather 'How does theorymatter?' and 'How do academic theorizing and research in the social sciences become tools not only to know the world and transform it [note the abstract masculinity lexicon], but to build by ourselves from below, the other possible worlds to face the current systemic and civilizational crisis?'[38]

Before reading *This Bridge Called My Back*, *yosotras* (I/we) had already begun to make ethical-epistemological-political-methodological[39] reflections, not from within the academy, nor from within feminisms, but in the midst of war in the heat of the 1994 Zapatista armed uprising. This struggle opened an ethical-political-epistemic dimension never before seen in Chiapas that has become very important glocally. To this we must add the many legacies we received from indigenous, Afro-descendant, popular, lesbo (trans) feminist, queer women resistances in Abya Yala and across the oceans. All this has helped me to visualize and name the different oppressions, dominations, violence, but also the joys that arise from the intersection of our race, class, sex–sexuality, gender, status, ethnicity, nationality and generational belonging. It has helped me to reflect on how we live these crosses inside our bodies and outside of them, when we have to be at the same time researchers, students, professors, university students, colleagues, artists, militants, activists, adherents, radiographers, mothers, sisters, wives, daughters, barefoot feminists without temple or guru. In 2012, while reflecting on all this, the following words were born from me for my colleagues and companions of the International Virtual Seminar "Creating Practices of Knowledge from the Gender, Movements and Networks":

> *Expando mis ideas.*
> *Busco llegar a sus corazones.*
> *Entusiasmarlas*
> *para juntas*
> *combatir el eterno no-tiempo.*
> *Ese que nos agobia.*
> *Que nos quiere saturadas, divididas,*
> *compitiendo entre nosotras.*
> *Separadas como individuas consumidoras,*
> *como máquinas productoras de papers, de hijos,*
> *de libros para quiensabe qué lector.*
> *Criadoras de profesionistas*
> *encampados en salones de clase*
> *con luz amarilla 24 horas.*
> *Profesionistas predestinados*
> *al desempleo calificado,*
> *a la precariedad,*
> *a convertirse en*
> *un frío número estadístico*
> *de la crisis sistémica y civilizatoria en curso.*

> [Expanding my ideas.
> I seek to reach your hearts.
> Excite you
> to bring us together
> fighting the eternal I have no-time.
> that overwhelms us.
> that wants us saturated, divided,
> competing among us.
> Separated as individual female consumers,
> as machines producing papers, children,
> books for who knows what reader.
> Breeders of professionals
> imprisoned in classrooms
> with 24 hours of yellowish light.
> Predetermined professionals
> to qualified unemployment,
> to precariousness,
> to become
> a cold statistical number
> of the systemic and civilizatory crisis in progress.]

Notes

1 Translation by Rosalba Icaza. Xochitl Leyva thanks Rosalba Icaza for connecting cultures and worlds, not simply translating words.
2 In Leyva (2015), I explain that this is the result of two major theoretical approaches: the Zapatista and the academic approach, which refers to "knowledge-practices". "Otherness" in Zapatismo means going beyond hegemonic powers and building alternatives beyond that power.
3 To get to know some of these communities, I have co-funded and/or contributed to the following sites: www.youtube.com/watch?v=PK-ONJGLM1U&t=1s, www.clacso.tv/gt_clacso.php?id_video=858 and http://glefas.org/xochitl-leyva-y-yuderkys-espinosa-en-contratiempo-audio/.
4 Vallenato is a musical genre originally from the Caribbean coast of Colombia. Its origin is a source of controversy, but it is believed that it was created by cowboys of the Magdalena Grande and the Since-Cordobesa *sabana*, who played the popular *decima* (tenth). These accordeon players were like minstrels who travel and sing stories from town to town while people rest, or during holy patrons' festivals. See https://sites.google.com/site/vallenato7/origen-del-vallenato, retrieved December 15, 2017.
5 Vallenato fragment from Omar Gelese, Valledupar, Cesar, Colombia.
6 This is a translator's endnote. "Abajo y a la izquierda" translates as "below and to the left" and is the Zapatistas' way of referring to a position that is critical towards institutionalization and elitism of 'official' leftist organizations and political parties in Mexico.
7 To give a unique definition of postcolonial feminism is not easy because of the internal diversity of the thinkers through time. But, it could be said that postcolonial feminism has been opposed to universal generalizations of white Western feminism. In particular, it has challenged the universalism of categories such as 'women' and 'gender' and the ways the latter interact with other systems of oppression and discrimination. These approaches emphasize the relation between women, gender and race as a product of colonial history that creates racial, power and class differences. For some, postcolonial feminism is part of the third wave of feminism and, as such, it puts emphasis on "Third World Women", their agency and voice, and their cultural and historical context.
8 Yuderkys Espinosa defines decolonial feminism in the following ways: "I tend to define decolonial feminism as a moment in construction and production of feminist ideas. It is articulated to the larger time of the production of the subaltern voice, a non-hegemonic voice, which has always been there but only acknowledged by a gaze that particularized it, made it specific and hence, disabled as a more general thought. This has consequences on the ways gendered historical oppression has been interpreted. Therefore, it is an open space for dialogue and continous revision, a fertile ground inhabited by many committed people. People and epistemologies that do not name themselves as feminists, or that do not want to be named decolonial and speak in terms of anticolonial, antimperialist, anticapitalists but that share as common objectives to challenge and oppose a racist imperial reason. It is also a moment in which we need to turn our gaze to the past, to what has been disregarded and destituted from historical epistemic legitimacy. I call this a return to comunity or the comunal", Yudekys Espinosa, interviewed by J. Barroso 2014, 22, retrieved January 15, 2018.
9 See http://sureste.ciesas.edu.mx/proyectos/pvifs/pagina_principal.html, www.worldcat.org/title/proyecto-videoastas-indigenas-de-la-frontera-sur/oclc/318914253, http://jkopkutik.org/sjalelkibeltik/, https://soundcloud.com/search?q=Xch%27ulel, www.encuentroredtoschiapas.jkopkutik.org and http://construyendosaberesendialogo.blogspot.mx/
10 This fragment was taken from www.cromos.com.co/personajes/actualidad/articulo-143499-detras-de-choco-jhonny-hendrix, retrieved December 15, 2017.
11 See Espinosa and Curiel (2015).
12 GLEFAS members define their group in their website as "integrated by activists and critical feminist thinkers that have decided to come together to promote a regional collective space from which we reflect and situate our gaze in a Latin American context. We promote feminist research, education and action and we are interested in encouraging

the production of historical and geopolitically situated conceptual frameworks for the development and strenthening of feminist, social-sexual, anti-racist, and anti-capitalist movements", cited in http://glefas.org/, retrieved December 13, 2017).

13 I use the term *neozapatistas* for networks created by local, national and international people in solidarity with and that identify with the political demands of the EZLN. For more information on this term, see Leyva (1998).

14 *The Other Campaign* (La Otra Campaña) was summoned in June 2005 by the Zapatista Army of National Liberation (EZLN) through the Sixth Declaration of the Lacandon Jungle. In the Other Campaign, civil society is called to organize itself into a national movement that, from below and to the left, promotes the construction of the other politics ("other" in relation to the oficial party-based and electoral democracy), the creation of a National Struggle Program and the creation of a new constitution.

15 See http://etimologias.dechile.net/?poder, retrieved December 15, 2017.

16 These are the author's own notes on the von Werlhof seminar that took place in Mexico City in November 2015.

17 Red Trasnacional Otros Saberes (RETOS); for more information, see www.encuentro redtoschiapas.jkopkutik.org

18 Red de Artistas, Comunicadores Comunitarios y Antropólog@s de Chiapas (RACCACH). For more information, see http://jkopkutik.org/sjalelkibeltik/

19 Website available at http://jkopkutik.org/sjalelkibeltik/

20 Centro de Investigación y Estudios Superiores en Antropología Social (CIESAS); see http://sureste.ciesas.edu.mx/xochitl-leyva/

21 In this section, all references are to be cited as endnotes so as not to cut the flow of the text.

22 Anzaldúa (1988b, p. 225).

23 This is a term by Cherríe Moraga (1988b: 1).

24 See SVI at www.encuentroredtoschiapas.jkopkutik.org

25 Damian Guadalupe's chapter can be read and heard here: http://jkopkutik.org/sjalelkibeltik/

26 Levins Morales (1988, p. 65).

27 Yamada (1988, p. 47).

28 Moraga (1988a, p. 22).

29 Levins Morales (1988, p. 65), Lorde (1988, p. 90), Moraga (1988a, pp. 27–28).

30 The concept of 'activados' or 'activitated people' has been developed by Gustavo Esteva, co-funder and member of the Earth University in Oaxaca; see www.unitierraoaxaca.org

31 There are many authors and books that have developed and discussed this concept, but for now I am only referring to Slaughter and Leslie (1999 [1997]).

32 Lorde (1988, p. 92).

33 Moraga (1988a, p. 21).

34 Ibid.

35 See Nardini (2014).

36 The article by Krizia Nardini (2014) offers a good summary of the feminist theoriest contributions.

37 See volumes 1 and 2 of *Prácticas otras de conocimientos. Entre crisis, entre guerras* (Leyva et al., 2015).

38 For more information, see Leyva (in press).

39 For more information on this personal-collective process, my own chapter can be read or heard at www.encuentroredtoschiapas.jkopkutik.org/. The chapter was published in English as Leyva (2012).

References

Anzaldúa, G. (1988a). Hablar en lenguas: una carta a escritoras tercermundistas. In C. Moraga & A. Castillo (Eds.), *Esta puente, mi espalda: voces de mujeres tercermundistas en los Estados Unidos* (pp. 219–228). San Francisco, CA: ism Press.

Anzaldúa, G. (1988b). La prieta. In C. Moraga & A. Castillo (Eds.), *Esta puente, mi espalda. Voces de mujeres tercermundistas en los Estados Unidos* (pp. 156–168). San Francisco, CA: ism Press.

Comité Clandestino Revolucionario Indígena-Comandancia General (CCRI-CG) – EZLN (2005) *Sexta Declaración de La Selva Lacandona*. Retrieved from http://enlacezapatista. ezln.org.mx/sdsl-es/

Cumes, A. (2015). Colonialismo patriarcal y patriarcado colonial: orígenes de un despojo continuado. In *La "india" como "sirvienta": servidumbre doméstica, colonialismo y patriarcado en Guatemala* (Chapter 2), PhD thesis in Anthropology. México: CIESAS.

Espinosa, Y. (2014) Feminismo decolonial: una ruptura con la visión hegemónica eurocéntrica, racista y burguesa. Interview with J. Barroso. *Iberoamérica Social: Revista-red de estudios sociales*, December 3, 22–33, retrieved from http://iberoamericasocial.com/feminismo-decolonial-una-ruptura-con-la-vision-hegemonica-eurocentrica-racista-y-burguesa/

Espinosa, Y. & Curiel, O. (2015). *Diplomado Feminismo Descolonial: Aportes y debates. Virtual Seminar*, May 11–August 10, retrieved from http://glefas.org/

hooks, b. (2004). Mujeres Negras: dar forma a la teoría feminista. In *Otras inapropiables* (pp. 33–50). Madrid: Traficantes de Sueños.

Imberton, G. (2014). Vulnerabilidad suicida en localidades rurales de Chiapas: una aproximación etnográfica. *Revista Liminar: Estudios Sociales y Humanísticos*, *12*(2), 81–96.

Jiménez, R. A. & Cardiel, L. (2013). El suicidio y su tendencia social en México: 1990–2011. *Papeles de Población*, *19* (77), 205–229.

Köhler, A., Leyva Solano, X., López Intzín, X., Martínez Martínez, D. G., Watanabe, R., Chawuk, J. et al. (2010). *Sjalel kibeltik. Sts'isjel ja kechtiki'. Tejiendo nuestras raíces. Weaving Our Roots*. México: Cesmeca-Unicach, CIESAS, PUMC-UNAM, IWGIA, Orê, Xenix Filmdistribution, PVIFS, RACCACH, CDLI-Xi'nich, Sociedad Civil Las Abejas, Sak Tzevul, OMIECH, Oxlajunti', MirArte, retrieved from http://jkopkutik.org/sjalelki-beltik/

Levins Morales, A. (1988). Y ¡ni Fidel puede cambiar eso! In C. Moraga & A. Castillo (Eds.). *Esta puente, mi espalda. Voces de mujeres tercermundistas en los Estados Unidos* (pp. 60–66) San Francisco, CA: ism Press.

Leyva Solano, X. (1998). The new Zapatista movement: political evels, actors and political discourse in contemporary Mexico. In V. Napolitano & X. Leyva Solano (Eds.), *Encuentros Antropológicos: Power, Identity and Mobility in Mexican Society* (pp. 35–55). London: Institute of Latin American Studies (ILAS).

Leyva Solano, X. (2012) Walking and doing: about decolonial practices. In J. Rappaport & L. Field (Eds.), *Collaborative Anthropologies 4*, 119–138.

Leyva Solano, X. (2015). Una mirada al tomo I. In X. Leyva Solano, J. Alonso, R. Aída Hernández, A. Escobar, A. Köhler, A. Cumes, R. Sandoval et al. (Eds.), *Prácticas otras de conocimiento(s): Entre crisis, entre guerras* (pp. 36–103). Mexico: Cooperativa Editorial RETOS, PDTG, IWGIA, GALFISA, Proyecto Alice, Taller Editorial La Casa del Mago.

Leyva Solano, X. (in press). Guerras epistémicas, academia(s) y movimientos anti y alter: desde el sur profundo para el planeta Tierra. In B d. S. Santos & M. P. Meneses (Eds.), *Conocimientos nacidos en las luchas: construyendo las epistemologías del sur*. Barcelona, Spain: Akal Editores.

Leyva Solano, X., Alonso, J., Hernández, R. A., Escobar, A., Köhler, A., Cumes, A., Sandoval, R. et al. (2015). *Prácticas otras de conocimiento(s): Entre crisis, entre guerras*. México: Cooperativa Editorial RETOS, PDTG, IWGIA, GALFISA, Proyecto Alice, Taller Editorial La Casa del Mago.

Lorde, A. (1988). Las herramientas del amo nunca desarmarán la casa del amo'. In C. Moraga & A. Castillo (Eds.), *Esta puente, mi espalda: voces de mujeres tercermundistas en los Estados Unidos* (pp. 88–93). San Francisco, CA: ism Press.

Moraga, C. (1988a). La güera. In C. Moraga & A. Castillo (Eds.), *Esta puente, mi espalda: voces de mujeres tercermundistas en los Estados Unidos* (pp. 18–28). San Francisco, CA: ism Press.

Moraga, C. (1988b). Introducción: en el sueño, siempre se me recibe en el río. In C. Moraga & A. Castillo (Eds.), *Esta puente, mi espalda: voces de mujeres tercermundistas en los Estados Unidos* (pp. 1–6). San Francisco, CA: ism Press.

Moraga, C. & Castillo, A. (1988). (Eds.) *Esta puente, mi espalda: voces de mujeres tercermundistas en los Estados Unidos.* San Francisco, CA: ism Press.

Nardini, K. (2014). Volverse otro: el pensamiento encarnado y la "materia e importancia transformadora" de la teorización del (nuevo) materialismo feminista. *Revista Artnodes: Revista de Arte, Ciencia y Tecnología, 14,* 18–25.

Rahnema, M. & Robert, J. (2011[2008]). *La Potencia de los Pobres.* San Cristóbal de Las Casas, Chiapas: CIDECI Las Casas/Unitierra-Chiapas, Serie Junetik Conatus.

Slaughter, S. & Leslie, L. ([1997] 1999). *Academic Capitalism: Politics, Policies, and the Entrepreneurial University.* Baltimore, MD/London: Johns Hopkins University Press.

Truth, S. (1851). *¿Qué acaso no soy una mujer?* Retrieved from https://voxafro.wordpress.com/2013/01/01/acaso-no-soy-una-mujer-sojourner-truth/

von Werlhof, C. (2015 [2010]). *¡Madre Tierra o Muerte! Reflexiones para una Teoría Crítica del Patriarcado.* Oaxaca, Mexico: Cooperativa El Rebozo.

Yamada, M. (1988). La invisibilidad es un desastre innatural: reflexiones de una mujer asiáticoamericana. In C. Moraga & A. Castillo (Eds.), *Esta puente, mi espalda: voces de mujeres tercermundistas en los Estados Unidos* (pp. 46–53). San Francisco, CA: ism Press.

5

ABOUT THE TRANSNATIONAL NETWORK OTHER KNOWLEDGES

La Red Trasnacional Otros Saberes (RETOS) between crises and other possible worlds[1]

RETOS

What is RETOS?

We are a space under construction, a collective effort articulated within a network of academic-activists and activists involved in various movements, organizations and groups that exist throughout the Americas/Abya Yala. We started the articulation we today call the Transnational Network Other Knowledges (RETOS for its acronym in Spanish) between 2008 and 2009 with four working groups, to which we added one more in 2010. These groups are called nodes in the network. The five nodes are based in Peru, Chiapas, Chapel Hill, Puerto Rico and Colombia. What united us was not a conventional research agenda but instead critical observations and common questions that emerged from the experiences of collaboration lived in our bodies, minds and hearts. These experiences led us to build a collective effort rather than a conventional or classic 'research project.'

The beginnings of RETOS

In April 2008, several of us met at an academic gathering and realized we had much in common, including that the various movements and initiatives with which we collaborated, worked or participated were not only fighting development projects or problems of capitalism, but were also creating imaginaries, practices, knowledges and world views with their own distinct logics as part of and a condition for their political work. In other words, they were also developing other ways of knowing reality, of living sexuality, of sharing and building knowledge, interacting with nature and so on.

Another thing we had in common was a shared desire to challenge the separation between research and action, between researcher and activist, between scientific knowledge and practical or popular knowledge. None of these dichotomies convinced us, nor did we practice them in our lives, given that we are researchers, educators, activists, militants, artists and communicators, primarily through alternative free media. Hence, we place value in 'walking together' in/with movements, and from there building awareness and knowledge in a different and collective way. Knowledge that has, above all, practical and political value.

One element that at that time we could not fully verbalize but that emerged through a series of conversations and RETOS meetings was the fact that the movements creating these 'new' political practices are also generating new knowledges and other forms of knowing/doing. These ways are not based on the certainty and dominance of a 'single truth,' but instead aim to find ways of knowing with a more experimental character, putting feeling, spirit and heart toward the center and thereby perhaps providing a space for multiple rationalities. We say "perhaps" because this is something we are exploring and wondering about collectively.

Through RETOS we want to develop new epistemologies, methodologies, ethical practices and languages of radical social transformation, those which to us seem relevant to the actual conjuncture of the current crises of modern civilization/Western capitalism in which we live.

Without doubt, one of the most visible characteristics of the present space-time is the centrality of uncertainty. In contrast to the dominant epistemologies of the social sciences, for us, uncertainty is not necessarily something negative. It can be a moment of opportunity to re-evaluate, develop and create other concepts and perspectives on the relationship between theory and practice. These uncertainties are manifest in fundamental questions about how we think and understand what is happening now and furthermore, how this leads us to develop/construct/propel other futures.

For these reasons, one of the urgent tasks for activists and activist-researchers in RETOS is to reconsider: 1) categories, 2) theories of social change and 3) the methodology/epistemology/ethics used to analyze and promote social transformation. This process challenges the conventional divisions between academia and social movements, between South and North, between practice and theory.

We believe in the importance of embarking on transnational articulations with local roots, weaving networks that not only investigate social and political movements, but that also do so for/with/from these movements. These articulations not only serve as corrective to mainstream academic ways and means, but also as part of a radical political practice itself. We believe that only through this kind of systematization, analysis and reflection we will be able to contribute to the construction of new tools to act and resist dominant academic practices today. We believe these tools include the creation of new political and social vocabularies that will permit new imaginaries and new ways of acting within current processes, opening the potential for radical social transformation.

Crisis, movements and alternatives

These days it is common to argue that the world stage at the beginning of the 21st century is defined by multiple crises. These crises tend to be classified and named as the 'ecological crisis,' the 'economic crisis,' the 'political crisis,' the 'food crisis' and the 'energy crisis.' Without doubt, RETOS was born in and of this context and we recognize the multiple interrelated crises in which we live. However, for us it is essential to understand that naming 'the crisis' in this way does not allow us to visualize others that are less recognized, but just as important, such as the 'cultural crisis' and 'epistemic crisis.' All of these are not conjunctural crises, but rather are the result of a long history of the organization of the modern colonial capitalist system and the relationship that it promotes between humanity and nature.

Faced with these crises, the social movements spanning the 21st century have developed deep cultural demands and practices that foreground other conceptions and practices of democracy, autonomy, body, nature and territory. While a number of them can be understood as movements with pre-figurative practices, others have practices that are more creative and/or experimental. All of them, however, invite us to think and propel profound changes in the organization of human life and relationships with nature.

The disputes around the meaning and practice of concepts such as democracy, development and politics that these movements have opened make us question the way we see and interpret reality. These disputes invite us to wonder about the role of movements in building alternatives to the crisis of Western modernity as a pattern of power and knowledge.

As knowledge practices are forged in fields of power, defending social movements as creators of knowledge retains high political significance. The theoretical practices stemming from social movements are generated in relation to historical regimes (epistemological and ontological) that they are struggling to transform. Therein, the importance of *knowledge-making practices* from movements emerges, on the one hand, from their situations and their unique places of enunciation while, on the other, from their struggle against the ruling (even repressive) regimes of truth or hegemony.

We believe that social movements push back against the field of knowledge by offering specific alternatives and meanings, such as sexual diversity or the concept and practice of 'buen vivir,' as well as by proposing different ethics or another frame of reference in which people can live their lives beyond competition and money. Through their practices, discourses and imaginaries, other movements deny the monopoly of truth assumed by the ruling regimes. For example, refuting that money is the most important determinant of value either directly – by explicitly opposing 'expert' discourses – or through the proliferation of a variety of alternative ways of knowing and being.

In the face of the multiple and multifaceted crises confronting us today, we affirm that epistemological/ethical/methodological changes in knowledge are part of broader and deeper cultural changes happening in different parts of the world, especially in (but not limited to) societies with colonial 'baggage.'

The path that RETOS is trying to build implies changing our understanding of what we are opposing and what we are promoting. We face the challenge of thinking differently from Cartesian logic that stems from Western colonial power that imposes a certain type of knowledge or way of knowing. That Western logic sets hard goals and unchangeable truths. Rather than this, we would open resonant spaces and allow for more processual and non-permanent connections.

The five basic premises of our work

First premise

In RETOS, we depart from a non-conventional premise that has become our guiding idea: those social movements and political actors which have been politically, culturally and epistemically marginalized by the dominant systems today are the historical forces that are developing and experimenting with practices, knowledges and wisdom with great potential to offer possible solutions to the multiple crises. That is, in their practices of resistance these movements and actors are creating and articulating alternative paths for the future.

For this reason, we look toward and work with/from/for subaltern actors, to systematize, to reflect and analyze together with them these new practices, ideas and imaginaries. We work 'from below' not because we romanticize these actors, or because we feel sorry for them, but because we believe that a view from below offers a perspective that cannot be seen by those on 'top,' nor by those in the middle or those looking 'from nowhere,' who have been legitimatized by calling themselves 'neutral.' We think the perspectives, practices and imaginaries of the subalternized/marginalized are important to act on in the present because they have been denied through repression, forgetting and disappearing.

Second premise

We work from movements to develop better epistemologies/methodologies/ethics/politics for understanding and for intervention in the present. From the beginning, RETOS has worked through shared affinities and common sensibilities, not from an idea of intellectual work supported by rational and instrumental questions.

In the different nodes that are linked through RETOS, we have developed less orthodox methods not based on defining the 'object of study' as a set of questions and method of analysis whose unique starting point or center are those debates and academic authorities. Rather, we have entered a process of reflection and sharing of experiences born from the various places where we work, from the different movements that we accompany or in which we take part. It is from there that concepts, tools, problems, challenges and ideas for working together are born.

In this process, we have actively worked to make visible, problematize and deconstruct the Cartesian 'subject-object' divide, which is the basis of most research approaches, even many that claim to be critical and progressive. It is necessary to stop assuming that there is a clear and simple distinction between the world of action/activism and the world of knowledge-production/academy. We have come to realize and understand that in today's world both academics and activists inhabit common problem-spaces characterized by an uncountable number of crises and uncertainties.

The question of the Cartesian divide is complicated because many of us have multiple identities all moving at the same time: we are activists, leaders, communicators, educators and much more. In acknowledging this, we do not ignore or erase by decree the differences and tensions between activism and academia, but rather we are working to identify the strengths of both worlds and what we have in common. Mostly we want to go beyond the prisons of identities and for that we are seeking, questioning, exploring, trying, creating and inventing how to act, live and respond from our various locations and sites, as historical subjects submerged in the multiple crises.

Third premise

The question or problem of the forms of organization appropriate to the present is common to all movements and activists with whom we work. This is directly related to questions about the nature and location of the political, including non-capitalist economies. In each of the spaces where we work, the traditional forms of organization, particularly political parties and the notion of 'a movement' with a single identity or problematic, have proven to be limited and, in some cases, deeply inadequate. Therefore, we try to experiment and work with various organizational forms that challenge hierarchy, privilege, the accumulation of power and the institutionalization of political entities. We value diversity and difference, but we are also aware that they can or are being co-opted and/or institutionalized for power. For this reason, we are trying to act from our bodies, minds, practices, hearts and imagination. Without question, many of us have learned from and been inspired by the political work of women, indigenous men in struggle and practice, and feminist theories. We also recognize, though, the contradictions and limitations in these realms. Moreover, several of us are increasingly combining our perspective as woman with gender struggles, thus further fertilizing our daily work, doing and knowing.

Fourth premise

In some of the nodes of RETOS we have seen the need to visualize, systematize and analyze the limitations, contradictions and tensions that live within our own movements, networks and organizations. This is not to discredit or destroy them, but to start from the inside to recognize these processes and from there to build real alternatives that are stronger and more effective against systems of oppression. Many of us believe that in this way we can avoid simplistic, triumphalist or romantic visions that add little to the construction of other worlds. A number of us are interested in building a self-critical, reflexive approach that allows us to see both the contributions and limitations, the progress but also the internal contradictions within movements, networks and organizations. With this we are trying not to fall into new or neo-colonial dichotomies, but instead to explore other ways of *being* and *doing* in the world.

Fifth premise

We believe that our searching requires new solutions within the spectrum of what we think and define the parameters of 'real' and 'possible.' Our searches also require new ways of naming problems and of thinking and organizing our societies, struggles and proposals. We believe that the parameters of the current system need to be rethought, and movements need to rethink themselves. It would be arrogant to think that they are not already doing so – they are doing it – so then we must ask: what are the organizational/epistemic/ethical/political challenges these movements are living? How are these challenges being faced and/or resolved? Can we share and learn from them in a more articulated way? Can we get a better understanding of the contemporary scene as well as develop (in network and/or collectively) new tools and strategies to intervene? Can we create/promote/build/ produce (in network and/or collectively) new insights into the kinds and forms of knowledge and knowledge-making practices necessary for radical transformation, liberation and emancipation, not only of peoples, but of all humanity?

This text was originally published as 'Acerca de la Red Trasnacional Otros Saberes (RETOS): Entre Las Crisis y Los Otros Mundos Posibles. Documento Para el Debate,' a working paper presented at the II Encuentro Internacional de la RETOS celebrated July 30–August 1, 2011 in CIDECI Las Casas/UNITIERRA-Chiapas, San Cristóbal de Las Casas, Chiapas, Mexico. It was published online at http:// encuentroredtoschiapas.jkopkutik.org/

Note

1 RETOS is the Red Trasnacional Otros Saberes (RETOS) and was founded in 2008. RETOS gathers academics, academics-activists, activist-artists, artists from Brazil, Chapel Hill, Chiapas, Colombia, Peru, Puerto Rico and the Netherlands working together to develop research and teaching practices attentive to epistemic justice; http://encuentro redtoschiapas.jkopkutik.org/

PART II
Voice

PART II

Voice

6

THE DECOLONIZATION MANIFESTO

Wanelisa Xaba

Part 1 – How to stop reproducing white supremacy

Decolonization as a tool for Black liberation is mostly articulated as a political ideology removed from our personal politics. On an intellectual level, Black activists understand that South Africa has not gone through the decolonization process. We understand the process of decolonization as the psychological, spiritual and the physical decentring of whiteness as a dominant tool of imperialism and the subjugation of people of color. However, the difficult work of personalizing decolonization and working on the different ways we have internalized white racism is a topic we shy away from.

As the clichéd feminist mantra asserts, the personal is political. The political is also personal, meaning decolonization is personal. Unfortunately, some Black activists are only comfortable pointing a finger at the system. We (myself included) do not want to consider that we have internalized white supremacy and reproduce violence on other Black bodies.

During #FeesMustFall, when womxn were raped or abused in the movement, men in the movement insinuated that the personal was lying or that they wanted to ruin the political credibility of the comrade (Ebrahim, 2016). Even during apartheid, prominent men in the fight for liberation were rumoured to be abusive husbands (Smith, 2010). Over the years, some womxn activists that were in ANC camps around the continent have also come out with their experiences of rape by men in the movement (Humphreys, 2006). The examples above demonstrate how we reproduce the system we fight against when we do not decolonize how whiteness has impacted how we think about gender, sexuality, consent and ability (ableism).

The way in which Black men in nationalist movements have dealt and continue to deal with incidences of rape and gender-based violence is an example of the 'selective freedom fighter' syndrome (Zondi, 2017). I use 'selective freedom fighter' to describe people who fight against white oppression but are comfortable with inflicting violence or defending violence inflicted on other Black people like womxn, non-binary people and queers.

Don't get me wrong, I am not saying that internalising white supremacy is our fault. We did not choose to exist in a world that devalues and perpetually traumatizes us as Black people. Unfortunately, most of us have been raised by parents who grew up under apartheid and raised us to hate ourselves. Some of us were taught to speak English instead of African languages in order to better assimilate into whiteness. Some of our white schools teach us that our hair is ugly and must be hidden at all costs, or extended families shame us for having dark skin (Daily Vox Team, 2016).

The media and public spaces encourage us to aspire to whiteness through messaging that portrays white people as pure, beautiful and intelligent, while simultaneously denigrating Black people as evil, ugly, violent and unintelligent (Daily Vox Team, 2017a). The church as a white supremacist, anti-queer institution, which is part of colonial imperialism, has also influenced how we think about womxn (Daily Vox Team, 2017b), gender expressions, sex, desire and sexuality. Black radical activists do not realise that sentiments like 'homosexuality is un-African' (McKaiser, 2012) are examples of how they have internalized conservative and hateful colonial constructions of sexuality and the gender binary.

All of us are products of 'the system.' However, as Black activists and Black people in general, we have the responsibility to examine the different ways white supremacy invades our intimate spaces, thoughts and behaviors.

The first step to unlearning whiteness is acknowledging that it festers within us. We must acknowledge that while we experience violence under white supremacy, we also reproduce it. This can be done by reflecting on the ways we relate to other Black people who hold marginal identities. If you are a heterosexual Black person invested in Black liberation, you have the responsibility to examine the ways in which you reproduce queer-antagonism. If you are an able-bodied person invested in Black liberation, you must continuously check your language or how you organize protest spaces that do not accommodate activists who are differently abled and/or who have mental illnesses. If you are a Black man who is invested in Black liberation, it is urgent for you to check your male privilege and your complacency in rape culture. It is being cognizant of class privilege and how socio-economic mobility and proximity to whiteness comes with power.

We also have the responsibility to be accountable to the broader community when we reproduce white supremacy. This can be done in acknowledging when we are told we are being violent, apologizing, educating ourselves and the continuous commitment to always do better. This is the personal work of decolonization – the continuous recognition of our violence and the commitment to unlearning whiteness within us. When we move decolonization from the headspace to the heart, we realize that decolonization holds us accountable to how we treat fellow Black womxn, fellow Black non-binary people, fellow Black not-in-our-tax-bracket people,fellow

Black queer people and even our partners. This is what I mean when I say decolonization is an intimate and personal journey – the commitment to unlearning the violent behaviors we have inherited from the enemy.

Part 2 – Colonization and the colonial subject

Recent popularized debates on decolonization and resistance against colonial legacies have underscored the African National Congress's failure to decolonize (the country currently known as) South Africa.

I say 'popularized' because recent movements speaking about decolonization often erase the ongoing work of decolonization done by collectives who are not in close proximity to whiteness.

I resist the notion of 'colonial/apartheid legacies.' The word 'legacy' implies something inherited from a previous order. I would argue that we still live under colonization and apartheid. It does not make sense to call for decolonization and simultaneously speak of apartheid legacies. Calls for decolonizing the university, the state, knowledge, land and reparations or the Black psyche are evidence that South Africa is still a colonial state managed by self-serving Black politicians. By extension, this also means Black people are colonial subjects in this colonial state. Therefore, it is important to understand and talk about how we are constructed and imagined in the colonial state.

In the previous section, I spoke about the necessity of making decolonization a personal journey. I also spoke about the need to recognize the elements of the enemy we have internalized and reproduce. Another element of understanding our internalization of white supremacy is understanding how whiteness imagines us as Black people and what purpose these constructs serve.

We as Black people are walking social constructs. As colonial subjects, we exist as canvases of the colonial white imagination. Edward Said has written extensively on the construction of the East as the 'Other' (Yang, 2014) in his book *Orientalism* (Said, 1979). Frantz Fanon writes about the construction of colonial society, the colonial subject and the hypersexualization of the Black heterosexual man (Pithouse, 2016). Chinua Achebe has written on the colonial imagination and representation of Africa as the 'dark continent' (Achebe, 1959). Feminists of color such as María Lugones have also written extensively on the colonial imagination of sexuality and gender (Lugones, 2008). The construction of the heterosexual cisgender nuclear family as the only healthy model of a family is part of the white imagination which looks down on complex and gender non-conforming African family structures (cf. Amadiume [1987] and Oyěwùmí [1997]).

In South Africa, Black people continue to exist as a product of colonial and apartheid white supremacist imaginations. The hypersexualization of cisgender Black men is an extension of the bestiality of Blackness.

The construction of Black people as lazy is an illogical and false colonial imagination because Black people have built and continue to build colonial societies (Biko, 2017). It is used as a smoke screen by white supremacist organizations, such as the Democratic Alliance, to deny structural racism and the exclusion of Black people. Hendrik Verwoerd's Bantu education policies also formed part of the white imagination of Black people as intellectually inferior (South African History Online, 2016). Biological and medical racism that assert that Black people are able to physically endure pain are racial constructs that serve to ease the white conscious for their brutality, centuries of hard labor and continuous medical experiments (Holloway, 2016). Our internalization of Blackness as strength dates back to the marketing of strong slaves at slave auctions as well as the normalization of Black oppression and struggle (Hutson, 2014).

Luckily for Black people, the white colonial imagination is lazy and uncomplicated. For example, the idea that there are millions of people and that they have to fit into two gender categories is very 'lazy.' Most importantly, the idea of gender, as we understand it within a colonial context, is the laziest construction in Western modernity. Another example of this lack of imagination: Black people are lazy. How can Black people be lazy when they wake up at 4:00 and 5:00 AM to clean your home, your streets and raise your kids? Dololo logic. Black people are stupid? How, when most of us are fluent in at least three to six languages and we constantly navigate multiple worlds? White people want a standing ovation for saying, "Sawubona," and "Thabo Mabeki."

As lazy and uncomplicated as the white imagination is, it is dangerous. It is dangerous because it becomes the norm and the truth. Remember the 'Fees Must Fall' student who was ridiculed for critiquing science (UCT Scientist, 2016)? The idea of decolonizing science and recognizing other indigenous forms of knowledges, which include science, seem laughable even to Black people because whiteness is the norm. In the colonial imagination, people of color have never produced knowledge (even though some of their 'science' they have stolen from people of color).

The normalization of whiteness is also linked to power and domination. Colonization as a system of subjugation constructs the subject in a way that makes it possible and justifies the colonization. The lie that white people are superior to Black people is not an arbitrary white supremacist belief but a powerful tool for subjugation. When Black people view themselves as inferior to white people, this sets up white people as the 'natural rulers' of society. In this case, the construction of Black intellectual inferiority is necessary for the consolidation of white power.

This makes it important to understand how whiteness imagines us in order to continuously disrupt it. When a student boldly claims that science must be decolonized, it is our duty to affirm her, defend her and educate ourselves on different indigenous knowledges. It is our duty to demand our university health science faculties teach indigenous medicine and that we have traditional healers lecture in our classes. To disrupt, disrupt and disrupt.

Despite this, even though as colonial subjects we exist as products of white imagination, we are not stagnant, we do not only exist as 'lazy' social constructs. We have internalized some of these constructs, however, in many different ways we resist and find new ways of reimagining Blackness. Poor Black womxn in the township and rural areas reimagine Blackness and resist every day. Black *trans, non-binary, intersex youth disrupt white colonial imagination every day. Brenda Fassie disrupts. Lebo Mathosa disrupts. When Zodwa dances with her Savanah at Eyadini she continues to disrupt. Even if all you do is breathe today, you resist and disrupt.

This text was originally published in two parts in the *Daily Vox*, 18 July 2017 (www.thedailyvox.co.za/decolonisation-manifesto-part-1-stop-reproducing-white-supremacy-wanelisa-xaba/ and www.thedailyvox.co.za/decolonisation-manifesto-part-2-colonisation-colonial-subject-wanelisa-xaba/).

References

Achebe, C. (1959). *Things Fall Apart*. New York: Anchor Books.

Biko, H. (2017). Racist stereotyping threatens SA, 19 April 2017, retrieved from *Mail & Guardian*, https://mg.co.za/article/2017-04-18-racist-stereotyping-threatens-sa/

Daily Vox Team. (2016). This young girl has had to change school three times because of her hair, 29 August 2016, retrieved from *Daily Vox*, www.thedailyvox.co.za/att-with-amira-patel-young-girl-change-school-three-times-hair/

Daily Vox Team. (2017a). 5 more racist ads that will make you go WTF, 4 February 2017, retrieved from *Daily Vox*, www.thedailyvox.co.za/5-racist-ads-will-make-go-wtf/

Daily Vox Team. (2017b). We need to foster safe spaces for the LGBTQIA+ community, 20 April 2017, retrieved from *Daily Vox*, www.thedailyvox.co.za/we-need-to-foster-safe-spaces-for-the-lgbtqia-community-alinaswe-lusengo/

Ebrahim, S. (2016). We've BEEN speaking against violence on womxn's bodies – Is anyone listening?, 15 December 2016, retrieved from *The Street*, www.thedailyvox.co.za/weve-speaking-violence-womxns-bodies-anyone-listening/

Holloway, K. (2016). Medical racism and the ignoring of black pain, 26 April 2016, retrieved from *Alternet*, www.alternet.org/personal-health/medical-racism-and-ignoring-black-pain

Humphreys, J. (2006). Women tell of rapes in ANC camps, 30 March 2006, retrieved from *Irish Times*, www.irishtimes.com/news/women-tell-of-rapes-in-anc-camps-1.1289890

Hutson, M. (2014). Whites See Blacks as Superhuman, 14 November 2014, retrieved from *Slate*, www.slate.com/articles/health_and_science/science/2014/11/whites_see_blacks_as_superhuman_strength_speed_pain_tolerance_and_the_magical.html

Lugones, M. (2008). The coloniality of gender. *Worlds & Knowledges Otherwise*, 2, 1–17.

McKaiser, E. (2012). Homosexuality un-African? The claim is an historical embarrasment, 2 October 2012, retrieved from *Guardian*, www.theguardian.com/world/2012/oct/02/homosexuality-unafrican-claim-historical-embarrassment

Oyĕwùmí, O. (1997). *The Invention of Women: Making an African Sense of Western Gender Discourses*. Minneapolis: University of Minnesota Press.

Pithouse, R. (2016). Violence: what Fanon really said, 8 April 2016, retrieved from *Mail & Guardian*, https://mg.co.za/article/2016-04-07-violence-what-fanon-really-said

Said, E. W. (1979). *Orientalism*. New York: Random House, Inc.

Smith, D. (2010). How the other David Smith rewrote the Nelson Mandela story, 16 September 2010, retrieved from *Guardian*, www.theguardian.com/world/2010/sep/16/young-mandela-david-smith

South African History Online. (2016). Bantu education and the racist compartmentalizing of education, 10 June 2016, retrieved from *South African History Online:*

Towards a People's History, www.sahistory.org.za/article/bantu-education-and-racist-compartmentalizing-education

UCT Scientist. (2016). Science must fall?, 13 October 2016, retrieved from *YouTube*, www.youtube.com/watch?v=C9SiRNibD14

Yang, J. (2014). What is Orientalistm, and how is it also racism?, 17 April 2014, retrieved from *Reappropriate*, http://reappropriate.co/2014/04/what-is-orientalism-and-how-is-it-also-racism/

Zondi, N. (2017). What Desai forgets to mention about Malema in "Julius vs the ANC," 16 April 2017, retrieved from *Daily Vox*, www.thedailyvox.co.za/desai-forgets-mention-julius-malema-julius-vs-anc-nolwandle-zondi/

7

THE LIABILITY OF FOREIGNNESS

Decolonial struggles of migrants negotiating African identity within UK nurse education

Roselyn Masamha

Introduction

Embarking on the task to decolonize is a complicated endeavour: it demands of us an openness and vulnerability that is decentring, which disrupts our established comfortable positions. Even as I am writing this account I feel enormous pressure to lighten experiences that are serious and painful, I feel compelled to endure the emotional labour of easing the discomfort of my readers. Throughout my writing, I am burdened by the issue of implication of colleagues I have worked with along the way. Somehow, I find myself prioritizing the *feelings* of the dominant powers I am seeking to challenge. This constant act of self-policing and self-censorship threatens the authenticity of my account. I agonize over the risk of this writing becoming an angry account of 'special pleading', which makes me acutely aware of the danger of reproducing those very same power dynamics that I am setting out to contest. Through writing, I am coming to understand the true extent of a colonized mind and the effects of internalizing inferiority; the frustration of having your own story stolen from you so that what you are left to tell is such a distorted and compromised version that sometimes even you cannot recognize, let alone identify with it. Stories are important. What is even more important is to safeguard their 'purity' because they offer a powerful and refreshing counter-narrative to what can often be quite oppressive expert knowledge. Mine is an account which has taken a long time to give, in part because telling my story goes against the grain. As a person who migrated from a developing country that was colonized by the British, a British education was a coveted *possession* and accessing a British education in Britain was a coveted experience. Therefore, exposing both these things for their limitations caused a cognitive dissonance, a conflict within, which was difficult to reconcile.

The efforts to decolonize knowledge production, which have erupted world-wide, gave impetus to this writing. Additionally, as an outsider in the privileged position of an educator, teaching on a nursing degree course that prepares nursing students for professional registration and clinical practice, I have a responsibility to actively engage with decolonizations and feminisms in global teaching and learning. The nursing students I now teach represent my former self, and my own discomfort with that which I used to hold in high regard means I cannot blindly teach based on approaches that are contradictory to what has become my world-view. I must do something different. Over the last five years as a lecturer working in higher education at universities within the United Kingdom (UK) teaching and supporting students, I am constantly reminded of the additional challenges faced by migrant students and recognize in them "that could be me – *that was me*".

What follows is an exploration of the interface of decolonization and migration in the postcolonial context of the UK. I start with an overview of structural social and political developments which form the backdrop against which my personal narrative is situated. I choose to share my personal educational journey as an African migrant nursing student in the UK who is now a lecturer because, as Nash suggests,

> While it is personal, it is also social. While it is practical, it is also theoretical. While it is reflective, it is also public. While it is local, it is also political. While it narrates, it also proposes. While it is self-revealing, it also evokes self-examination from the reader.
>
> *(2004, p. 29)*

As a lecturer who has navigated the landscape of migrant student-foreign practitioner-nursing lecturer, having been on the receiving end of a colonizing education, I believe I have a unique understanding of one who has been in the experience. This understanding better enables me to inform teaching approaches that take into account the position of migrant students and begin to make active efforts to understand their worlds. I will also draw on interview material collected in the context of my research which explores the impact of competing perspectives of teaching and learning for international students.

My research focuses on a case study of Zimbabwean qualified nurses recruited to undertake nursing education in the UK, who shared their reflections of their UK nursing education. As research participants who had completed their nursing education, they were in a better position to reflect on their clinical education in its entirety. Within this research I embody the complex position of being both the researcher as well as the researched, with my personal narratives forming part of the data for analysis. The shared worldview between myself and the research participants created connections that resulted in richer data. I used an heuristic enquiry approach (Moustakas, 1990), which starts with my own personal narratives and then invites people who have navigated similar journeys to share their experiences. The result is a collective remembering with narratives akin to the concept of wounded storytellers (Frank, 1995), identifying with the desire to share knowledge in the hope of something positive coming from a 'wounding', albeit of a different sort – a lived experience. The use of my personal experience is not to purport homogeneity across all experiences of African migrant student nurses in the UK, but rather to put it up against the experience of others, open to challenge and debate while simultaneously making it available for resonance with other diaspora experiences (Brah, 1996).

My aim is to make an impact on migrant students, native students, nurses in practice who assess student nurses' practical performance and lecturers, who in this context I believe to be the main stakeholders of the teaching and learning exchange at a grassroots level; that is, in the classroom and the practice area where nursing education is seen to formally commence. For the migrant student, I aim to provide something that recognizes and acknowledges experience, for both resonance and challenge, something to hang that sense of dislocation onto. For the native student, I aim to stir a curious awareness, a prompt to interrogate those taken-for-granted norms. For the educator, I aim to stimulate a consciousness of practice and provide opportunities for meaningful, considered change. For the research participants, to provide an opportunity to re-inscribe themselves as knowledgeable citizens whose contributions are embraced as valid knowledge. The experiences shared will serve as practical examples of some of the literary debates and global discussions which may appear to some as abstract, and thus difficult to connect with.

Context

In the UK, an increasing ageing population with more complex health needs has resulted in higher demand for nurses and consequently a shortage in labour (Buchan, 2003). International recruitment was one of the UK government's responses to demand for workers within the health and education service sectors, and this included recruitment from Zimbabwe (Tinarwo, 2011). Within nursing in particular, from a workforce point of view, the UK is unable to meet its National Health Service (NHS) and private healthcare provision requirements without extending recruitment beyond its borders (Adhikari & Melia, 2015). There is a business case for opening up borders which is, however, precariously positioned alongside pressure to tighten those same borders. The resultant competing tensions have made migration discussions highly topical in political, economic and social conversations. The presence of people of different cultures in the same space presents some challenges, to which a number of diversity initiatives and efforts to promote multiculturalism were made. However, the dominant discussions about migration and migrants have centred on a perception of how this has compromised, not enriched, the historical, cultural and social fabric of the country. Education establishments, workplaces and communities themselves have become contested spaces in which migrants co-exist alongside the native population, which is subject to media representations that have a tendency to situate migrants in a particular (often negative) way. Migrants themselves are rarely given a voice or an equal platform from which to contribute to these discussions.

Most research on migration has also tended to follow a similar pattern of being 'on and about migrants', rather than *with*. However, insights into migrant experiences cannot be generated through scholarly thinking alone, and central to this are narratives of those whose stories we seek to represent. Through the use of personal narratives as a form of enquiry (Richardson & St Pierre, 2000), I will give an account of my educational experience as an African migrant in the UK. I also draw from stories of other participants in my research, with recognition that I cannot do justice to their contributions within this one chapter. The use of personal narratives both as a term and a method is a deliberate act to trouble the positioning of academic writing that is infused with personal perspective and experience as somehow less valid within the knowledge hierarchy. My motivation to write has always been to engage rather than instruct, thus making myself clearly present in my writing has been a significant part of that engagement. Most of what is advocated to be 'good academic discipline' involves an expected distancing of yourself from your writing in an effort to make it more objective. It has, however, been my experience that the often-discouraged intentional presence fosters connections. Additionally, an acknowledgement of bias and an exercising of reflexivity allows for an interrogation of subjectivity. In my research, participants have shared their stories, which are often discredited as counter-narratives to prevailing discourses. I have been less concerned with the accuracy of the stories that they told and focused more on the kind of discussions that the stories generate. From these discussions emerge theories and, on this basis, there is an argument for the inclusion of migrant stories into mainstream literature. There needs to be an acknowledgement of the fact that these stories are a form of knowledge in their own right, from which we can develop theories. Migrant stories enable us to develop new complex understandings, providing experiences in context connected to the person, rather than starting with ill-informed hypotheses deduced from data removed from the person in the experience.

I will engage in scholarly personal narratives (SPN) to analyse the experiences and implications of occupying a migrant status in nursing education. Holdstein and Bleich (2001) define SPNs as an approach which allows for the incorporation of the full range of human experience into formal scholarly writing. Nash (2004) draws attention to the role of SPNs in the wider education agenda by encouraging us to go further than merely using very revealing and provocative personal stories to 'hook' the reader. Nash (2004) proposes that we use our personal stories as a source for exploring bigger educational, social, cultural and political issues. Through sharing my personal story, I hope that I can, at least in part, move you as readers outside of yourselves to view your external worlds in a different way. I hope to be able to expand your imagination and enable you, as suggested by Spivak (1990), to think new thoughts.

My story . . .

I am a black Zimbabwean woman. I was an international nursing student during the time that the UK was embarking on an international recruitment drive, not dissimilar to what is happening currently in order to meet the staffing requirements within healthcare service provision. Zimbabwe, at the time, was one of the countries identified for international student nurse recruitment long before its prevailing narrative was reduced to a single story of corruption, despot governments and human rights defection. I make this point here because its salience will become evident as this account unfolds. My transition into the UK adult education context was problematic, which you could argue was to be expected for a seventeen-year-old fresh from high school and in a foreign country. However, it was the nature of this 'problematic condition' that impressed upon me the need to investigate it further. Unpicking the exact nature of the problem was to become a preoccupation of mine for some time, and eventually found itself as a doctoral research project.

Background

I grew up in a family dominated by education professionals where the importance of a good command of English was more than a little emphasized. Even informal conversations at the dinner table were routinely vetted for correct past participles! While I fully acknowledge that when I moved to the UK I had transition difficulties that I may not have been able to clearly articulate, I was fairly certain that these difficulties were not about my English language proficiency. Yet any discussions about challenges faced by international students were often oversimplified to being about language difficulties despite the fact that there was actually no agreed definition of what constituted English language proficiency. This oversimplification detracted from the need to investigate international students' challenges further. The real issue for me lay in the politics of knowledge, the impact of skewed media representations of migrants in general and Zimbabwe in particular. Additionally, there was the 'liability of foreignness', a term that I explain in more detail further in this account – all the while dealing with the challenge of persistently navigating the paradox of being an invited but somewhat unwanted guest, thus feeling like a trespasser in the academy – what Puwar (2004) refers to in the book title as 'space invaders, bodies out of place'.

UK nursing education experience

I recall my nursing education experience to be a marginalizing one. I remember particularly being struck by the irony of how excluded I felt while on a course that was teaching me to be an advocate of inclusion (for people with learning disabilities). How was it that the very process that professed to be teaching me to be inclusive was in itself excluding? This marginalization was less about individual prejudices than it was about systems, processes, approaches and practices that were normalized in a way that was both unfamiliar to me and forced any alternatives to the margins, a concept I later came to understand as everyday racisms (Essed, 1991). Essed (1991) provides a structure within which to understand the silenced experiences of contemporary, nebulous discriminations, which are covert in their manifestations and obvious only to the person experiencing it. Understanding how everyday racisms are experienced and recognized, as well as how the knowledge of their occurrence is acquired, is essential.

My personal experience of education in the UK revealed that my skills and knowledge were always situated within the paradigm of foreignness, and my legitimacy as a knower was to be continuously defined by this. The challenge was always to get people to see beyond the foreignness and accept, as valid knowledge, the contributions I had to offer. I realized that my African identity dictated the legitimacies that were extended and withheld in relation to knowledge production – put quite simply, being African had implications for what I was allowed to know, what I was expected to know and not know. A case in point concerning what I was deemed to know was that whenever the word 'culture' was mentioned, there was an expectation that I would know all about 'culture' as if I was the embodiment of all things cultural. Again, when there was mention of 'race', attention was turned to me, suggesting that I represented all things racial. The latter seemed to be fuelled by my apparent visibly racialized identity, which in itself is a distortion, as all human beings have a visible racial identity. To emphasize the visibility of mine is to set whiteness as the norm, as suggested by Thompson (2001). In these two instances of culture and race, the knowledge legitimacies were not only extended but they were expected. Yet, in other instances, those same legitimacies were withheld by both my peers in small group discussions and also by teachers in the wider classroom discussions. Puwar (2004) attests to this by highlighting that people who are ethnically marked are positioned as signifiers and representatives of specific interests, seen in particularly confined terms that lock the body with a set of ideas. Members of the dominant culture often fail to see them as more general representatives of universal concerns. I found this selective permission to have one's contribution accepted and valued to represent a peculiar shift from being excluded to being included conditionally.

Science and technology, for example, were domains in which I was assumed not to have any knowledge, a manifestation of the indignities of coming from a country with a poor international profile and whose representation does not extend beyond poverty, chaos and primitive living. Being an African in the UK redefined for me what it means 'to know'. I quickly became familiar with the fact that people had very biased and narrow constructs of what knowledge looks like and the kind of person that can embody it. I came to learn that the knowledge construction zone is highly policed and tightly patrolled by assumptions, perceptions, stereotypes and biases. These systematically determine permissions, legitimacies, statuses, validities and opportunities given to particular people at specific times. So subtle are the mechanisms which operate in this area that they are barely noticeable, while so routinely and unconsciously practised, rendering the problem invisible to most.

One of the ways to make a seemingly invisible problem visible is to apply a frame. Frames enable us to incorporate new facts into how we conceptualize a problem (Crenshaw, 2016). In this instance, I propose 'liability of foreignness', first coined by Hymer (1960) as a frame to help ensure that migrant students do not fall through the cracks of our social justice movements.

Liability of foreignness

Aside from clinical knowledge and skills, nursing as a practice identifies social performance as a professional activity (Willetts & Clarke, 2014). For someone not socialized in the local culture, it is almost impossible to engage competently in this social performance. My Africanness meant that I endured what I will refer to as the liability of foreignness. This is a term borrowed from the business world, where it is used to capture the inherent disadvantage that foreign firms have in comparison to local ones, largely due to their non-native status (Mezias, 2002). In a nursing education context, native students have the advantage of having accumulated their native economic, legal, cultural and social knowledge at no cost, while foreign students lack this form of embeddedness (adapted from Hymer, 1960). Foreign students can find it difficult to truly understand the host country's 'sticky' unwritten laws and its cultural and social regulations, and how these affect day-to-day interactions (Szulanski & Jensen, 2004). The resulting disadvantage manifests in an increased number of misunderstandings, reduced confidence and a perception of incompetence.

In such situations, however, educators often default to a student deficit model on the basis that if a particular approach has worked for a protracted period of time for a number of students, on the occasion that it does not work it is most likely the student's problem. This position sees educators reticent to interrogate their long-standing methods and acknowledge that a non-native student may require a revised approach, that non-native students may have knowledge that is framed in a different way and warrants a different approach to assessment. Oftentimes it is a learning problem of institutional actors rather than a learning problem with students, which unfortunately tends to be the more typical interpretation. At the most basic level it is about an ability to understand how different students learn. One of the most serious effects of deficit thinking is that it reinforces stereotypes and, in the process, people who are already disenfranchised are further marginalized.

African identities in the context of knowledge

Asante (2006) advocates for the development of a critical theory based on African agency, which seeks to advance a coherent theory rooted in the experiences of African people. There is a need to disrupt the taken-for-granted beliefs that shape dominant forms of knowledge while ascribing value only to a select type of knowledges, which in turn silences other equally relevant and valuable knowledges. According to Pasura (2014), Africans are the least studied major ethnic group in the UK, and until their experiences have been investigated in more depth the wider implications of their disadvantage will remain unclear. Exploring the experiences of black African migrant nurses in particular is pertinent, as their lives are shaped by the interplay of a host of variables that distinguish them from second and third generation migrants and makes their experiences unique (Herbert et al., 2008). Exploring these issues is critically important at this point in time in global and professional history because of the persistence of approaches that pathologize certain cultures (Brah, 1996). There is need to develop a complex understanding of what is actually happening.

The media representations fed to the public about migrants meant that being a foreigner carried negative connotations. As a foreign migrant student, participation in class was to invite further unnecessary attention. Lack of context, a different accent and variation in pronunciations meant that contribution to discussions just emphasized all the more that I did not belong. Silence, on the other hand, provided a sense of security however false and misguided. A sense that I could fade away into the background and fool myself that if I was quiet enough we could all pretend that I was not there. This was based on an erroneous belief that this invisibility would foster an acceptance, by virtue of the fact that I was not imposing my already inconvenient presence onto those that had a 'right' to be there. When other foreign students contributed to discussions, I cringed and wished they would stay quiet. On reflection, I am confronted by the extent to which I had internalized the 'trespasser' identity to the point of wanting to silence others. Hall and du Gay (1996) encourage an exploration of the obvious, as well as hidden, power structures that force the internalization of inferior positions in an uncritical way. Of course, what happened was that this silence further isolated me whilst simultaneously feeding into the commonly held perception of the 'ignorant African'. I learned, as stated by black feminist poet Audre Lorde, that "your silence will not protect you" (1984, p. 41). For me, engaging with decolonizations is as much a process of learning as it is unlearning. This internalization of an inferior position was not only based on being a foreigner/migrant in the UK, but also has its roots in being a colonial subject. This inferiority is a layered inferiority which has to be unpacked if one is to successfully wage a resolute and uncompromising struggle within decolonization.

Thiong'o (1986), in a dated but nonetheless still pertinent text on decolonizing the mind, made a cutting and powerful observation of what he termed a 'cultural bomb', noting that, of its strongest effects, was an aim "to annihilate a people's belief in their names, languages, heritage of their struggle, unity, environment, capacities and ultimately in themselves" (Thiong'o, 1986, p. 1). It makes us see our past as unworthy and therefore makes us want to distance ourselves from it and instead identify with that which is furthest removed from ourselves, such as other people's languages rather than our own. Thiong'o went on to say that it makes us want to identify with that which is "decadent and reactionary, all those forces which would stop our spring of life, even planting serious doubt about the moral rightness of struggle" (1986, p. 1), additionally presenting possibilities of success as beyond reach, then (in response to the resultant despair and despondency) dominant powers presenting themselves as the solution to which we must show praise.

My Africanness

Similar to the reflections by Apprey (2008), my time in the UK revealed that people do many things with my Africanness. Some use it as an opening gambit to conversation, which normally takes the form of the question "So – where do you come from?" This question, however innocently asked, serves to emphasize the fact that I do not belong, confirming my outsider status. Finney and Simpson (2009) make a nuanced observation of British othering, positioning it as a functional aspect of British national identity. They propose that, since British culture finds it difficult to define itself, it becomes easier to assert that which is not British, making rejection of difference an active part of expressing national identity. One of the characteristics of a nation that will have deemed itself to be a superior power is the desire to make everything like itself, making everyone conform to its own definitions of normalcy or risk becoming an outsider. In the UK, the colonial process (on the few occasions that it is spoken about) is often presented more in partnership terms and having being less about domination, but rather as a beneficent and civilizing influence (Tiné-Fischer & Mann, 2004). This 'beneficial' view of colonization compromises the British public's understanding of the true impact of colonization, of its exploitative and oppressive nature. There is a need to address this distorted view of colonization so as to reduce the risks of current decolonization efforts leading to a 'negative moment'. Mbembe (2015) describes this as a moment when new antagonisms emerge while old ones remain unresolved.

My Africanness is also used by some to effect what Adichie (2009), in a TED talk titled 'The Danger of a Single Story', calls a "patronising well-meaning pity", one borne out of an uncritical consumption of the corrupted narrative that sees all migrants as an undifferentiated mass of refugees fleeing poverty and catastrophe – of which the plight of the poor African woman attracts even more sympathy, at least in the first instance. This then swiftly moves to resentment of one who is perceived to have nothing to give and everything to take. Possessing any valuable knowledge is therefore perceived as unlikely, and the only authorized utterance is that of eternal gratitude for having being rescued from a troubled place. My experience exposed me to the fact that there is still a widely and commonly held view of African women as helpless, dependent and subservient. This view is incompatible with possession of valuable knowledge or an ability to make a claim to knowledge which can be incorporated into mainstream discussions. Yet, all over Africa, there are progressive women advancing all manner of complex initiatives, creating and sharing new highly valuable knowledges. The dominance of a narrative of the 'helpless African woman' is addressed in part by Adichie (2009) in her talk on the 'The Danger of a Single Story', where she identifies the problem of stereotypes, not so much that they are untrue, but that they are incomplete, positing a single story as the all-defining story.

Some of the participants in this research shared questions and comments they encountered while in clinical practice, albeit from elderly patients, but nonetheless indicative of a particular perception of Africa. The subsequent failure of their mentors to offer support to redress these perceptions in itself quite telling: "Did you get those clothes at the airport when you arrived?" "Did you know of cheese before you got here?" "It must be really nice for you, to be able to now live in a brick house." "How come you speak English so well?" "So, how do you keep yourself safe from all those wild animals?" From the staff and colleagues, a common question in slightly different forms was "How do you know that?" – usually preceded or followed by "I thought you said you only moved here recently?" Such questions led me to reflect on a decolonization definition by Mbembe (2015), which posits decolonization as the elimination of this gap between image and essence, placing emphasis on the restoration of the essence to the image, allowing it to exist in itself and not in something other than itself, which is usually distorted, clumsy, debased and unworthy.

Claims to knowledge superiority

On June 4, 2017, following the terrorist attacks in London, UK Prime Minister Theresa May, in her address to the nation stated that "People should be persuaded that the Western way of thinking is superior" (Stone, 2017). Although this address was situated in a specific context, there were several objections to this statement. I have since found that the available reference to this speech has been modified to express a less controversial view. In making this statement, Theresa May implicated all of us who are not Westerners in that casual British arrogance that renders anything non-Western inferior. On what basis was this assertion being made? For this assertion to have been made by a well-travelled authority who engages with a diverse range of international leaders was, in a word, careless. If, after all the exposure that being prime minister affords an individual, such beliefs remain unchanged, there is little hope for the average member of the public who may have little or no exposure to other cultures. Of even greater concern is that if we position the government as a parent institution of which educational institutions are a subset that draw from a central understanding, is it any wonder that academic institutions have a tendency to invalidate non-Western knowledges? At this point, I am reminded of the proverb "Fish rots from the head", which is of unknown origin, but metaphorically refers to the concept that corruption (and, in this instance, I mean corruption of ideas) starts from the leadership and filters to the citizens and the organizations below.

Intersectionality: a case of nursing knowledge and African knowledge

There is an intersectionality aspect to African women in the UK undertaking nursing education in respect to knowledge. Crenshaw (1991) put forward the term 'intersectionality' to capture the fact and effect of multiple oppressions on the same individual, which highlights that our complex identities shape how we experience exclusion. Real inclusion demands that we pay attention to intersectional vulnerabilities, which in this case relates to the statuses of being a nurse and of being an African woman.

In addition to all the issues highlighted which emphasize the 'inferior' position of African knowledges, nursing as a profession has had its own troubled history and challenges in terms of defining its body of knowledge and positioning itself at the same level as other professions. Most of this is steeped in its representation by a high proportion of females, seen historically as handmaidens to doctors, who were traditionally mostly male. To a large extent, the public image of nursing having its basis in the shadow of medicine remains. Willetts and Clarke (2014) stress that this struggle continues today, despite nursing having met all the criteria required to be identified as a profession which includes a systematic body of theory, a regulatory body that monitors conduct and performance, a code of practice and a professional authority. Aranda and Law (2007), however, warn that the continued focus of educational preparation as the only characteristic defining nursing as a profession fails to give recognition to other attributes that contribute to what constitutes profession and professional identity. Nursing identities, like African identities, are multifaceted and should not be reduced to one-dimensional entities, but rather should have their multidimensional natures represented accurately.

Nursing education in the UK is comprised of 50 per cent theory, taught in the universities, and 50 per cent practice, assessed in the clinical areas. These clinical areas are contested spaces that serve and are serviced by members of the general population. In these spaces the intersectional experience manifests, first, in an undermining of clinical advice given to a patient by a nurse. Patients and relatives often seek confirmation from the doctor, who usually reiterates the same information, but their professional status means the same clinical advice carries more weight and the patient is then satisfied. Additionally, for me, my race made my 'foreignness' obvious at first encounter, which I felt set a pretext for how my knowledge and practice were perceived.

Any discussions on race dynamics were often silenced by diversity and multiculturalism rhetoric, which declare the clinical spaces 'race neutral' (Mapedzahama, Rudge & Perron, 2012). Furthermore, such discussions are often viewed as divisive and antagonistic to cohesion and integration efforts. The challenge, as put forward by Smith (2007), is to rethink policy beyond the official rhetoric of equality and diversity initiatives, and instead critically examine and interrogate the co-existence of cultural diversity and racial prejudice – particularly in spaces that have historically been predominantly white.

Adult learning theories

The widely accepted adult learning theories are built on a premise that adult learners should be self-directed, independent and autonomous. All these are Anglo-European values rooted in privileging self-sufficiency and individualism, which tend to be found in cultures where competitive individual achievement results in a high status (Flannery, 1994). In reality, while use of initiative, self-direction, active participation, research and critical analysis are recognized as integral parts of adult and professional learning within UK universities, most developing countries' educational systems are not informed by the same ideas. Consideration needs to be given to the fact that the practices of rational argument, engagement with established knowledge, challenging published information and critical analysis are not naturally occurring but are built through particular socialization processes (Moja, 2004). Developing critical thinking, problem solving and constructivist thinking is a challenge for any student. For Zimbabwean students, that endeavour is complicated by a history of colonial imposition of a hierarchical education system that demanded compliance, rather than questioning (Weiler, 2001). Contrary to popular belief, colonization is not something that happened hundreds of years ago. It happened in my lifetime and I am not particularly old; the colonialism legacy is only just unfolding.

Personal experience attests to the difficulties encountered with student-led activities, which crossed the traditional boundaries of learning and what constituted being taught. Far from being empowering and motivating, this approach often prevented full participation and ultimately resulted in feelings of exclusion and learning from the margins. Although observations of this have been made decades ago, thoughtful engagement with these observations continues to lag behind. Wertsch (1991) identified that if students are not sufficiently orientated to this new form of learning, their knowledge and experience may never be shared and this newly found freedom to be an active participant in the adult education process may prove to be disempowering and undermine efforts of well-intentioned instructors. Consequently, under-prepared students may never become full participants in the learning process (Wertsch, 1991).

Points for reflection

In the UK, the question "Why do *foreign* students demand a decolonization of the university curriculum and complain about Eurocentrism when they are here in our country?" is often asked. My response to this would be that an active engagement in international recruitment and globalization further reinforced the university as a globally public space which exists for the common good to which all students must be able to claim rightful ownership. Belonging is central to an ability to exercise that ownership and not feel like a trespasser. Mbembe (2015) reminds us that this belonging is nothing to do with native charity, hospitality or tolerance; it has nothing to do with having to assimilate into a culture that is not yours as a precondition of participation in the public life of the institution. Universities are the very spaces in which challenging academic debates should be embraced and facilitated, the platforms from which new understandings should be fostered and nurtured.

While it is not possible to legislate for open-mindedness or instil changes of perception by command, I hope that this reflection has revealed what some of the problems of a colonizing education look like and how the problems present. In my view, such reflections, when shared, can be helpful in progressing from conversations to generating theories that can shape future practice. If we continue to uncritically follow traditional and established practices which fail to take account of the changing landscape of the student body, if we put into practice only certain theories of adult learning, if we choose to do only what is comfortable and avoid the disconcerting nature of change, then we are in effect perpetuating and participating in marginalization. Unwittingly or not, we are all implicated by the practices that we partake in. As educators, we need to recognize the barriers to full and equal participation as something to be subverted and dismantled, rather than overcome. Challenging established systems is not an easy task; however, as authorities (of a level) in university contexts, we have an active role to play in challenging the processes and practices that uphold traditions of privilege, selective inclusion and discrimination.

Decolonization involves both a doing as well as an undoing, which ensures that we do not attempt to scaffold new understandings based on misinformed foundations. We need to understand the complexities of what effect colonizations had in the first instance in order to systematically address what we now know and see as the impact.

Decolonization is not about reversing what happened in the past, nor is it about what is sometimes called 'obsessing over the past'; rather, it is acknowledging the past and not trying to dismiss, understate or deny it. The present does not emerge out of itself – it has a 'before', and making active efforts to understand this enables us to progress into the future informed and better equipped to view situations in a more balanced way. We may not have all the answers or be able to generate an immediate resolve, but even basic awareness is progress.

Concluding remarks

Decolonization involves making specific and active efforts to give voice to those who would otherwise never be given a platform or indeed not feel able/empowered to take up what may be seen by others as an available platform. I purpose myself to seek out every opportunity to allow all the research participants in my research to have their voices not only heard but also validated. I have learned more about decolonization by engaging with them and taking time to acknowledge and understand their experiences and perspectives. There are many things we can learn from each other. Contrary to popular belief, decolonization is actually beneficial to all parties, so it is not about doing favours for anyone. Rather, it is about affording ourselves the full knowledge spectrum.

A good understanding of decolonization safeguards against including conditionally, accepting only partially under specific conditions. There is a need to unmask and confront misconceptions and fully embrace difference. On a personal level, this includes a reimagining of Africa as a place that has challenges and some adversities – yes – but also as a place that produces valuable outputs of a wide spectrum, of which knowledge is one of the outputs. Decolonization is not about replacing the existing centre with a new centre, but rather an acceptance of the existence of multiple realities, none of which need to take centre stage or have a greater value than another. On a practical level, a useful simple position to adopt when confronted with something unfamiliar is to say, "that's different", and then proceed to try and understand another perspective allowing yourself an education, as opposed to "that's weird!", which closes off any discussion and rejects any other position that is not the same as your own while at the same time asserting a dominant perspective as the common-sense right approach.

Liability of foreignness as a frame is useful to have as part of an educator's toolkit. In application, this should generate questions for us as lecturers, such as: "How does this student's being foreign affect their education?" "What impact does their unfamiliarity with the environment and context have on their learning?" "What reasonable adjustments do I need to make to my teaching?" "How can I create an environment conducive to optimize engagement?" "What does belonging look and feel like?" "How can I foster it?" "In what ways can I provide effective support?" Such questions are not only beneficial to migrant students, but for all students. If we "get it right" for international students, we "get it right" for everyone.

In keeping with my aim to engage stakeholders at grassroots levels, and in addition to my own views, I drew some suggestions from the research participants. I attempt to strike the very delicate balance of achievable changes/steps which can be done fairly easily, while at the same time avoiding 'sticky plaster' solutions to what are clearly complex issues that warrant depth of consideration. As a starting point are what I have called "Post-it notes to my lecturers and peers/fellow students" (see Chapter 13).

Acknowledgements

I would like to acknowledge the contributions of my supervisors (Helen Bradbury and Dr Rebecca O'Rourke) to my research as part of a Doctorate in Clinical Education through the University of Leeds, UK. The ideas in this chapter have been developed as part of my research journey.

References

Adhikari, R. & Melia, K. M. (2015). The (mis)management of migrant nurses in the UK: a sociological study. *Journal of Nursing Management, 23*(3), 359–367.

Adichie, C. N. (2009). The danger of a single story. *TED Global*, retrieved November 27, 2017, from www.ted.com/talks/chimamanda_adichie_the_danger_of_a_single_story

Apprey, M. (2008). Identity and difference: race, racialization, and otherness in the intersubjective field in clinical practice. *2008 Annual Conference of the Association of Clinical Pastoral Education*, Charlottesville, University of Virginia, pp. 38–55.

Aranda, K. & Law, K. (2007). Tales of sociology and the nursing curriculum: revisiting the debates. *Nurse Education Today, 27*(6), 561–567.

Asante, M. K. (2006). A discourse on black studies: liberating the study of African people in the western academy. *Journal of Black Studies, 36*(5), 646–662.

Brah, A. (1996). *Cartographies of Diaspora: Contesting Identities.* London: Routledge.

Buchan, J. (2003). *Here to Stay? International Nurses in the UK*, vol. *43.* London: Royal College of Nursing.

Crenshaw, K. (1991). Mapping the margins: intersectionality, identity politics, and violence against women of color. *Stanford Law Review, 1*(1), 1241–1299.

Crenshaw, K. (2016). The urgency of intersectionality. *TED Women*, retrieved November 27, 2017, from www.ted.com/talks/kimberle_crenshaw_the_urgency_of_intersectionality

Essed, P. (1991). *Understanding Everyday Racism: An Interdisciplinary Theory.* Newbury Park, CA: Sage Publications.

Finney, N. & Simpson, L. (2009). *Sleepwalking to Segregation: Challenging Myths About Race and Migration.* Bristol, UK: Policy Press.

Flannery, D. D. (1994). Changing dominant understandings of asults as learners. *New Directions for Adult and Continuing Education, 61,* 17–26.

Frank, A. W. (1995). *The Wounded Storyteller: Body, Illness and Ethics.* Chicago, IL: University of Chicago Press.

Hall, S.,& du Gay, P. (Eds.). (1996). *Questions of Cultural Identity.* Thousand Oaks, CA: Sage Publications.

Herbert, J., May, J., Wills, J., Datta, K., Evans, Y. & McIlwaine, C. (2008). Multicultural living? Experiences of everyday racism among Ghanaian migrants in London. *European Urban and Regional Studies, 15*(2), 103–117.

Holdstein, D. H. & Bleich, D. (2001). *Personal Effects: The Social Character of Scholarly Writing.* Logan, UT: USU Press Publications.

Hymer, S. H. (1960). *The International operations of national firms, a study of direct foreign investment.* Massachusetts Institute of Technology, Department of Economics: MIT Press.

Lorde, A. (1984). *Sister Outsider: Essays and Speeches.* Trumansburg, NY: Cross Press.

Mapedzahama, V., Rudge, T. & Perron, A. (2012). Black nurse in white space? Rethinking the in/visibility of race withing the Australian nursing workplace. *Nursing Inquiry, 19*(2), 153–164.

Mbembe, A. (2015). Decolonizing knowledge and the question of the archive. #Rhodes Must Fall Public Lectures, University of the Witswatersrand, South Africa.

Mezias, J. M. (2002). Identifying liabilities of foreignness and strategies to minimize their effects: the case of labor lawsuit judgments in the United States. *Strategic Management Journal, 23*(3), 229–244.

Moja, T. (2004). Globalization: a challenge for curriculum responsiveness. In H. Griesel (Ed.), *Curriculum Responsiveness: Case Studies in Higher Education* (pp. 21–38). Pretoria, South Africa: South African Universities Vice-Chancellors Association.

Moustakas, C. (1990). *Heuristic Research: Design, Methodology, and Applications.* Newbury Park, CA: Sage Publications.

Nash, R. J. (2004). *Liberating Scholarly Writing: The Power of Personal Narrative.* New York: Teachers College Press.

Pasura, D. (2014). *African Transnational Diaporas: Fractured Communities and Plural Identities of Zimbabweans in Britain.* London: Palgrave Macmillan.

Puwar, N. (2004). *Space Invaders: Race, Gender and Bodies Out of Place.* New York: Berg.

Richardson, L, & St. Pierre, E. A. (2000). Writing: a method of inquiry. In N. K. Denzin & Y. S. Lincoln (Eds.), *Handbook of Qualitative Research* (pp. 959–978). Thousand Oaks, CA: Sage Publications.

Smith, P. (2007). Overseas-trained nurses, diversity and discrimination: perceptions, practice and policy. *Journal of Clinical Nursing, 16*(12), 2185–2186.

Spivak, G. C. (1990). *The Post-Colonial Critic: Interviews, Strategies, Dialogues* (S. Harasym, ed.). New York: Routledge.

Stone, J. (2017). Theresa May: London terror attack shows Britain too tolerant of extremism. *Independent*, retrieved January 30, 2017 from www.independent.co.uk/news/uk/politics/london-bridge-terror-attack-theresa-may-tolerance-of-extremism-terrorism-islam-a7771836.html

Szulanski, G. & Jensen, R. J. (2004). Overcoming stickiness: an empirical investigation of the role of the template in the replication of organizational routines. *Managerial and Decision Economics, 25*(6–7), 347–363.

Thiong'o, N. W. (1986). *Decolonising the Mind: The Politics of Language in African Literature.* Nairobi, Kenya: East African Educational Publishers.

Thompson, A. (2001). A summary of whiteness theory, retrieved from www.pauahtun.org/Whiteness-Summary-1.html

Tinarwo, M. T. (2011). Making Britain "Home": Zimbabwean Social Workers' Experiences of Migrating to and Working in a British City. PhD Thesis, Durham University, School of Applied Sciences.

Tiné-Fischer, H. & Mann, M. (Eds.). (2004). *Colonialism as a Civilizing Mission: Cultural Ideology in British India.* London: Anthem Press.

Weiler, J. (2001). Promoting the dialogue: role of action research at Belvedere Technical Teachers' college, Zimbabwe. *Educational Action Research, 9*(3), 413–436.

Wertsch, J. V. (1991). Sociocultural setting and the zone of proximal development: the problem of text-based realities. In L. T. Landsmann (Ed.), *Culture, Schooling, and Psychological Development* (pp. 71–86). Norwood , NJ: Ablex.

Willetts, G. & Clarke, D. (2014). Constructing nurses' professional identity through social identity theory. *International Journal of Nursing Practice, 20*(2), 164–169.

8

DECOLONIAL FEMINIST TEACHING AND LEARNING

What is the space of decolonial feminist teaching?

Françoise Vergès

> According to the school, life is perfect when it allows itself to be treated as dead, to be cut into symmetrical conveniences.
>
> *(Tagore, 1933)*

> It seems that the only way to communicate with the white world is through the dead, dry leaves of a book.
>
> *(Means, 1980)*

Writing about learning and teaching often brings back personal memories of school; a mix of joy, humiliation, boredom, sadness, friendship, grueling repetition, home-work . . . Since school occupied a good part of our childhood and adolescence, it is not surprising that it is a period that remains imprinted in our memories. Then, for some of us, teaching and learning as decolonial feminists become a *theory in practice*, a process of unlearning and learning, of pedagogy from below, of *education* as a method to work collaboratively. Let me start my contribution with a remark and a citation. The remark: writing about teaching and learning brings back my own memories of school in Reunion Island in the 1960s and 1970s, where French language, history and culture were forced upon children of a post-slavery post-colony; racism and white ethnocentrism dominated. The citation is the powerful and troubling utterance by Audre Lorde: *"the master's tools will never dismantle the master's house"* (Lorde, 2007 [1984], p. 111; italics added) Powerful, because it has an uncanny intuitive force and can be applied to any discipline from art to philosophy to language; Troubling, because if the master's tools are not appropriate, what tools are available when capitalism has shown its capacity to colonize even the radical field, to turn revolutionary slogans into advertisements? The remark and the citation will serve as threads through which I will look at feminist global teaching and learning, which for me are intertwined, and suggest some ways to implement a decolonial pedagogy.

Pedagogy, which had been progressively contaminated by the corporate lingo of "outcomes," is again at the heart of the reflection of radical politics. Experimentations can be found everywhere, building an important library of alternative pedagogies, feminist, indigenous, from below, of the oppressed . . . The multiplication of syllabi that are either taught in universities – see the Black Lives Matter syllabus (Roberts, 2017) – or in programs that bring together body and mind – see, for instance, the "Māori Movement," a health and wellbeing program that brings together the traditional training of the Māori warriors (both male and female) into a modern interpretation (see Māori Movement, n.d.) – demonstrate the continuous search for methods of teaching and readings that encourage thinking transversally and across borders of disciplines and countries (American Philosophical Association, n.d.).[1]

However, before going further, it is important in any reflection on education to acknowledge the long tradition of radical teaching and learning. Ethnic minorities, workers, women, colonized and indigenous peoples answered, and continue to answer, to their exclusion from official institutions and curricula by setting up their own institutions, curricula and methodologies. National liberation movements gave education a central role in the construction of the new imagined community. They proposed a *pedagogy of emancipation*. They argued that decolonization could never exclusively mean liberating the land, as colonialism had produced contempt for oneself and one's own people's culture and history; thus, freeing oneself of the white mask glued on black and brown skins was a condition for a new world to be. The new nation required a pedagogy to decolonize the self and the community. Learning meant first *unlearning* what colonialism and racism had instilled in the self. The expression "creating a new man [sic], a new world, a new humanism" were at the core of decolonized education, whose goal was to undo the psychic damages of racism and propose new curricula, which in turn would develop new forms of inquiry (see, for example, Césaire, 2001 [1955]; Fanon, 2005 [1961], 2007 [1952]). The architecture of schools and universities sought to reflect that ideal: modern and decorated with art, celebrating the nation. Yet, programs of decolonized national education ended up readopting Western models and chose to ignore the devastating effects of patriarchy, sexism, homophobia and ethnic or linguistic nationalism upon learning and teaching. Hence, discontent quickly grew among students in independent states. More recently the issue of decolonizing the institution and the curriculum has come to the fore (South Africa, India, United States . . .): students reject censorship, learning by rote, corruption, colonial methodology and sexual harassment.

In the second half of the twentieth century, feminists criticized in the West an education that ignored the contributions of women and that has instilled normative notions of gender among girls, hindering their aspirations and their hopes. Feminists of color added the critique of racism that pervaded Western education and criticized the universalistic ideology of white feminism. Feminists and people of color pushed through the doors of academia and imposed their own departments, introducing their authors, narratives, forms of writing and researching and maps of knowledge. Curricula that looked at the intersections between race, gender, ethnicity, indigeneity, sexuality and class have been developed. Yet, the question of feminist teaching and learning remains an open one.

It would take too long to cite the names of the women and men who have distinguished themselves in that endeavor in Asia, Africa, the Caribbean, the Americas, the Indian Ocean and Europe. But it is to this long tradition that we should turn to imagine decolonization and feminism in global teaching and learning in the twenty-first century. The current context is one of privatization of institutions of teaching, of e-teaching, of assault on humanities and social sciences, of new forms of imperialism and capitalism, of renewed xenophobia, of the abuse of feminism by imperialism and of "femonationalism," to use the term coined by Sara Farris (2017). Private institutions – either by creating online or tangible institutions – are multiplying and big corporations with budgets higher than many states in Africa, Asia, or even Europe, are investing into teaching. The context is also one of increasing demands by students to decolonize education and the curriculum, to make school and university places free of abuses of power, of white supremacy, of sexual harassment, homophobia and transphobia. Teaching and learning today can also not ignore the increased planetary threats on human life that will fall first on poor and racialized groups worldwide. Thus, the task of imagining a decolonial feminist theory of learning and teaching will have to take into consideration critical queer theory, the critique of new forms of colonization and dispossession and the ways in which racial capitalism now operates. It would have to understand the reasons of the discontent with education.

As the fascination with the Western and white world is fading and its idea that education was about enlightening peoples caught in darkness is weakening, we should not, however, underestimate its capacity to harm or its power to transform anything into a commodity for consumption, even in the world of education. The ideology of the economy of speed and of fast results is pervasive and social inequalities are increasing. One of the first tasks may be to devitalize the power of that ideology. It seems to me that one of its pillars is the discourse about an inherent 'lack' – among women, gay, lesbians, trans, blacks, Muslims, and peoples living outside the West – that prevents them being 'full' human beings. It has a long history and has been a point of convergence between patriarchy and colonialism, capitalism and progressivism. It is a perverse but powerful discourse: it instills in the individual the belief that, from its birth on, she/he is lacking something – whether in terms of beauty, character, mental, moral or physical abilities – but that if she/he follows some rules defined by white power, she/he should be able to *catch up* some day with what is most desirable: the moral and physical qualities attributed to a white person. But, in fact, the person who has been marked as 'lacking' will never be able to catch up and be caught in an endless *race* for an unattainable goal. In his history of racist ideas in America, Ibram X. Kendi (2016) calls this ideology 'uplift suasion':

the idea that if blacks followed the rules of white society, they would be treated as equal. It is racist, he writes, because it accepts the opinion that blacks are originally inferior and it puts the burden of race relations squarely upon them (Kendi, 2016, pp. 124–125). Uplift suasion has its own feminist version in which the vocabulary of choice and freedom is central. "Be all you can be" – the slogan of the U.S. military translates that ideology well. But if the benchmark is the Western white individual male, his love for technological solutions and his abuse of power upon women, peoples of color and nature, then attaining that goal would mean losing what makes you someone, a being among other beings. However, the 'catching up' ideology remains strong and pervades teaching and learning. Its measure is a 'success' whose criteria have been defined by experts; far from being a neutral term, success here stands as measuring one's conformity to capitalist principles framed in terms like 'outcomes,' 'pragmatism,' 'freedom' and 'entrepreneurship,' terms that would need to be unpacked. Should education be understood in relation to this understanding of success? 'Success' is its measure, but success is far from being a neutral term, it has been constructed as and it is important to challenge it, to rethink what success in education can be, what the objectives of teaching and learning are. In other words, one of the decolonial feminist mottoes could be "beware of the seductive traps of the institution" – whether in the ideas of what a 'good' teacher must be or in the competitive world of higher institution. What the late African-American feminist critic Barbara Christian argued in "The Race for Theory" in 1987, playing on the two meanings of 'race,' still resonates. Christian wrote:

> [I am] more concerned with . . . the race for theory, in relation to its academic hegemony, and possibly of its inappropriateness to the energetic emerging literatures in the world today. The pervasiveness of this academic hegemony is an issue continually spoken about – but usually in hidden groups, lest we, who are disturbed by it, appear ignorant to the reigning academic elite.
> *(Christian, 1987, p. 53)*

In this race, teaching and learning lose their force; they become a device for supporting one's ego and narcissism and their methods are fixed, forbidding play and discovery. Against this, Christian opposed a method *in situ*, where the unexpected is not feared:

> I, therefore, have no set method, another prerequisite of the new theory, since for me every work suggests a new approach. As risky as that might seem, it is, I believe, what intelligence means – a tuned sensitivity to that which is alive and therefore cannot be known until it is known.
> *(Christian, 1987, p. 62)*

If "decolonization is a historical process," as Frantz Fanon wrote, then decolonial feminist teaching and learning is a process of self- and collective discovery, attuned to the demands for social justice, antiracist, anti-imperialist and anti-capitalist struggles.

Experience/practice I: learning/resisting amnesia in school

I grew up and went to school on Reunion Island in the 1960s and 1970s. Reunion is one of the French 'overseas territories', i.e., lands that belonged to the French colonial empire (slavery and post-slavery) and have remained within the space of republican France. The island is situated on an African/Asian axis, in the Indian Ocean world, a culturally and socially shared space centuries before the arrival of Europeans. Reunion, which had no native population, became a French colony in the seventeenth century and was populated by enslaved men and women from Madagascar and the eastern coast of Africa, as well as settlers from France. Slavery was abolished on December 20, 1848 and the French state brought indentured workers from China, India and Africa to replace the enslaved men and women in the sugar plantations. Migrants also came from Gujarat, China and other countries of the Indian Ocean Rim. Colonial racism, social inequalities and economic dependency upon the colonial state organized society. Creole became the common language. On March 19, 1946, when the colonial status was abolished and the island became an 'overseas department' high rates of infant mortality, illiteracy and poverty defined society. The French state was then reorganizing its empire, configuring new forms of domination in the context of the Cold War and global decolonization. Fearing the loss of all its colonial territories, the state targeted any form of dissent and discontent in overseas territories and launched a 'postcolonial' program of assimilation in which school was an important element. Teachers were brought from France carrying the ideology of its republican coloniality: the idea that with the end of the Algerian war, France was done with colonialism and racism and that the principles of the Republic – liberty, equality, fraternity – had never really been violated.

During my school years on Reunion Island, using Creole language was forbidden and punished; we never learned a thing about the history, geography and culture of our country; the history of slavery which had been central to the racial, social and cultural organization of the island for almost three centuries was not given its due place; we never read about the Indian Ocean world; and practically were taught nothing about the crimes of French colonialism. For most our teachers, the only country that mattered was France. They were almost all white, male and French (they were called *zoreys*, a derivation of a Tamil word meaning 'boss'), earned higher salaries than in France and received other financial and social benefits – a legacy of the colonial status. They never wondered about their privileges; they took them as natural.

At school, where I was a 'good' enough student, though often punished for my recalcitrant behavior, I learned *nothing* about my world and the larger world that did not fit the French narrative of 'grandeur' and civilizing mission.[2] But I received another education with my parents who, were both anticolonial communist and feminist activists and avid readers of literature and essays. They took their children to political meetings and encouraged them to be passionately curious about the world – how it was socially constructed, what the consequences of colonialism, imperialism and capitalism were. I learned why mountains have Malagasy names (they were the names of maroons, female and male); I learned why the Indian Ocean mattered, about decolonization, about the Algerian war of independence. At home, we received radical journals from China, Cuba, Madagascar, France and Mauritius . . . My mother took me to the only independent cine-club and I saw movies of Italian realism, of the Soviet Union, of the French *Nouvelle Vague* . . . In other words, early on I learned that school was a "manufactory specially designed for grinding out uniform results" (Tagore, 1933, n.p.); one you had to go through by trying, as best as you could, without being destroyed by it. I also understood that, though the French school system was racist, it was nonetheless important that Réunionnais children had access to it. There was no reason for eschewing the republican principle of equality in French schools in a French overseas department, but what kind of equality could it be in a colonial situation? Anticolonials had another understanding of equality, and even though sending Réunionnese kids to a school meant that they would not be allowed to speak their language nor to learn about their history, even though French school was designed to make them fail, fighting for access to school for all and for a more appropriate schooling was (and still is) a social struggle.

Today, in spite of some progress, the denial of Creole and Reunion's history and culture has produced (in 2007) an 'illiteracy' rate of 21 percent among people between 16 and 65, and 14.8 percent of those under 16. I put illiteracy is between quotation marks because, although it is true that 21 percent of people cannot write or read in French, the term hides its causes – slavery, colonialism, racism. Meanwhile, the University of Reunion has no department of African or Asian Studies, or of Feminist and Queer Studies . . .

What I learned from that experience is that teaching amnesia is an important tool for an education that must create a strong disconnect between the child and the world; one that must kill curiosity and repress any learning through the senses. Tagore gives an interesting example of that imposed disconnect:

> I well remember the surprise and annoyance of an experienced headmaster, reputed to be a successful disciplinarian, when he saw one of the boys of my school climbing a tree and choosing a fork of the branches for settling down to his studies. I had to say to him in explanation that "childhood is the only period of life when a civilized man can exercise his choice between the branches of a tree and his drawing-room chair, and should I deprive this boy of that privilege because I, as a grown-up man, am barred from it?" What is surprising is to notice the same headmaster's approbation of the boys' study-ing botany. He believes in an impersonal knowledge of the tree because that is science, but not in a personal experience of it.
>
> *(Tagore, 1933, n.p.)*

Gradually, personal and sensory experience is abandoned at school and holding and reading a book becomes the *only* sensual experience for most students.

It is striking that the remark by a young Indian at the beginning of the twentieth century meets one made by a young Réunionnese in the 1970s, and could still be made today. School is teaching disconnect with one's world, one's senses and one's capacity to understand phenomena from one's experiences. Meanwhile, alternative schooling, be it feminist, revolutionary or indigenous, has always paid attention to sensual learning and children's physical and mental wellbeing. The Black Panther Party started to feed breakfast to poor black children; Tagore established a school and later a university at a place in the poor, rural hinterland of Bengal, Shantiniketan; social movements everywhere have opened night schools for workers and activists. There is indeed a long radical tradition of teaching and learning in which feminism has developed its own curriculum borrowing from others and inventing.

Experience/practice II: thinking/learning with the senses

In 2014, I was one of the teachers at a week-long summer school in a country of the Global South with my friend, the anthropologist Aarti Kawlra. Ph.D. students, who had been selected from a wide range of institutions, listened to lectures, worked in groups and spent a day in a local workshop. I chose to accompany the students going to a village of weavers. Each student was assigned to a woman weaver to learn how to weave. The eldest weaver offered to teach me. I tried and was absolutely unable to even put together the weft, always breaking the thread. The woman gently slapped my hand, shaking her head at my clumsiness, patiently showing me how to do it without breaking the thread. I suddenly decided that I did not want to learn. In fact, I felt humiliated by my transformation into a pupil. After a while, I realized how my petulance was ridiculous and an expression of my incapacity to put myself in the shoes of a totally ignorant pupil. I went back, the elder woman smiled at me – she had certainly understood why I had left and decided to be generous rather than contemptuous. It was when I finally suspended any conscious thought, when I stopped acting like a student at school and started imitating the dance of her fingers that I succeeded. Even though I knew about the importance of imitation in crafts, I had forgotten that this was how I had learned to sew clothes: by looking at how pants, dresses, skirts were made and trying to imitate their pattern. I made mistakes, lost pieces of fabric, but got there eventually.

Another memory came to mind: growing up, I had spent hours in the kitchen, fascinated by the process of cooking, the transformation of vegetables and meat into a fragrant dish. Whenever I asked when to add onions or spices, the answer was: "Just look, you'll see." It was not smell or measuring spices with extra care that would make me a cook but learning to touch and see, a way of seeing that taught me exactly when to put in spices, how to cut onions for that one recipe . . . The gaze was central to cooking – cooking books were a genre of literature, the sheer pleasure (like novels) of bringing images to mind.

These memories and experiences became central during that summer school because they intersected with other remarks and observations. The classroom as a workshop became a topic of reflection and practice. By the end of the week, when Aarti and I asked students to describe what they had observed about the concrete conditions of the workshop (fruits, tea and coffee every morning, lunch set up at noon, rooms being cleaned, a different setting for dinner every night) and of the day they had to spend in a workshop (who had cooked lunch, who had brought it?), they protested – it had not been part of their assignment, they said. Since we had not asked them to pay attention to these arrangements, it was unfair to expect them to have something to say. Aarti and I were astonished.

Education teaches students to take the world for granted. Becoming disconnected is a requirement in a higher education whose goal is to transform one into an 'academic.' It is not that teaching and learning must become a commentary on current affairs only, but the connection between the world and the topic at hand should not be ignored. Arrangements, ways of teaching and learning, built upon racial and gendered divisions, are naturalized. For instance (something that is very important to me), the spatial arrangement of a room is rarely questioned, but why are the rows of students facing the teacher the same around the world, with the deep-seated meanings attached to being in the first or last row? I always tell students to observe the spatial arrangement of a classroom; they will automatically learn something about gendered, racial, and social hierarchies. Even though no law imposes a classroom spatial arrangement, we assume that it is the way it is, but why?

In academia, why do articles signed by ten to twenty authors never occur in social sciences and humanities, whereas it has become commonplace in life sciences? Why are social sciences and humanities defined by the 'author'? There was a time when feminist texts were never signed individually; feminist academia brought with it the aura of the author. Somehow, academia could not accept collective and collaborative scholarship and writing.

Postcolonial or decolonial teaching and learning are not enough to encourage change if it is not grounded in an active perception of the environment, if it does not rest on the fact that work in social and human sciences has to be done collaboratively, if it does not constantly reflect on the conditions that made teaching and learning possible, or impossible, or difficult. Though I cannot envision the end of the fabrication of *the* theorist in social sciences and the humanities – I went myself from never signing texts to becoming an 'author,' so no moral judgment here – I would nonetheless like to encourage more collaborative and collective ways of writing, teaching and learning.

Experience/practice III: museums, spatial arrangements, objects

When I was discussing slave trade and slavery in non-academic spaces to audiences of white people, I noticed that, even though they were often attentive and curious, they had difficulty making connections with their own society. Debates would inevitably turn to 'modern slavery' in Saudi Arabia or to exceptional cases in Europe. Colonial slavery was in the past: sad, but with no concrete impact on their world.

When I discussed racism, the legacy of slavery and colonialism in the overseas departments, one of their arguments got me thinking: none of their ancestors had been slave traders or slave owners, they were poor and disenfranchised, their families had never benefited from slavery. I thought about concrete ways to answer these remarks. In 2012, I proposed to the curator of the Paris Triennial, Okwui Enwezor, that he organize guided visits in the Louvre museum entitled "The Slave in Le Louvre: An Invisible Humanity."

The Louvre's collection is framed between two important dates for the history of colonial slavery: 1793, the date of its opening, and 1848 (after which art collections are in the Musée d'Orsay). The date of the first abolition of slavery in a French colony, Saint-Domingue, was 1793, triggered by the insurrection of the enslaved, which had started in 1791. The second and final abolition of slavery in the French colonies came in 1848, after Napoleon had reinstated slavery in 1802.

I wanted to visit the Louvre to search for the ghostly presence of the enslaved women and men, by looking at the ways in which the products of their work had entered social and cultural life, at how they had become objects of representation and status, at the ways in which sugar, coffee, tobacco, cotton, chocolate (and teapots, coffee pots, sugar bowls) had entered the representations of European individuals and social life. Indeed, the products of slavery and colonialism had gradually entered European lives in very intimate ways regardless of the direct involvement, or not, of one's ancestors in slavery. All Europeans became addicted to coffee, sugar and tobacco, but they had to ignore that they came from bonded labor. The products of slavery affected social manners (receiving with coffee, tea, sugar, sweets), the ways society started to think about love, birth, weddings, femininity (sugar, cakes, candies), and masculinity, bad manners and revolution (tobacco). A racialized producer/consumer division became naturalized. Through invisible but very concrete ties, the French were joined to the history of enslavement – slavery was the condition upon which pleasure and enjoyment were obtained.

By teaching the presence of slavery through the products that made European life 'sweeter' and how consumption became separated from production, I proposed a method of reading that would bring back the multi-layered dimensions of material and visual culture. For workshops or seminars with teachers or students, I also developed a reading of the banana, a familiar and ubiquitous fruit given to babies, children and the elderly, and known for its nutritious value. I traced its journey from New Guinea, where it has been domesticated to the rest of the world; its link with slavery, with rituals to ancestors in so many cultures, with mythology, with construction and clothing (leaves for roofs, fiber for weaving clothes), with music and dance (Josephine Baker being an iconic figure), its relation with the male sexual organ, and with the creation of the 'banana republics' (these countries of Central America where the U.S. company United Fruit received support from the CIA to crush unions, organize military coups and impose its prices); the campaigns to bring the banana into the U.S. home with Carmen Miranda, the nice and sexy Latina opposed to the guerilla and the unions; the diseases and health problems brought by high levels of insecticides and pesticides – cancer, leukemia, depression, miscarriages; the search for a genetically modified banana, the agro-business complex . . . The idea was to learn about geography, world history, gender, race, imperialism, North/South relations, and racial capitalism from a fruit to which everyone could relate, and to suggest that this could be done with other plants or objects. This simple device has been very successful. It proposed a methodology that would dismantle the master's house.

The master's tools

"What does it mean when the tools of a racist patriarchy are used to examine the fruits of that same patriarchy?" Lorde (2007 [1984], pp. 110–111) asked, speaking from her experiences as a black lesbian feminist in the United States in the 1960s to 1980s. She answered: "It means that only the most narrow perimeters of change are possible and allowable" (2007 [1984], p. 111). The master's tools "may allow us temporarily to beat him at his own game, but they will never enable us to bring about genuine change," she concluded, and women who defined the master's house "as their only source of support" would lose the fight (2007 [1984], p. 112).

Though Lorde's argument has often been understood as raising the question of the possibility of emancipation, I take it as a practice of healthy suspicion, of learning and teaching "without guarantees," as Stuart Hall (1986, p. 28) would say. However, I want to suggest that Lorde's utterance brings the following question to mind. Is education, as we know it, *impossible*? Have learning and teaching been so affected by the universalist and patriarchal Eurocentric vision of education as a 'civilizing mission' that they cannot be saved, that they have to be reimagined? The Enlightenment ideal that has become hegemonic contends that a 'good' education inevitably leads to an adequate and conscious understanding of one's situation and consequently to Reason and individual emancipation. Sensory education can therefore not be integrated, as it threatens the process, and the text must become the dominant medium through which knowledge is attained; the architecture of the classroom must set up a hierarchy between those who possess knowledge and those who do not, and it is gender-, class- and race-based. That ideal, we know, informed much of the colonialist and imperialist ideology and it continues to inform the dominant ideology of education. It is top/down; it instills a deep disconnect between oneself and the world; it teaches competition and individualism; it institutes a strong separation between disciplines, but also between the humanities and life sciences at a moment when the need to bring multiple understandings of the world – the social, the cultural and 'nature' – is more urgent than ever. The question is not to drop reading – on the contrary, one must learn and teach the pleasure of reading – but to forsake some arrangements and methods that kill curiosity and the desire to learn and teach as practice *in situ*.

In a speech given in July 1980, Russell Means, the *American Indian* leader (as he wants to be called) qualified European schools as "indoctrination mills":

When I speak of Europeans or mental Europeans, I'm not allowing for false distinctions. I'm not saying that on the one hand there are the by-products of a few thousand years of genocidal, reactionary, European intellectual development which is bad; and on the other hand there is some new revolutionary intellectual development which is good. I'm referring here to the so-called theories of Marxism and anarchism and "leftism" in general. I don't believe these theories can be separated from the rest of the European intellectual tradition. It's really just the same old song.

(Means, 1980, n.p.)

Means did not trust "education," he did not believe it could emancipate Native Americans. Rather, it would transform them into "apples" (red outside, white inside) – the same process that made people who were black or brown on the outside white on the inside. This deep suspicion of education as a process of whitening echoes Audre Lorde's warning about the master's tools. But Means' words also reiterate the remarks of the poet, philosopher and educator Rabindranath Tagore, who declared in 1933 that the regular type of school is a "manufactory specially designed for grinding out uniform results" and who shared a mistrust for the gap created by education between the sensorial world and knowledge. It led to the following feeling: "I have been obliged to act all through my life as if I were born in a world where there are no trees" (Tagore, 1933, n.p.).

Despite claims to the contrary, transforming education into a technique with a predictable and positive outcome has not been successful. Feminist decolonial ways of teaching and learning have to undertake the challenge of weaving colonial/ imperial binaries with multi-species entanglements beyond listing notions such as complexity, openness, hybridity and intersection. It is not an easy task, but it is an urgent one. As decolonial feminists, we need to hold onto many threads: unpacking the fabrication of binary formations yet explaining the strategic necessity of constructing an us vs. them; working with nature and life scientists while continuing to unveil the racial and gendered history of nature and life sciences; pursuing a critique of the coloniality of power and racial capitalism; nurture antiracism, anti-imperialism; fight against queer and trans★ phobia; listen to the dispossessed.

What does all this have to do with *decolonial feminist* teaching and learning? Decolonial feminist teaching and learning belongs to the historical struggle for decolonization – in other words, to the long road to liberation of the mind, the self and society. Teaching and learning must be thought of as processes that are constantly revised, questioned and transformed. But, first, it must teach autonomy and confidence. Decolonial feminism being about dismantling the master's house, the coloniality of power and all systems of abusive power, its method rests on the theories of emancipation from mental slavery that so many racialized and indigenous activists and scholars have written about, but also on collective liberation. It is about teaching and learning about struggles for social justice, against capitalism and imperialism and against racism, which is destroying so many lives of young people as schooling contributes to structural racism. As Sonia Sanchez has written:

"I cannot tell the truth about anything unless I confess being a student, growing and learning something new every day. The more I learn, the clearer my view of the world becomes" (Sanchez, 2010, p. 17).

Notes

1 Even though the *Diversity and Inclusiveness Syllabus Collection* page only brings together syllabi from North America, it provides syllabi on a variety of topics.
2 Hence, I remember learning about volcanoes by learning about extinct volcanoes in France, but not about the active volcano on my island.

References

American Philosophical Association. (n.d.). *Diversity and inclusiveness syllabus collection*, retrieved from www.apaonline.org/page/diversitysyllabi
Césaire, A. (2000) [1950]. *Discourse on Colonialism*. New York: Monthly Review Press.
Christian, B. (1987). The race for theory. *Cultural Critique, 6*, 5–63.
Fanon, F. (2005 [1961]). *The Wretched of the Earth*. New York: Grove Press.
Fanon, F. (2007 [1952]). *Black Skin, White Masks*. New York: Grove Press.
Farris, S. R. (2017). *In the Name of Women's Rights. The Rise of Femonationalism*. Durham, NC: Duke University Press.
Hall, S. (1986). The problem of ideology. Marxism without guarantees. *Journal of Communication Inquiry, 10*(2), 28–44.
Kendi, I. X. (2016). *Stamped from the Beginning. The Definitive History of Racist Ideas in America*. New York: Nation Books.
Lorde, A. (2007) [1984]. *Sister Outsider: Essays and Speeches*. New York: Crossing Press.
Māori Movement. (n.d.). Retrieved from www.maorimovement.co.nz/using-maori-movement
Means, R. (1980). *Revolution and American Indians: Marxism is as alien to my culture as capitalism* (speech), retrieved from www.filmsforaction.org/news/revolution-and-american-indians-marxism-is-as-alien-to-my-culture-as-capitalism/
Roberts, F. L. (2017) *Black Lives Matter syllabus*, retrieved from www.blacklivesmatter syllabus.com/black-lives-matter-fall-2017
Sanchez, S. (2010). *"I'm Black When I'm Singing, I'm Blue When I Ain't" and Other Plays*. Durham, NC: Duke University Press.
Tagore, R. (1933). *My school* (lecture), retrieved from www.swaraj.org/shikshantar/tagore_myschool.html

9

ATELIER IV MANIFESTO

Françoise Vergès (curator)
Gia Abrassart, Bénédicte Alliot, Kader Attia, Paola
Bacchetta, Jean-François Boclé, Odile Burluraux,
Jephthe Carmil, Gerty Dambury,Myriam Dao, Lucie
Dégut, Alexandre Erre, Fabiana Ex-Souza, Nathalie
Gonthier, Yo-Yo Gonthier, Antoine Idier, Marta Jecu,
Léopold Lambert, Carpanin Marimoutou, Myriam
Mihindou, Laura Huertas Millan, Kat Moutoussamy,
Frédéric Nauczyciel, Pier Ndoumbe, Pascale Obolo,
Yohann Quëland de Saint-Pern, France Manoush
Sahatdjian, Melissa Thackway, Mawena Yehouessi,
Mikaëla Zyss

This is a text written collectively in June 2017 following the fourth edition of a workshop I organize annually and which I have called "L'Atelier." It was on dystopia/utopia. The argument was that in the Global South dystopia is not a literary genre like in the West but a condition of life brought on by the slave trade, genocides, enslavement, colonialism, imperialism, forced labor, forced sterilizations, destruction of the environment . . . Thus utopia, being now dismissed in the West for having produced failed dreams and catastrophe, is the expression of a possibility, whose objective is not the creation of a utopian community but the rejection of the death sentence expressed in "There is no alternative." Conversely, decolonial feminist teaching and learning is a practice that encourages imagination and action.

"Let us rip down the curtain that masks the possible. The mighty, the masters of Capital and of the Empire tell us that their current dystopia is the norm and they have us believe that they control time. Paraphrasing Frantz Fanon, we declare that "we must shake off the heavy darkness" into which we are plunged "and leave it behind." We want to imagine a utopia, one that will give us energy, the force to contest, an invitation to emancipatory dreams and represent an act of rupture: daring to think outside what is presented as "natural," "pragmatic" and "reasonable." We do not wish to build a utopian community, but to breathe creative force back into dreams of indocility and resistance, justice and freedom, happiness and kindness, friendship and wonderment.

The world dislocates our lives and threats are accruing. It is as if every single thing must enter the vast racist, murderous and misogynist global supermarket and become merchandise. Cultural appropriation masquerades as diversity. History has become a vast bric-a-brac and the postcolonial an enchanted world in which one can go shopping for images, sounds, memories, bodies and objects that people in cultural institutions then dispose of as they like without taking into account the buried histories, scarred memories, forgotten genocides.

In an unbearable turnaround, oppressors claim to be victims. Since some have declared the "end of History," everything can be manipulated. Once the end of history is declared, there is no longer any need for peace, nothing to stop us entering a permanent state of war. Time is said to have come to a standstill and history believed to no longer be a process of contestation and aspirations, but rather a moment trapped in eternal repetition, an eternal return of the same. Historical revisionism produces new amnesias. On the one hand, the ambient anti-intellectualism flatters the basest of tastes; on the other, a disembodied art is passed off as subversive. The notion of "decolonization" itself is losing its meaning.

Yet, everywhere, a new day is dawning, spaces are opening, voices are rising and the old word "solidarity" is again full of hope and meanings. This is why we want to give back their strength to dreams and hope, to a space that is open and terrestrial, to imagine a soaring timeframe. The fear of being labeled mad will not lead us to abandon the idea of utopia. Hot-air subversion is of no interest to us. We are, however, open to the thousand tiny gestures, to actions that, everywhere, are organizing resistance and transmission, spreading knowledge and understanding, suggesting other temporalities and spatialities than those of the masters.

In these reconfigurations, the figure of the Maroon, those men and women who refused the long night of oppression, strikes us as primordial. To escape, if only for an hour, a day, a night, or years, to create, against all odds, a space of freedom is the lesson they bequeath to us. Making a reified icon of the Maroon would be to betray their memory. It is a danger that looms for all figures of freedom and, before we know it, we would risk seeing this figure set in stone on the fronts of museums. We take our imperative of constantly being on the move, in motion, inventing new, free territories, from the Maroons. The night welcomes our dreams and opens up still unexplored paths.

We claim the right to be unfinished and contradictory. We want to creatively redefine the visual traces of history, to explore the past to analyze the present and imagine the future.

Our utopia must remain a never-achieved goal; it must instill a permanent state of curiosity."

ATELIER IV – June 10–12, 2017

PART III
Institutions

10

WHAT A NEW UNIVERSITY IN AFRICA IS DOING TO DECOLONIZE SOCIAL SCIENCES

Jess Auerbach

It's not often that you get to create a new university from scratch: space, staff and curriculum. Yet that's exactly what we're doing in Mauritius at one of Africa's newest higher education institutions. And decoloniality is central to our work.

I am a member of the Social Science Faculty at the African Leadership University. Part of our task is to build a canon, knowledge and a way of knowing. This is happening against the backdrop of a movement by South African students to decolonize their universities, Black Lives Matter protests in the United States, and in the context of a much deeper history of national re-imagination across Africa and the world.

With this history in mind our faculty is working towards what we consider a decolonial social science curriculum. We've adopted seven commitments to help us meet this goal, which we hope will shift educational discourse in a more equitable and representative direction.

Seven commitments

#1: By 2019, everything we assign our students will be open source

Like most institutions of higher education in Africa (and across much of the world), ALU's library is limited. Students often deal with this by flouting copyright and piracy laws and illegally downloading material. We don't want to train our students to become habitual law breakers, nor do we want them to accept second-tier access to commodified knowledge.

Our aspiration is that by 2019 everything we assign in our program will be open source. This will be achieved by building relationships with publishers, writers and industry leaders, and negotiating partnerships for equitable access to knowledge. This will ensure that a new generation of thinkers is equipped with the analytic tools they need.

It will also move towards undoing centuries of knowledge extraction from Africa to the world that has too often taken place with little benefit to the continent itself.

#2: Language beyond English

Students who read, write and think in English often forget that knowledge is produced, consumed, and tested in other tongues.

We commit to assigning students at least one non-English text per week. This will be summarized and discussed in class, even when students are unable to read it themselves. Our current class is comprised of students from sixteen countries who between them speak twenty-nine languages. English is the only language they all share. Exposing students to scholarly, policy and real-world work that's not in English means they are constantly reminded how much they don't know.

As we grow, students will also be expected to learn languages from the continent: both those that originated in colonialism (Arabic, English, French, Portuguese), and those that are indigenous (Zulu, Wolof, Amharic).

#3: 1:1 student exchange ratio

Having cross-cultural experiences, particularly as an undergraduate, has become an important part of demonstrating work readiness and social competency in a 'globalized' world. Yet scholars have shown that globalization is often uneven. Strong currencies enable such experiences, so those who benefit usually come from Europe and North America.

This has had huge implications for higher education, where 'student exchange' usually takes place at a ratio of 10:1 – ten Americans or Norwegians, for instance, exploring South African townships, for one Ghanaian who might make it to the Eiffel Tower.

In Social Sciences, the body is the research tool and the mind the laboratory in which experiments are undertaken. We support as much exchange as possible across the broader institution. Our commitment when it comes to student exchange is strictly 1:1 – one ALU student goes abroad for every one exchange student we welcome into our classroom.

#4: Text is not enough

Africa's long intellectual history has only recently begun to be recorded and stored through text. If students are exposed only to written sources, their knowledge is largely constrained to the eras of colonization and post-coloniality.

To instill a much deeper knowledge and more sensitive awareness to context and content, we are committed to assigning non-textual sources of history, culture and belief: studying artifacts, music, advertising, architecture, food and more. Each week students engage with at least one such source to attend to the world around them in a more careful way.

#5: We cannot work alone

Social scientists often assign themselves the role of 'deconstructor': unpacking power, race, capitalism and consumption with glorious self-righteous abandon. My colleagues and I recognize that we cannot work alone and require our students to play a central role in contributing to the university's outputs.

We design our curricula in such a way that students are compelled to create, iterate, work with feedback, apply that feedback and critically appraise it. We want them to collaborate with as wide a range of other people as possible, stretching them to use language and the tools of analysis that they acquire in their training with real-world implication. For example, students recently worked with our legal, policy and learning teams to write the university's statement on diversity.

#6: Producers, not only consumers

The students who choose to come to the university bring with them tremendous insight and experience. These are often developed and augmented by spending time in the quintessential multi-cultural environment of the campus and dormitories. That allows certain fusions, tensions and commonalities to emerge much more clearly than they might in other places.

By working and living within this environment, it's essential that students start contributing to discourses surrounding Africa as early as possible. It might take years to know how to write a publishable scholarly article, but an op-ed, podcast or YouTube video is not quite so demanding. This allows students to get accustomed to their voices contributing to and shaping public dialogue in and about Africa.

#7: Ethics above all

Social Sciences both reflect and shape the world. Our program, then, is committed to the principle of 'do no harm,' and also to be an impetus for good.

Students will learn to think and act to the highest ethical standards, and to feel confident in asking the same of others working with them. This is essential in bringing into being a world in which Africa's place is both central – as it has arguably always been to global capitalism – and respected.

Collaboration

It's early days at ALU. There's a lot we still need to do, and it will take time for us to build the institution into what we collectively envision. These seven commitments are an important foundation for the Social Sciences. We're inviting responses and collaborations through our blog, through email or through collaborations with our students.

This text was originally published in *The Conversation*, 13 May 2017 (https://theconversation.com/what-a-new-university-in-africa-is-doing-to-decolonise-social-sciences-77181). These commitments have received well over 100,000 hits online and sparked global dialogue, and Jess, and her colleagues and their students, remain deeply committed to them. Based on an institutional "pivot", however, on 12 June 2018 the entire Social Science Faculty announced their resignation from ALU. The work continues in a changed form. Please see our website https://decolonizedsocialscience.wordpress.com/ for further updates.

Further reading

ALU. (2017a). About us. *ALU*, retrieved from www.alueducation.com/about/

ALU. (2017b). Our campuses. *ALU*, retrieved from www.alueducation.com/

Britz, J. J. & Lor, P. J. (2007). A moral reflection on the information flow from south to north: an African perspective. *De Gruyter*, 4 December 2007, retrieved from www.degruyter.com/view/j/libr.2003.53.issue-3/libr.2003.160/libr.2003.160.xml

Czerniewicz, L. (2016). Is it piracy? How students access academic resources. *The Conversation*, 16 March 2016, retrieved from https://theconversation.com/is-it-piracy-how-students-access-academic-resources-55712

Echezona, R. I. & Ugwuanyi, C. F. (2010). African university libraries and internet connectivity: challenges and the way forward. *Library Philosophy and Practice 2010*, retrieved from www.webpages.uidaho.edu/~mbolin/echezona-ugwuanyi.htm

Fairbanks, E. (2015). Why South African students have turned on their parents' generation. *Guardian*, 18 November 2015, etrieved from www.theguardian.com/news/2015/nov/18/why-south-african-students-have-turned-on-their-parents-generation

Ferguson, J. (2006). *Global Shadows: Africa in the Neoliberal World Order*. Durham, NC: Duke University Press.

Maldonado-Torres, N. (2017). Outline of ten theses on coloniality and decoloniality. *Frantz Fanon Foundation*, retrieved from http://frantzfanonfoundation-fondationfrantzfanon.com/IMG/pdf/maldonado-torres_outline_of_ten_theses-10.23.16_.pdf

Mburu, L. (2017). Language, power, exclusion and decoloniality in Africa. *Decolonized Social Science and Undergraduate Learning*, 27 May 2017, retrieved from: https://decolonizedsocialscience.wordpress.com/

Stebleton, M. J., Soria, K. M. & Cherney, B. T. (2015). The High Impact of Education Abroad: College Students' Engagement in International Experiences and the Development of Intercultural Competencies. *Frontiers*, 1–24.

Sunday News Online. (2016). Decoloniality in Africa. *Sunday News*, 11 December 2016, retrieved from www.sundaynews.co.zw/decoloniality-in-africa/

11

COLONIALITY OF POWER, KNOWLEDGE AND MODES OF (DES) AUTHORIZATION

Occupation practices in Brazilian schools and universities

Marta Fernández and Andréa Gill

By the end of 2015, more than two hundred secondary schools in São Paulo were being occupied by student movements against the 'reorganization' plan of the public-school system proposed by the state government to improve educational performance in line with the growing neoliberalization of learning and teaching worldwide. According to the key proposals for reform, the public schools of São Paulo – in the economic heart of Brazil – were to be restructured in terms of learning cycles that would separate students by age group (6–10 years; 11–14 years; and 15–17 years) (Governo do Estado de São Paulo, 2017). The declared objectives purported to offer a pedagogical model better suited to the needs of each stage of individual development, as well as to reduce conflicts between students of different ages and facilitate the overall management of school spaces (Governo do Estado de São Paulo, 2017). Without prior consultation with students, parents/guardians, teachers and administrators, the Secretariat justified the measure by means of the statistical survey data developed by the State of São Paulo. It argued that units that serve students of only one age group would improve the capacity and efficiency of schools to prepare students for a global modern competitive society through more technical, disciplined and individualized learning models (Governo do Estado de São Paulo, 2017).

The case presented by the Secretariat to justify the reorganization policy was challenged by numerous education research practitioners who warned that the isolation of the age variable negated its intersection with other key factors, such as the socioeconomic conditions of students, the support of teachers and staff, class sizes and resources, among other forces that reflect the inequalities of a highly segregated postcolonial society (Campos & de Souza, 2015). Against the authoritarian and technocratic ways in which the proposals were developed, São Paulo's secondary school students spearheaded a series of protests that involved a varied and creative repertoire of collective tactics such as petitions, marches, blockades, solidarity concerts, public lectures, debates and the paralyzation of classes (Campos & de Souza, 2015). When these tactics proved insufficient to pressure the government to revise its plan, the students, inspired by the recent mobilizations of the Chilean student movements, among other growing practices of resistance against neoliberal and conservative reform, decided to occupy their schools en masse.

The students' movements were articulated in terms of a sense of *luto*, a kind of mourning in the face of the threats expressed by the reorganization plan and the projected closing of ninety-three schools in the region (Santiago & Fernández, 2017). Public mourning was chronicled and channeled into the spirit of *luta*, a collective struggle that had among its tactics a funeral procession on the National Day of the Dead aimed at guarding one of the schools that was marked for closure (Santiago & Fernández, 2017). Tactics, in turn, metamorphosed into a sustained practice of occupation, as the students' grief was not heard in political terms by government decision-makers and the media. As one of the students pointed out, "occupying was the solution that we found to be heard by those who often ignore us, or even pretend to have no knowledge of us" (Campos, Medeiros & Ribeiro, 2016, p. 112). With no public debate or consultation, the reorganization plan was deemed in violation of the legal principles that secure the democratic management of public education and the right of parents, guardians and students to participate in the decision-making processes of public policy (Campos et al., 2016).

Although this chapter seeks to focus on the 2015 occupation movements of São Paulo's secondary schools and what they reveal in terms of the political, economic, social and cultural conditions that reproduce our society as a whole, it is important to first situate these practices within the transnational movements that helped to articulate the students of São Paulo and, in turn, students in secondary schools and universities throughout the country. One of the marked influences on these occupation movements were the Chilean occupation movements. In 2006, they staged the 'Rebellion of the Penguins,' alluding to the traditional uniform worn by the students during school hours.

The Chilean 'penguins' mobilized at a national level, occupied nearly all of the schools in the country to demand free and quality public education, as well as the wholesale overhaul of the neoliberal educational model architected during the dictatorship of General Augusto Pinochet. The imposed model had drastically reduced public spending on education, while instituting the management of schools as companies and municipalizing the once federal responsibility for education. As is the case in peripheries variously situated throughout Latin America and beyond, this downloading of responsibilities ends up penalizing the most precariously positioned schools, contributing to the systematic reproduction of inequalities in Chilean society. The influence of the Chilean process predominantly marked the methods mobilized by the students of the São Paulo occupations. More than a direct application or emulation of models of resistance, as one student of the

Fernão Dias State School put it in December of 2015, "we went in search of material, to understand how the entry into the schools, the occupation, the dynamics, and the assemblies could be" (Campos et al., 2016, p. 85).

While the 'Rebellion of the Penguins'[1] inspired movements of resistance and critical reflection on the precarization and mercantilization of the educational system in Latin America, it was the manual produced by Argentine students of the Frente de Estudiantes Libertarios/Libertarian Students' Front in 2012 entitled *Cómo tomar un colegio* (*How to Occupy a School*) (2015)[2] that offered a practical and operational orientation on how to organize cleaning committees, security, meals, and press relations. Once the Fernão Dias Paes State School in Pinheiros, in the western zone of São Paulo, initiated its occupation, the movement quickly spread throughout the state education system by the sharing of information, experiences and rallying calls through social media networks like WhatsApp and Facebook.

The qualified victory of the students of São Paulo, who by the end of 2015 succeeded in stalling the execution of the reorganization plan of the then governor, Geraldo Alckim, did not usher in the end of the struggle for democratic and quality education in Brazil. When São Paulo's students vacated their schools, occupation as a political tactic was increasingly adopted, throughout 2016, by students of public school systems and public and private universities throughout the country in a political context modified by the coup that ousted President Dilma Rousseff and brought President Michel Temer to power in August of that year. In this continually changing and volatile context, new demands emerged alongside the fight against the proposed constitutional amendment (PEC 241) that would freeze public spending on health and education for the next twenty years as well as against the proposal of the Escola sem Partido/School without Political Parties. The latter was drafted to regulate a 'neutral' form of teaching free of ideological considerations through the censorship and permanent vigilance of teachers and pedagogical materials used in the classroom.

The student movements of São Paulo, markedly inspired by its Chilean and Argentine counterparts, are situated within a broader movement of the occupation of public spaces that has grown as a strategy of political resistance against the precarization and mercantilization of virtually all aspects of life. In general, they present themselves as horizontal movements, not defined by fixed leadership or representative practices that experiment with new modes of participative politics. As a result, government responses tend to oscillate between a silencing and a non-recognition of this political form of organization, accompanied by the disproportionate use of police/military force to suppress the 'invasion' of public spaces by non-legitimated forces (Gimenes, 2016). However conflicting the dynamics and objectives of these insurgent social and political movements that seek more participatory modes of engagement, they stand before us as a challenge to modern ways of conceiving politics and societal relations of power more broadly (Gimenes, 2016).

Times of intensified transformation and dispute tend to come accompanied by waves of conservatism, galvanized by those unwilling to cede their place and privilege.

This is no exception in Brazilian postcolonial society, where the occupation of schools comes at a time following heated debates and initial experimentation with affirmative action programs. Reflecting on ongoing and multifaceted efforts at decolonizing Brazilian society, founded more than half a millennium ago through a European slavocratic regime that naturalized cultures of servitude and inequality, decolonial thinkers throughout Latin America have pointed out the key role of the educational institution in reproducing inherited structures and relations of power. Ana Amélia de Paula Laborne (2014), reflecting on the Brazilian case, cites Santiago Castro-Gómez on the decolonial turn that has spread throughout Latin America:

> The social sciences function structurally as an 'ideological apparatus' that internally sanctioned the exclusion and disciplining of those who did not conform to the profiles of subjectivity that the state needed to implement its politics of modernization. Externally, the social sciences legitimized the international division of labor and the inequality of the terms of interchange and commerce between the center and the periphery, that is, the enormous social and economic benefits that European powers obtained through domination of their colonies.
>
> *(Castro-Gomez, 2005, p. 179 cited in Laborne, 2004, p. 157; our translation)*

Within the pluriversal proposals of decolonial thinkers, Laborne (2014) also brings to the fore the following affirmation by Boaventura de Sousa Santos: "It is not simply a new knowledge that we need; what we need is a new mode of producing knowledge. We do not need alternatives; we need an alternative way of thinking to the alternatives" (Santos, 2008, p. 20 cited in Laborne, 2014, p. 158; our translation).

In the context of the struggle for curricular reform and the inclusion of African history and Afro-Brazilian culture into the elementary and secondary school curriculums (Bill 10639), Nilma Gomes, education research practitioner and leader within the Brazilian anti-racist movements, describes this process of decolonization and democratization as the movement toward the construction of a 'post-abyssal thought'. So as to open space for non-hegemonic forms of knowledge and learning, she advances the decolonial critique regarding how dominant epistemic models fix, on one side of the abyssal line of being, scientific thought, and on the other, 'the rest' (beliefs, opinions, intuition, magic or other subjective modes that at best serve as an object for scientific investigation) (Gomes, 2012, p. 732). In her words:

> This process does not imply the creation of more dichotomies, but rather the challenge of an egalitarian co-presence in which the Other is seen not only as the recipient of the universal knowledge and rights produced by the Western world. Beforehand, s/he is also a producer of knowledge and other forms of justice, as well as an interlocutor and integral part of the whole process. S/he may even diverge and propose alternatives.
>
> *(Gomes, 2012, pp. 732–733; our translation)*

To live this egalitarian co-presence, all those involved need to be retrained to occupy their place and dialogue from that which is perceptible for them. This process goes far beyond a deconstruction and reconstruction on individual terms; what is called for is an objective decolonization of the conditions from which our society is thought. This is what is at stake in the decolonization of education and the varied politics of transformation for which it opens the way.

In this spirit, the central argument of this chapter is that the occupation movements within Brazilian secondary schools, and the occupation of universities across the country that followed, destabilize not only modern claims to knowledge, but also the very processes of (des)authorization that enable such practices to reproduce society as it is. Inspired by a decolonial perspective, the chapter works from an understanding that modernity has always been colonial, since European modernization did not found itself on a genealogy endogenous to the continent. As effaced from the master narratives of Eurocentered social sciences, it depended on the 'discovery' of the Americas in the sixteenth century to constitute itself both inter-subjectively as a locus of civilization, progress and rationality, as well as materially, in terms of the exploitation of resources, the expropriation of colonized populations and the profits of enslaved labor (Quijano, 2005). That is to say, European hegemony came to command not only physical and material resources, but also minds – subjectivities, cultures and the production of knowledge – repressing and rendering invisible the heterogeneous cosmologies and genealogies of non-European societies. Through these imbricated processes, (post)colonial societies, racialized as inferior in their very constitution, were ousted from the history of the cultural production of humanity. Their representatives continue to be excluded from spaces of power and decision-making today, through hierarchies that are reproduced internally by way of markers of 'europeness' (read: whiteness).

In this sense, occupation movements, in all of their diverse manifestations, can be encountered as processes of dispute and contestation over the terms of the game – that is, who gets to decide what, through what narratives and relations of power. As movements that struggle for the effective decolonization of the structures of society, as well as minds, spirits and bodies, they reveal the political, economic, social and cultural conditions that reproduce the inequalities of contemporary society, which is the focus of the chapter presented here. More than exploring the limits and possibilities internal to these movements, which are in the process of being experimented and narrated by the students themselves, this chapter aims to explore the conditions that the occupations reveal about the society in which it is situated and that the educational system is put in place to reproduce.

However, this new way of living and doing politics is still being read by political decision-makers and members of traditional political parties, as well as repressed by the state and its allies (as seen in the direction of public schools today), in and through a modern/colonial grammar that is incapable of capturing and dialoguing with this hitherto unexperimented form of doing politics. The lessons that they hold for us remain to be deciphered and depend on our ability to make legible their many contestations and disputes.

Following this introductory section, the chapter is divided into three parts. In the first section, we explore how occupations put into question the modern notion of a progressive and unidirectional temporality that separates the past, the present and the future in discrete ways so as to grasp the terms of a politics of transformation. In the second section, we seek to shed light on the impacts of occupations on our sense of space centered on the separation of public and private that position and (des)qualify political subjects, to rethink the possibilities of citizenship itself. In the third section, we analyze how occupations problematize practices of (des)authorization through the policing of bodies/ minds and the knowledges that are consequently produced to relocate politics and the political.

To capacitate ourselves for such a reading, we employ here an imbricated lens to understanding oppression, which takes gender, race, class, sexuality, dis/ ability, nationality, religion and territory, together with numerous collective markers that position us hierarchically in relation to others, as structural principles. Methodologically speaking, this implicates a move beyond an intersectional approach based on identitarian categories. Similarly, it is a move beyond a deconstructive reading that remains within the internal logic monologically set by hegemonic forces, toward a recentering that (dis)locates the objective positions from which we examine and engage with society. As educators committed to a pedagogy of transformation, we offer here a preliminary reflection regarding these localized struggles toward the decolonization of learning and teaching.

This reflection was written while we were witnessing the occupation of our university campus at the end of 2016. As a private university, what was put into dispute were the very boundaries between public and private and the (im)possibilities of political engagement. Although our university institution would not be directly affected by the government cuts, all of the social supports that (dis)enable students, staff and faculty to live their lives in and beyond the campus would be affected. Part of the motivation for initiating this work in progress came from our conversations with students in the context of the occupation of our university in 2016, as well as from ongoing conversations through the growing everyday occupations by bodies long excluded from the governing institutions of a post-colonial society.

In addition to the conversations with students that served as inspiration for the work here presented, we predominantly analyzed materials produced by those involved in the occupation practices, published in news articles, social media and a scattering of academic reflection, as it is, after all, a recent phenomenon. That said, those whose voices are given more space to reverberate, even within critical counter-movements, prevail as a reflection of the racialized gendered hierarchies that mark society as a whole. The objective here is not to analyze the internal hierarchies reproduced by these student movements, but instead to see how these movements have been received by society at large and what this has to say about processes of decolonization and democratization in context.

Occupation: politicizing the present, past and future of a politics of transformation

In the 2015 occupations of the São Paulo schools, the protagonism was secured by political subjects historically marginalized within structures of power: students of public elementary and secondary schools, in large part youth from the periphery (Campos et al., 2016). Despite stigmatization by the media and government decision-makers as ignorant and naive, and even as vandals and criminals, they rendered visible the false precepts of the reorganization policies proposed by the Secretariat of Education to the public. The term 'reorganization' itself was contested by the students: "How does the governor want a reorganization, considering that not even what we presently have is organized?" (Campos et al., p. 31). Indeed, Brazilian public school students have long faced overcrowded classes taught by teachers with precarious wages and exhausting working hours, in addition to a series of infrastructural problems such as the absence of libraries, laboratories, athletic fields and basic resources such as toilet paper and water (Campos et al., 2016). Thus, students took to occupying spaces long *abandoned* by the Brazilian governing elite.

What became clear in the process of the students' occupation is the autonomist character of their political mobilization, refusing interference from older and more experienced leaders, government decision-makers, parents and other authority figures. In turn, the students became the targets of a series of discourses that disempowered them and depoliticized their demands, as had also occurred throughout the 'Penguin Rebellion' in Chile. Instead of being referred to as occupants, students were called 'invaders' and mainstream narratives portrayed students as doing nothing but vandalizing property, using drugs, dating and cutting classes (Campos et al., 2016). When the subject of the constitutional amendment of PEC 241 (stipulated to freeze investment in education for a twenty-year period) was introduced into the debates, President Temer disqualified the occupation movements by stating that the students did not even know what a PEC is (Uribe, Amora & Prado, 2016). On the other side of the same paternalistic coin, it was common to assume that students were not the real agents of the occupations, but that they were being manipulated by leaders of teachers' unions and left-wing political parties driven by ulterior motives beyond those of the students.

However, such strategies of infantilization, criminalization and disqualification of the student movements were daily contested through the students' discourses, but above all through their practices. On the reorganization plan, one of the students wrote, "with our strength and unity, let us overturn this ignorance" (Campos et al., 2016, p. 36). The public school, generally represented as a space of need and of disadvantaged, disinterested and passive students, was resignified as one of agency and inventiveness. Students asserted their autonomy and the non-partisan character of their movements and transformed the space of their schools into a formative place of debates and workshops that dealt with varied topics, such as race, gender and sexual orientation, as well as in-body exercises, such as capoeira, dance and marital arts, among other activities (Campos et al., 2016). What constitutes knowledge itself was a/effectively redefined in practice.

The articulation of a paternalistic narrative, based on the reproduction of fixed and hierarchical boundaries between children and adolescents on the one hand, and adults (parents, politicians, school directors, etc.) on the other, was put into check by the occupation movements of secondary school students, which served as an example and inspiration for university students throughout Brazil. In fact, numerous secondary school students began to participate in lectures and debates at universities, sharing their knowledges and experiences of occupation. They thus challenged the assumption in the reorganization project that the separation of students by age group is pedagogically positive. In turn, the youth in São Paulo succeeded in challenging the modern imaginary that positions them as the future, the hope of the nation, thus rearticulating the question depicted on the posters widely circulated by the Chilean school, Javiera Carrera: "How to be the future if we are not the present?" (Brugnoli, 2006).

In such a presentist spirit, the student occupation movements differed from other political movements, of the Marxist-inspired revolutionaries who preceded them, by prioritizing tactics over strategy (Bates, Ogilvie & Pole, 2016). Although a specific agenda (the struggle against school reorganization) was the fuse from which occupations spread throughout São Paulo, students did not propose fixed or predefined political strategies that would close the movement to negotiations and possibilities in everyday social relations. Throughout the occupation process, it became clear that the students prioritized the process in relation to the results, and sought to forge, within the struggle itself, the social forms and relations to which they aspired more broadly.

The students' refusal to be led by any leader or political party in the name of a predetermined future, and the emphasis on an open political form did, in fact, create a series of clashes between the occupiers and government leaders and leftist parties that often insisted on representing and speaking for the students. That said, the many demands of the São Paulo occupation movement did not pre-exist the political practice, but rather were articulated and rearticulated in and through debate and the daily coexistence between them. Initially centered on the fight against the reorganization plan, the movement was strengthened by emergent demands such as the demand for free and democratic classes, transparency in accountability, effective participation of the community in school decisions, and the improvement of school infrastructure (Campos et al., 2016). Girotto (2016) shows us that the students were taking up the right to participate in the construction of their schools, to think about its practices, principles, methodologies and actions, evidencing in the present the future for which they were fighting. Against modern developmental narratives of maturation, which only make responsible those deemed apt to take charge in any given context, the student occupation movements redefined the terms of political subjectivity.

In the occupations of São Paulo's secondary schools, the gendered division of labor was put in check in everyday relations. The female students refused to assume conventional gender roles, demanding that everyone take part in the cleaning and cooking commissions. In fact, many female students ended up on the security commission and at the front lines of dialogues and clashes with the military police at the gates of their schools and on the streets. In the documentary *Lute como uma menina* (*Fight Like a Girl*) (Colombini & Alonso, 2016), they censured the lack of debate about feminism in school classrooms – a subject considered taboo in the current political climate of transformation/conservation – and explained how in a few weeks of occupation they started to engage with gender, race and class issues that made more sense in their daily lives than many of the classes that they traditionally had to attend. The school's obligatory classes were denounced for the traditional methods of copying content from the board and memorizing material to reproduce in exams. Alternatively, in the occupations, students participated in lectures, debates and artistic interventions that spoke directly to them and helped them make sense of the intersectionality of the oppressions of gender, race and class that inform their daily lives.

The student occupation movements demonstrated to a wary public that revolution and social change had to be lived rather than projected toward an uncertain future in ways far from empty idealism.[3] The experience of occupation, as it was centrally emphasized, cannot be conceived from up high by minds located at a distance from the spaces of transformation; the struggle is to be experimented by those who accept to live it and (re)create their ideas in the field and negotiate the inevitable contradictions.[4]

The choice to *live* a new society within the microcosm of the school is far from an easy undertaking, since students already enter these relations predisposed to think about time, space, social relations and politics in and through the hierarchies and exclusions of our modern/colonial imaginary. As we are always already (pre)occupied with values and prejudices, all learning implies, simultaneously, an unlearning or relearning. After all, as published on the Really Open University website,

> We are always in occupation; of time, of space, of our values, ethics and beliefs. Everything around us is also occupied at every single moment, there is no bit of space or time that is not laced with values and content.
>
> *(2010)*

On the Facebook page of Aparecido Damo Ferreira State School, we are invited into this relearning process: "It is not easy to learn to listen, to speak without being aggressive, to have horizontal relationships, to work together. Especially because we are taught to obey and not to think" (Campos et al., 2016, p. 133).

bell hooks, building on three decades of collaborative research that developed an intersectional approach to learning and teaching, proposes the transformative potential of education as the continual process of "learning a new language" (hooks, 2010, p. 24). That is to say, the key to an engaged pedagogy is not the development of new, original or transcendent ideas that leap from brilliant minds, but the process of rearticulating that which is present somewhere in our bodies, everyday perceptions and relations, which enables us to read and respond to the worlds that we inherited, toward a kind of self-determination, each in and from their place (hooks, 2010).[5]

In the documentary *Anjos Rebeldes* (*Rebel Angels*), one of the feminist occupants invites us to rethink education in these terms:

> In the education [that we receive] inside the school we are accustomed to look and to sit each one behind the other . . . There are people who have been studying here for four, five years and I say, "Damn, I never saw you and now I can look into your eyes, I can deal with you, I can understand you, I can see you" . . . We learned to see in here.
>
> *(Vasconcellos, 2015)*

In this sense, occupations redefined previously existing relationships as, prior to the occupations, students were distributed mainly in groups for personal interests and along the divisions that mark postcolonial society, such as age, gender, sexual orientation, race and class (Campos et al., 2016). In the occupations, new relations of intersubjectivity were forged and an understanding of each other as students of the public school system was brought to the forefront (Campos et al., 2016). From these repositionings, students negotiated the prison-like structures of public schools, with their "vigilant and punishing" walls and gates, in new ways, to self-protect against systematic police repression and violence.

In finding a new voice, the student occupation movements demonstrated a marriage between practices of self-government and self-determination. In addition to redefining their place in society, the ostensible commitment to horizontal decision-making processes meant that each activity or decision became an experience of democracy.[6] The transformation petitioned by the students was not aimed exclusively at a transformation of the state or its institutions, but at a broader political change in local and personal relations. In this way, students expanded the sphere of politics, beyond state institutions and political parties. The message of the students is that political life also exists outside the so-called representative parties and institutions and that it is necessary to democratize not only the state, but all aspects of life.

In this spirit, the student occupation movements offered us an invitation to rethink the feminist mantra that the personal is political. Politics, in this sense, is not defined exclusively in relation to the realm of instrumental reason – the so called adult world idealized through the codes masculinity, whiteness, among other Eurocentric standards of authority. As within the occupation movements, it works through varied ages and socioeconomic experiences, as well as gendered and racialized realities that make potent and a/effective mode of engagement. It thus remains for us to rethink in and through what conditions we seek to articulate a politics of social, economic, cultural and intersubjective transformation.

Citizenship redefined: beyond the logic of public/private space

Although schools are qualified as public spaces, the sense of the public is not given, but produced daily by the students themselves. Occupation movements, in general, denounce that places traditionally understood as 'public,' as is the case with the state, have been colonized by capital, operating in the interests of a select group of stakeholders as opposed to those of society (Quijano, 2005). Schools are not exempt from this logic of privatizing public space, a case in point being the exclusion of students from the decisions that directly affect them. For the students, the proposed reorganization privileges in the interests of big capital, such as those of the real estate market and other profit-oriented endeavors (Girotto, 2016), in detriment of the pedagogical goals that the Secretariat of Education is entrusted to defend.

By occupying their schools, the students were thus not entering a pre-existing public space, but producing the public space itself, reconfiguring it intersubjectively and materially. The presence of the students in the school for an extended period consequently triggered a process of reappropriation, both concretely and symbolically (Campos et al., 2016). The space of the school ceases to be an alienated space, but becomes a space in construction produced both by the shared meanings that the students attributed to it and by interventions in its material environment. Walls, once symbols of policing and discipline, gained color through graffiti and artistic interventions that invited a new sense of place and belonging (Campos et al., 2016). Even school symbols and commemorative statues were dethroned. At Fernão Dias State School, the first school to be occupied in São Paulo, the statue of a founding colonizer, after whom the school is named, was covered by a garbage bag (Resk & Italiani, 2015).

The very sense of belonging was redefined, as the caring and cleaning for the school grounds constituted in large part this sense of proprietorship and the possibility of a genuine reorganization of the shared space (Campos et al., 2016). The conditions that enable and service one's coexistence became evident in a collective designation of response-ability. Notions of private property were consequently resituated in the course of occupations, as students found school and sporting materials hidden in classrooms. For example, the Facebook site of the Romeu de Moraes State School reported: "We played soccer, volleyball and other sports using old balls and we were always told that they were the only ones. We were searching and found this . . . a lot of brand new balls, even table tennis nets (. . .)" (cited in Campos et al., 2016, p. 144; our translation).

While students constructed the school as a public space not ruled by privatized interest, they notwithstanding referred to such spaces as 'homes,' in affective terms of family. In this spirit, they imploded the modern dichotomy between public and private spaces. The school was seen as a qualified extension of their homes, since it was based on a division of labor that sought to resist the inequalities that affect women and girls in the traditional patriarchal family. This cultivation of solidary affective relations is not an invention of the occupation movements, but their politicization re-channeled their potential and stood in stark contrast to the proposed reorganization plans that treated students as numbers decontextualized from their cultural and socioeconomic surroundings. Such connections were constantly emphasized on the Facebook sites of occupations. Students of the Carlos Gomes State School, for instance, said:

there is our house . . . our home . . . I love even the "aunts" in the canteen . . . you cannot forget your home . . . your home and all your family . . . they are not of blood but of the heart . . . there we are not friends . . . we are a family and I know that if we all act together . . . they will not get us out of there . . . they cannot do that.

(cited in Campos et al., 2016, p. 33; our translation)

Eduardo Donizeti Girotto (2016) draws our attention to how the reorganization plan conceives the schools and its subjects as homogeneous, distributed in a homogeneous spatiality, giving form to an abstract narrative centered on numbers and statistics that silence the voices of the diverse political subjects engaged. The political geographer shows us that the reallocation of 700,000 students as foreseen in the plan would imply a profound change in the socio-spatial relation among students, as well as between students and the schools (Girotto, 2016, p. 1123).

The student occupation movements made manifest a totalizing narrative of education and society, exposing the arbitrariness of a project that does not recognize them as subjects (see Girotto, 2016). In the course of occupations, students resignified the spaces of the schools, resisting the apathetic bureaucracies that positioned them as objects of intervention and evaluation. They constructed themselves as political subjects, producing new curricula, filling those spaces with their visions, priorities and relations (Girotto, 2016). Furthermore, the networks of solidarity that emerged among the students ensured that any future public policy that sought to disentangle them would prove even more difficult to implement.

The movements also succeeded in creating relations of mutual trust and support with the communities where the schools were located. Neighbors and families proved to be essential to ensure the survival of the occupations, as they donated food and supplies, offered workshops and classes, and repaired buildings. Antonia Campos, Jonas Medeiros and Márcio Ribeiro (2016) show us that this spirit of solidarity helped to protect the occupations from the abuses of police forces and groups opposed to the occupations. During the invasion of the Maria José State School by an opposing group of parents, police officers and the school principal, for instance, cellular phone messages were sent by residents of the area, which were in turn forwarded to Facebook supporters. This brought journalists, lawyers and supporters to the school to pressure, report and register violent police action.

The reorganization plan treated students as atomistic beings detached from their families, neighborhoods, classmates, teachers and staff. In its plan to relocate students, the government did not consider students with special needs and the availability of parents to accompany young children (usually accompanied by their eldest siblings), the danger of the route to reach the new schools (especially for girls) or overall increases in personnel costs (Campos et al., 2016). Moreover, outsourced employees, mostly black women whose work makes the day-to-day functioning of the schools possible, would lose their job ties, and threatened with relocation far from their homes, while teachers and staff would lose the ties that they have built for years with students (Cruz, 2015).

In sum, the production of space experimented by the student occupation movements not only defied the formal boundaries of public and private spheres of interest, but moreover proposed a form of proprietorship that goes beyond modern notions of ownership and juridical accountability. It cannot be overemphasized how the process of taking care of one's place reveals the conditions that sustain it and opens up the possibility for redefining socioeconomic and political relations. Herein lies an important lesson that feminists, perhaps most forcefully feminist economists, such as Gibson-Graham and Marilyn Waring, have sought to offer as an antidote to the myths of individuality constituted on the terms of a white hetero-centered masculinity of the middle to upper classes, whose image continues to mold the norm and standard for political, economic and cultural subjectivity in the modern/colonial eurocentric tradition.

These lessons imprinted by the student occupation movements, with their redirecting of our attention to the present, have inspired the subsequent occupation practices at Brazilian universities. It remains to be seen how such practices of horizontality, autonomy and solidarity have spilled over into the homes and neighborhoods of the engaged students, politicizing spaces traditionally conceived as 'private' and rendering legible the relations of power that cut across distinct registers of society. The question that then remains goes well beyond the often-rehearsed dilemma of modern critical thought. Instead of asking, "What is political?" we are invited to ask, "Where is politics?"

(Des)authorizing voices: re-situating the place of the mind/body in structures of power/knowledge

The partial victory of the student occupation movements of São Paulo, which managed to postpone the reorganization plan at the end of 2015, was considered the most important political defeat of the then governor of São Paulo, Geraldo Alckmin. The approval ratings of the governor plummeted, especially among older and lower-income women (Campos et al., 2016). Campos et al. (2016) suggest that this significant drop in popularity was in part driven by the mothers and grandmothers of public school students, testifying to the capillarity of political struggle in society.

The occupations initiated by secondary school students in São Paulo multiplied throughout Brazil in 2016, influencing more than 1,000 occupations of public schools as well as public and even private universities. In this new political climate, the occupations were mobilized by a common national agenda, the fight against the constitutional amendment (PEC 241) proposed by the government's economic team that intended to stagnate federal spending for twenty years, including on education, together with the Escola sem Partido (School without Political Parties) initiatives that aim to criminalize critical debate within schools. Again, the authoritarianism of the reforms presented through a presidential act without dialogue with teachers, administrators and students is a reflex of broader efforts to (dis)qualify public engagement (Revista Educação & Sociedade, 2016).

More than a violation of an abstracted procedural order, the resistance of the students generates discomfort, by forcing their presence, protagonism and emotive voice into traditionally adult, white, masculine and rationalist spaces, dominated by government decision-makers, technocrats who formulate laws and academics who produce knowledge at a comfortable distance. The problem of subaltern voice has never been one of an inability to speak, but of the inability to be heard (Spivak, 1989). To be heard, the students' dissent would need to be translated into the hegemonic language of respectability defined as instrumental to the order of masculinity and the myths of individuality propagated by ahistorical claims to whiteness as the universal standard of humanity; instead, they represented excess, noise, and ultimately, disqualified bodies.

Decolonial thinkers such as Anibal Quijano (2005) and María Lugones (2015) argue that the separation between mind and body has its roots in the fifteenth and sixteenth centuries, from the Christian idea of the primacy of the soul – object of salvation – as opposed to the body – object of repression – for example, during the Inquisition. With Descartes, in the first half of the seventeenth century, the dualistic Christian approach gave way to the secularized idea of the radical separation between the mind, endowed with reason as the producer of knowledge, and the body to be controlled and contained by the power of reasoning (Quijano, 2005). Ramón Grosfoguel (2016) shows us with the Cartesian axiom of 'I think, therefore I am' how the Christian God came to be replaced by a sovereign 'I' as the producer of a truth transcendent of mundane relations in time and space. From this secularized foundation of knowledge, the idealized 'I,' shaped in the image of the propertied white man of a westernized modernity, invests the attributes of God, projecting himself as capable of producing a universal and disinterested knowledge. The mind acquires, with Descartes, a place equivalent to that of the eye of God, that is, as a disposition unconditioned by the body and other particular conditions of existence (Grosfoguel, 2016).

This dualism inherited from a colonial modernity, in turn, is constituted in practice through racialized and gendered hierarchies that (dis)qualify the subjects in question; bodies marked by femininity and blackness become key signifiers of inferiority and objecthood, as controllable and exploitable objects, projected as closer to nature (Lugones, 2015; Quijano, 2005). Consequently, knowledge produced from inferiorized non-white, non-masculine political bodies is excluded from the canon of the modern/colonial knowledge structures of Westernized universities that continue to impose the Cartesian legacy as the only criterion for validating knowledge production (Grosfoguel, 2016).

Such ideas gave rise to what Ramón Grosfoguel (2016) calls 'epistemic racism/ sexism'; that is, the epistemic privilege of Westernized white men over the knowledge produced by other political bodies, generating the inferiorization and disqualification of voices critical in relation to colonial and patriarchal projects. Westernized white men are given the privilege of defining what is truth, what reality is and what is best for others (Grosfoguel, 2016). Speaking from Westernized universities, such subjects have the monopoly of truth and universal knowledge. However, insofar as they are, in fact, producing knowledge from private and privileged spaces and bodies, their knowledge is, in Chakrabarty's terms, "provincial" – hence the necessity to study masculinity, whiteness, and other dominant markers of authority that fix the line between the authorized and the disauthorized (Chakrabarty, 2000; Grosfoguel, 2016). As Robbie Shilliam (2013), inspired by Frantz Fanon, points out, such universalism is situated and derived from structural places of racial privilege as defined by the codes of whiteness, namely in the image of white men who are the only subjects represented as unmarked by gender, race and other signs of particularity, partiality or 'difference' (Fanon, 1967).

As the standard of authority and knowledge, the markers of whiteness and masculinity define the 'I' that can achieve certainty in the production of knowledge through what Grosfoguel (2016) identifies as the method of solipsism; that is, through an inner monologue of the subject with himself, isolated from social relations with other human beings. In critiquing the Cartesian foundation of modern thought and politics, decolonial thinkers argue that the 'I' is always situated in particular, concrete social relations, which precludes any production of monological, antisocial and non-situated knowledge (Grosfoguel, 2016).

For postcolonial and decolonial thinkers, such as Gayatri Spivak, Quijano, Grosfoguel, and Lugones, Westernized universities are focused on producing a supposedly incorporeal and de-situated knowledge when, in fact, they are speaking from a racially and gendered privileged place. In light of such perspectives, the Escola sem Partido (School without Political Parties) project that incited the occupations in 2016 is to be read not as neutral and non-doctrinal as it presents itself, but as a political instrument of a particular worldview: white and masculine, embodied in and by the Brazilian State.

Bill 867/15, Escola sem Partido (Schools without Political Parties), starts from the assumption that there is a political indoctrination within Brazilian education and that teaching must be based on rules of neutrality. This neutrality must be posted on the walls of the classrooms and guide the elaboration of textbooks, as well as regulate selection processes at higher education. The project came at a time of transformation of Brazilian public and private universities, which, through affirmative action programs, have expanded the presence of poor and black students. One of the effects of the greater access of black students to the Brazilian universities is the formation of collectives and movements that increasingly dispute the hegemonic narratives enshrined in the curriculum. As such they contribute to the decolonization of the university, both within and beyond the classrooms. It became clear that the project is aligned with the racist foundations of the Brazilian state that historically, through its institutions including education, has been reproducing modern/colonial structures. In the documentary *Lute como uma menina* (*Fight Like a Girl*), one of the students criticizes the teaching that prevailed prior to the occupations, emphasizing how before the occupation they had only ever heard of the Portuguese (Colombini & Alonso, 2016).

As one of the most influential figures of the history of the Brazilian black movements, Abdias Nascimento (1980) brought our attention to how the educational curriculum begins Brazilian history at the moment of colonization and begins the history of Afro-Brazilians at the moment of enslavement by the Europeans. Such resistance to decolonize schools and other sites of early citizen formation ends up reinforcing what Nascimento (2009) refers to as a cultural genocide and epistemicide of Afro-Brazilians in diaspora, constantly dislocated, marginalized and annihilated by the white Brazilian postcolonial elite. In practice, the debates about race, class and gender relations that took center-stage in the 2015 occupations of São Paulo schools would not have space to continue under the Escola sem Partido (School without Political Parties) initiatives. This depoliticizes these questions as 'moral' dilemmas, and downloads and decides that the place for moral discussions is in the traditional family nucleus. Whether in terms of the much-feared 'gender ideology' that is seen to threaten heteronormative sex-based roles, or in terms of the insertion of African history and Afro-Brazilian culture in the curriculum that is seen to threaten the values of Western society, schools are charged with reproducing society as it is, as it currently benefits a glocal elite.

According to Rosane Borges, professor at the School of Communication and Arts at the University of São Paulo (ECA/USP), the adoption of this project brings into focus the monocultural, patriarchal and white supremacist ideology that for a long time has presented itself as the only conception of the world (Neto, 2017). For the coordinator of the Black Nucleus for Research and Extension of UNESP, Juarez Xavier, the project promotes the concealment of the genocide of black and indigenous peoples of the country who are denied a place of protagonism in official discourses and decision-making processes (Neto, 2017).

The occupation of schools and universities in Brazil must therefore be read, first and foremost, as a movement toward the decolonization and democratization of structures of knowledge and power, fostering critical reflections on what and how we teach our citizens to engage with/in society. In these ways, they have revealed not only the limits, but also the very conditions of possibility of the current education system, as well as the fears projected onto the future for which it is meant to prepare today's youth.

Finally, the student occupation movements have challenged the modern/ colonial dichotomy between mind and body, as they teach us that critical reflexivity is much more than the production of a theoretical or intellectual knowledge. Rather, it is embodied, affective, collective and intersubjective (Neary & Amsler, 2012). The occupations, even when not staged en masse, make their presence felt through the everyday occupations of poor, black and markedly feminine and queer bodies seen as 'out of place.' These are the occupations that make alternately legible bodies that were educated to contain and control themselves so that those who belong to the order of whiteness and masculinity may reinforce their myths of superiority that require the inferiorization of its 'others.' Universities, sacred spaces of the mind – of invisible bodies made colorless, genderless and free of particularity – where society's decision-makers are trained to occupy spaces of power, are now being forced to renegotiate its pacts and rethink its measures of (des)qualification and (des)authorization of subjects of knowledge and power.

Final considerations

The chapter sought to explore the occupation of Brazilian schools and universities as contributions to the process of decolonization of modern/colonial structures. Focusing above all on the 2015 occupations of state public secondary schools in São Paulo, we argue that this new way of doing politics – experimental, affective and responsive – questions the modern production of knowledge, authority and space/time relations. The occupations open up new possibilities to reflect critically on the racist and sexist structures that underlie the contemporary Brazilian state and society as well as other postcolonial countries.

Although the São Paulo student movements achieved a qualified victory in stalling the proposed 'reorganization' of state public schools, numerous other occupations did not achieve their stated objectives. Constitutional amendment PEC 241, for instance, was approved in December 2016 amidst much political turmoil. Nevertheless, we should not judge the success or failure of these movements through the modern/colonial grammar that we seek to undo, which understands gains and losses exclusively in relation to the state, its elites and institutions. As we have seen, occupations expand the sphere of politics, and our very understanding of the political.

The permanent struggle for a radical democracy, based on horizontal relations of presentation, is both an objective and a practice and, in this sense, an anticipated future – a future in the present. Students move between the well-demarcated times of modernity by experiencing the present and abating the idea of the future as a promise, and of the young as the future of the nation. Students struggle to make present, to have their voices be heard in the framework of a nation built on the exclusion of poor, black, feminine and peripheral bodies. The presence of such bodies, loaded with emotions, pains, stories, knowledges and critical awareness placed into hitherto inaccessible spaces marked by hierarchies of race, class and gender, has problematized the figure of the sovereign subject producer of knowledge, or of the subject who, in Cartesian terms, 'thinks, therefore exists.' Moreover, by their presence, the modern/colonial structures that position us in relational terms are destabilized: when one relocates, all must relocate.

The opening of universities to subjects of knowledge traditionally marginalized by the Brazilian state has put in motion a process toward pluriversality, that is, towards interepistemic dialogue. Yet, more than explore the limits and possibilities internal to these movements and presences, which is a work in process, we have looked to the occupations – by student movements, collectives and bodies contesting the terms of their (dis)qualification – as an ongoing process of the decolonization of structures of knowledge and power. Whether contesting a crooked look that tells people where they do and do not belong, the bibliographies and criteria of evaluation or the wholesale 'reorganization,' reappropriation and resignification of spaces and positions of decision-making, the decolonization of education is a permanent political dispute for the society that we are committed to recreate.

Notes

1 Viralized by way of Carlos Pronzato's documentary by the same name (*A Rebelião dos Pinguins*, 2007).
2 Translated, adapted and disseminated via social media networks by the collective O Mal Educado (The Poorly Educated).
3 For example, on the Facebook site of the occupation of the Saboia de Medeiros State School, the rallying call reads: "get up and fight, wake up and put into practice the whole revolution that you want to happen" (cited in Campos et al., 2016: 113; our translation).
4 On the same Facebook page: "Here we not only learn to fight for our rights, but to live them ... It has not been easy to often agree disagreeing ... to accept opinions, differences ... to help others and forget a little bit about our 'I'" (Campos et al., 2016: 133; our translation).
5 For additional strategies towards the same end see Illich (1985), Mignolo (2012) and Freire (2007).
6 Even the most prosaic decisions, such as what to make for lunch or dinner, were submitted to the collective reflexive process of the organized assembly (Campos et al., 2016).

References

Bates, D., Ogilvie, M. & Pole, E. (2016). Occupy: in theory and practice. *Critical Discourse Studies*, *13*(3), 341–355.
Brugnoli, Francisco. (2006). Como ser el Futuro si no somos el presente? *Facultad de Artes: Universidad de Chile*, retrieved June 22, 2017, from www.artes.uchile.cl/noticias/39287/como-ser-el-futuro-si-no-somos-el-presente-cartel-en-reja-colegio#
Campos, A. M., Medeiros, J. & Ribeiro, M. M. (2016). *Escolas de luta*, vol. 16. (Veneta, ed.) São Paolo, Brazil: Escolas de Luta.
Campos, L. R. & de Souza, S. F. (2015). Educação Quilombola e Decolonialidade: Um Diálogo Intercultural. *Anals do XII Congresso Nacional de Educação – EDUCERE. 1*, pp. 37313–37330. Curitiba: Editora Universitária Champagnat.
Casconcellos, B. (Dir.). (2015). *Anjos Rebeldes* [motion picture]. Brasil.
Castro-Gómez, S. (2005). Ciências Sociais, violência epistêmica e o problema da "invenção do outro". In E. Lander (org.), *A colonialidade do saber: eurocentrismo e ciências sociais* (pp. 227–278). Buenos Aires: CLACSO.
Castro-Gómez, S. & Grosfoguel, R. (Eds.). (2007). *El giro decolonial: Reflexiones para una diversidad epistémica más allá del capitalismo global.* Bogotá, Colombia: Siglo del Hombre Editores.
Chakrabarty, D. (2000). *Provincializing Europe: Postcolonial Thought and Historical Difference.* Princeton, NJ: Princeton University Press.
Colombini, F. & Alonso, B. (Dirs.). (2016). *Lute como uma menina* [motion picture]. São Paulo, Brazil.
Cruz, D. (2015). Façamos de cada escola um quilombo. *PTSU*, November 26, retrieved June 15, 2017, from www.pstu.org.br/facamos-de-cada-escola-um-quilombo/
Fanon, F. (1967). *Black Skin, White Masks* (R. Philcox, trans.) New York: Grove Press.
Freire, P. (2007). *Pedagogia do Oprimido.* São Paulo: Paz e Terra.
G1 São Paulo. (2015). Após suspensão da reorganização, escolas começam a ser desocupadas. *G1 São Paulo*, July 12, retrieved June 10, 2017, from http://g1.globo.com/sao-paulo/escolas-ocupadas/noticia/2015/12/apos-suspensao-da-reorganizacao-escolas-comecam-ser-desocupadas.html
Gimenes, C. I. (2016). Ocupar e resistir: entre o político e o pedagógico nas escolas ocupadas. *Blog DA*, November 2, retrieved June 15, 2017, from https://blogdaboitempo.

com.br/2016/11/02/ocupar-e-resistir-entre-o-politico-e-o-pedagogico-nas-escolas-ocupadas/

Girotto, E. D. (2016). A dimensão espacial de escola pública: leituras sobre a reorganização da rede estadual de são paulo. *Educação Social*, *37*(137), 1121–1141.

Gomes, N. L. (2012). Movimento negro e educação: Resignificando e politizando a raça. *Educação Social*, *33*(120), 727–744.

Governo do Estado de São Paulo. (2017). Reorganização Escolar é adiada para garantir o diálogo com comunidade escolar em 2016. *Governo do Estado de São Paulo Secretaria da Educação (SEE)*, retrieved June 18, 2017, from www.educacao.sp.gov.br/reorganizacao

Grosfoguel, R. (2016). A estrutura do conhecimento nas universidades ocidentalizadas: racismo/sexismo epistêmico e os quatro genocídios/epistemicídios do longo século XVI. *Educação Social*, *31*(1), 25–49.

hooks, b. (2010). *Teaching Critical Thinking: Practical Wisdom*. New York: Routledge.

Illich, I. (1985). *Sociedade sem escolas*. Petróplis, Brazil: Vozes.

Laborne, A. (2014). Branquitude e colonialidade do saber. *Revista da ABPN*, *6*(13), 148–161.

Lugones, M. (2015). Toward a decolonial feminism. *Hypatia*, *25*(4), 724–759.

Mignolo, W. (2012). Globalization and the geopolitics of knowledge: the role of the humanities in the corporate university. In K. L. Kleypas & J. I. McDougall (eds.), *The American-Style University at Large: Transplants, Outposts, and the Globalization of Higher Education* (pp. 3–40). Lanham, MD: Lexington Books.

Mignolo, W., Giuliano, F., & Berisso, D. (2014). Educación y decolonialidad: aprender a desaprender para poder re-aprender. Un diálogo geopolítico-pedagógico con Walter Mignolo. *Revista del IICE*, *35*, 61–71.

Nascimento, A. (1980, December). Quilombismo: an Afro-Brazilian political alternative. *Journal of Black Studies*, *11*(2), 141–178.

Nascimento, A. (2009). Quilombismo: um conceito emergente do processo histórico-cultural da população afro-brasileira. *Afrocentricidade: Uma abordagem epistemológica inovadora*, *4*(1), 197–218.

Neary, M. & Amsler, S. (2012). A new pedagogy of space and time? *Journal for Critical Education Policy Studies*, *10*(2), 106–138.

Neto, S. (2017). Escola sem partido, escola com racismo: "chegamos ao limite daquilo que os brancos estão dispostos a negociar." *Almapreta*, December 24, retrieved June 21, 2017, from www.almapreta.com/editorias/realidade/escola-sem-partido-escola-com-racismo-chegamos-ao-limite-daquilo-que-os-brancos-estao-dispostos-a-negociar

Pronzato, C. (Dir.). (2007). *A Revolta dos Pinguins* [motion picture]. Chile.

Pronzato, C. (Dir.). (2016). *Acabou a paz: isso aqui vai virar o Chile!* [motion picture]. São Paulo, Brazil.

Quijano, A. (2005). Colonialidade do poder, Eurocentrismo e América Latina. In *A colonialidade do saber: eurocentrismo e ciências sociais*. Buenos Aires, Argentina: Consejo Latinoamericano de Ciencias Sociales.

Really Open University. (2010). *What do we mean by "strike, occupy, transform"? Really Open University*, February 24, retrieved June 14, 2017, from http://reallyopenuniversity.wordpress.com/2010/02/24/what-do-we-mean-by-strikeoccupy-transform/

Resk, F. & Italiani, R. (2015). A história da escola ocupada que fez 93 ficarem abertas. *Estadão*, December 6, retrieved June 17, 2017, from http://sao-paulo.estadao.com.br/noticias/geral,a-historia-da-escola-ocupada-que-fez-93-ficarem-abertas--imp-,1807504

Revista Educação & Sociedade. (2016). Uma Reforma Apressada, Falha e Antidemocrática. *Educação Sociedade*, *37*(137, December), 921–925.

Santiago, V. & Fernández, M. (2017). From the backstage of war: the struggle of mothers in the favelas of Rio de Janeiro. *Contexto Internacional*, *39*(1, January), 35–52.

Santos, B. d. S. (2007). Para além do pensamento abissal: das linhas globais a uma ecologia de saberes. *Revista Crítica de Ciências Sociais*, *79* (November), 71–94.

Santos, B. d. S. (2008) *A gramática do tempo: para uma nova cultura política*. São Paulo: Cortez.

Schucman, L. & Cardoso, L. (2014). Apresentação Dossiê Branquitude. *Revista da ABPN*, *6*(13, June), 5–7.

Shilliam, R. (2013). Black redemption, not (white) abolition. In A. B. Tickner & D. L. Blaney (eds.), *Claiming the International: Worlding Beyond the West* (pp. 141–158). New York: Routledge.

Spivak, G. (1989). Feminism and deconstruction again: negotiating with unacknowledged masculinism. In T. Brennan (ed.), *Between Pyschoanalysis and Feminism* (pp. 206–223). London: Routledge.

Uribe, G., Amora, D. & Prado, M. (2016). Temer critica ocupações e sugere que alunos nem sabem o que é uma PEC. *Folha De S. Paulo*, November 8, retrieved June 23, 2017, from www1.folha.uol.com.br/educacao/2016/11/1830376-temer-critica-ocupacoes-e-sugere-que-alunos-nem-sabem-o-que-e-uma-pec.shtml

Vasconcellos, B. (Dir.). (2015). *Anjos Rebeldes* [motion picture]. Brazil.

12

LEARNING FROM PRISONS

Decolonial feminism and teaching approaches from prison to university

Elena Vasiliou

Introduction: embodying an epistemic 'betweenness'

This project owes its inception to my involvement with prison education and the impact this experience has had on my subsequent involvement in academia. Indeed, the trajectory of this research is shaped by the experiences I accumulated teaching in prisons for a period of four years. A fifth year followed when, along with teaching in one institution, I pursued enrolment in another: the university. Shuttling between prison and university generated some anxiety. I found myself dealing with the pressure to reconcile spaces that seemed irreconcilable and even incompatible. The PhD in Gender Studies (still ongoing) was a degree that I wanted to pursue. I was motivated by my involvement in prison teaching and inspired by a wish to explore my topic through alternative theoretical models. My experiences working in a prison setting had already changed the perspective I had acquired as an undergraduate Psychology student. My reflections on issues of incarceration, punishment, knowledge and education were revised significantly as a result of that experience. Moreover, theories of gender and decoloniality, even queerness, formed a fitting and useful frame for my reflections. Most importantly, these theories validated, on the one hand my need for an embodied approach to my investigation and, on the other, a need to see the prison not simply as an object to be investigated, but rather as a place capable of producing knowledge. Reversing the usual approach toward prisons and establishing a process of learning *from* prison is not easy when your education gives you the tools to interpret prisoners and prison settings under diagnostic criteria[1] or under specific schemes of knowledge. In other words, I began to see the necessity to exercise a disobedience against my discipline and some mainstream forms of prison science and explore the potential for reconceiving prisons as places for generating different forms of knowledge that invite reflection on issues of social, racial and epistemic politics.

Significantly, these forms of knowledge offer insights into how epistemic politics have come to affect society at large.

Decoloniality has a specific historical background and its own sociopolitical context (Quijano, 2000). Therefore, any attempt to bring and apply notions from, say, Latin America to Cyprus,[2] which is situated in between the East and West, could fail completely (Yaşın, 2000). This article recognizes the issues and ambiguities inherent in that effort. What follows is more an exercise on border thinking,[3] or an epistemic experiment and, as such, possibilities and openings strive against limits and failures.

The most important limitation in this research is the complicated relationship of Cypriots (both Turkish Cypriots and Greek Cypriots) with the concept and the practices of coloniality. In July 1878, the British arrived in Cyprus. The innovations introduced by the new colonial masters were integrated into the Ottoman rule, which created a mixed administrative system with 'eastern' and 'western' elements (Andreou, 2015). Independence came in 1960, but it was under the 'supervision' of three countries (the United Kingdom, Turkey and Greece). Fighting between the two main communities culminated in the Turkish invasion of 1974 and the island has remained divided since then. The two separate ethnic communities with their different realities approach their 'mother countries,' Greece and Turkey respectively, on a spectrum ranging from admiration to rejection. On the one hand, Greek Cypriots consider themselves to be more European than Greeks, especially when it comes to issues like higher living standards, 'civility' and their more functional civil service. At the same time, we can identify an 'atrophy of civil society' and 'clientelist neocorporatism' as the main features of the Greek-Cypriot community (Mavratsas, 2003). According to Yiannos Katsourides (2013), Cypriots desist from all forms of political activism and they don't have an interest in political participation except for voting. The result is that ideas of resistance or civil disobedience influence few people in Cyprus.[4] On the other hand, Turkish Cypriots feel squeezed between a domineering and overpowering 'mother country' that threatens to swallow them and the Greek-Cypriot Republic of Cyprus, which has rejected them since 1963 (Trimikliniotis, 2012).

According to Boaventura de Sousa Santos (2016), we can observe from the very beginning an internal colonialism in Europe. If we understand colonialism as "a system of naturalizing differences in such a way that the hierarchies that justify domination, oppression and so on are considered the product of the inferiority of certain peoples and not the cause of their so-called inferiority," then internal colonialism is questioned in Cyprus only in very rare cases (Santos, 2016, p. 18). According to Vassos Argyrou (1996), modernity in Cyprus is a legitimizing discourse. The recognition by Greek and Turkish Cypriots of a feeling of cultural inferiority in relation to Westerners is part of this discussion. But, instead of leading to a questioning of that domination, and to the theorizing of an "epistemology of the south," in line with Santos, in Cyprus this cultural inferiority has created a situation where colonialism has been internalized as a necessary step on the way to achieving modernity (Argyrou, 1996, p. 26).

This internalization is well described by Indonesian feminists Adriany, Pirmasari and Satiti, who narrate the feeling of discomfort when they transferred from Indonesia to the UK to study (2017). Their seemingly 'private' feelings are a clear reflection of the structural lack of representation of their experience as Indonesian women in mainstream gender and feminist theories. As a young scholar from the periphery approaching feminist and gender theories from a particular sociopolitical background, I can recognize and connect with their arguments. The distance between mainstream feminist and gender politics and theories from the day-to-day living of women (or people who identify as women) in Cyprus is substantial, even if in the last few years the sociopolitical climate in Cyprus has been changing rapidly. According to Maria Hadjipavlou (2010), first, no independent feminist movements have penetrated Cyprus. All attempts at gaining a foothold for feminism in the country originated from mainstream male-dominated parties. Second, the domination of the "Cyprus problem" has put all other issues on the back burner, including gender and environmental issues, gender violence, and minority rights (Hadjipavlou, 2010, p. 247). For example, abortion was legalized in south Cyprus in 2018, but in north Cyprus it is still illegal. Last, but very important, the discourse on the naturalization of violence against women can be traced back to the passive mentality of Greek Cypriots mentioned above (Verloo, 2011). That mentality is also at the root of the absence of civil culture in Cyprus, which makes it difficult to address issues of gender inequality publicly (Verloo, 2011).

To sum up before moving on, just as when universities in Europe and South Africa demanded decolonialization (de Jong, Icaza, Vázquez & Withaeckx, 2017), I believe it is critical to explore decolonial schools of thought from a specific context where a political, or epistemic, demand for such theories or actions is absent or invisible (Santos, 2016). In order to understand that absence we need to make a shift from mainstream feminist European discourses to the concept of coloniality of gender as proposed by Lugones (2008), which is a shift to a more reflective way of thinking focused on embodiment. Moreover, the theoretical and practical territory covered by education and punishment—or prisons and universities—is too large for the scope of the present chapter. However, this short-scale research has allowed us to situate the politics of knowledge and the politics of punishment in a particular sociopolitical and geographical context. My chapter is a minoritarian discourse, which nevertheless suggests some insights into complicated issues (Deleuze & Guattari, 1986). In that light, my concerns are the following: to contribute to a shift from a mainstream/traditional drive to study prisons as marginal spaces to a desire to learn from the margins. Second, in order to learn from prisons, we need to exercise a radical responsiveness and an embodied way of learning. Third, a critical rethinking of the value of weakness as a strength in teaching can contribute to ideas of decolonial teaching and feminism in and across prison and academia. Lastly, the separation of the production of knowledge from European epistemic premises is not independent from the separation of politics of punishment and of education. To de-link from these modes of knowing along the lines of Mignolo's (2011) and Dussel's (1993) arguments, which I will outline below, it is important to bend the concept of epistemic disobedience across disciplines and within disciplines.

Decolonial pedagogy: toward a de-linking of the education/ punishment-based colonial approach

In *Discipline and Punish*, Foucault refers to education and punishment in the following terms: "But, in its function, the power to punish is not essentially different from that of curing or educating" (1995, p. 303). How we can understand prisons as places that educate and (neoliberal) universities as places that punish? How do the processes of gendering and racializing participate in the processes of educating and/or punishing? How have Western universities embodied from the very beginning the racist and sexist structures that are the foundation of that complicated relationship (Grosfoguel, 2013)? It is precisely here where decolonial schools of thought can contribute to an alternative understanding and praxis of the process of education. We need to identify a number of shared moments in order to understand how punishment and education constitute a duality in a similar way in which "modernity/coloniality expresses a *duality*," in the words of Rosalba Icaza (2017, p. 28). After recognizing that duality, we need to develop procedures and methodologies to de-link the following: educational processes from punishment practices, and epistemological theories from imperial/modern knowledge. One small part of that attempt is the implementation of the prison educational program I will describe later in this chapter.

Drawing from Dussel (1993), who refers to the myth of modernity and equates modernity with Europeanization, I will touch upon the main elements of that myth in order to underscore the link between punishment and education, both based on colonial structures. Modern European civilization not only presents itself as superior, but also establishes this constructed superiority as natural. Early criminologists like Cesare Lombroso are perfect examples of this bias at work (Gibson, 2002). According to Dussel, those feelings of superiority are externalized as a mission to educate those whom they consider inferior. The obstacles to the Europeanization/ civilizing impulse are removed with violence. Elements of epistemic violence are also part of this process.[5] This violence constitutes the operative event of victims who take the role of a sacrifice in the name of civilization. The results are twofold: first, there is a feeling of remorse directed at those who are perceived to be barbarians, or primitive or inferior; second, the relief projected by the 'civilizers' masks the guilt they experience for their actions. The last stage of this process is a repercussion modernity considers unavoidable (Dussel, 1993).

According to Mignolo (2011), the power of the state and its control over the production of knowledge are the twin pillars of the colonial matrix of power. That matrix of power consists of four connected fields: control of the economy, of authority, of gender and sexuality and of knowledge and subjectivity. The result of that control is racial, gender, ethnic, national or class discrimination, which has riddled historical and geo-political discourse for centuries. Mignolo suggests:

"Decolonial thinking and doing focus on the enunciation, engaging in epistemic disobedience and delinking from the colonial matrix in order to open up decolonial options" (2011, p. 9).

The call for epistemic disobedience in order to disconnect from the colonial matrix of power is very important because it lets us challenge heteronormativity, gender and racial discrimination in society. The concept also builds a coalition between the notion of disobedience and the notion of the 'episteme.' Epistemic disobedience is a way to disconnect epistemical knowledge from colonial knowledge, an approach followed by the prison education program presented below.

María Lugones' criticism of contemporary and mainstream feminist theories is also very important when considering the de-linking from modern/imperial knowledge (Lugones, 2008). Three elements from her approach are very useful for engaging with decolonial schools of thought in and across academia. The first is a shift from an abstract and neutral way of knowing to learning/teaching as a somatic and spiritual process. The second of Lugones' criticisms is the realization that the oppression/resistance dynamic must go beyond a monolithic understanding of oppression and resistance. Such a monolithic understanding is grounded in a Western binary assumption about autonomy and agency on the one hand, and vulnerability and victimhood on the other. Instead, oppression and resistance must be understood as a continuum. The stories of imprisonment told by women (and men) reveal that victims and perpetrators are not identities but positions in a very complicated system of power. Finally, Lugones argues that a politics of coalition is necessary if we want to shift from a Western way of thinking to a more collaborative way of learning/teaching/living (Lugones, 2008).

A "paradoxical" failure[6]

Meanwhile, the intersection of the politics of punishment and the politics of knowledge creates a paradox. According to Ruggiero and Ryan, academic disciplines that engage with penal theories contribute to "a passive trajectory" (2013, p. 6). In criminology, for example, voices for a more radical, or new, understanding of criminology have been recurring since the 1970s. The common feature of all of these voices is a recognition that criminology is growing as a scientific or research endeavor,[7] but that it is out of touch with public and policy discourses. Part of this paradox can be traced back to the discussion surrounding the failure of prisons to reform prisoners (Foucault, 1995). This discussion has existed since the establishment of prisons. Over the years, it has taken different forms and has had different focuses (Nilsson, 2003). The high rates of suicide or attempted suicide, recidivism, the excessive consumption of psychiatric medicines, the marginalization of ex-convicts and the racializing of the crime are some major factors that reinforce the idea that prisons have failed as a system. Mathiesen describes prison as "a fiasco" (2005, p. 137) and Nilsson (2003) refers to that failure as an accepted truth among criminologists and sociologists.

The paradoxes also connect with the fact that the poor go to prison and the rich go to university. Wacquant (2009) and Earle (2011) refer to an inverse relationship between prisoners and university students.[8] When prisoners are incarcerated, they enter a system which excludes upward social mobility. The opposite happens (or was happening until the recent past) for university students. According to Earle, "Universities offer the opposite, a positive credential, a degree certificate that lights the road to higher salaries, safer jobs and more satisfying work – the professions – even the middle class!" (2011, p. 21).

To understand why prisons are failing but growing in number, we must first rethink the trinity of political, epistemic and legal discourses and practices surrounding incarceration and punishment, as well as the ambiguities inherent in the way we talk about rationality. That said, a call for a critical rethinking regarding the expansion of incarceration systems and mechanisms by hegemonic mainstream disciplines like criminology and psychology, which follow Eurocentric structures of knowledge, is not enough. We must first distinguish between criminality and mental illness. Criminality and mental illness are not only acts or phenomena; they are not for criminologists and psychiatrists what language is for linguists. Linguists and sociologists deal with material with a subjective dimension (i.e., language, society, gender, sexuality, etc.), but criminologists and psychiatrists deal with material that they most often do not admit or consider to experience themselves.[9] For this reason, we can note the absence of a lived experience in their knowledge of their subjects. This absence explains why, when thinking about prisons, it is necessary to think beyond the established disciplines and to differentiate between the ideology of humanism, the meaning of punishment and the construction of a knowledge base that is constantly shifting.

University and prison: a chronicle of crossing borders

What follows is an exploration of how decolonial thinking goes hand-in-hand with teaching. As far as the praxis of teaching goes, I will discuss from the point of view of a person who has basic education in psychology and understands prisoners from a different epistemic lens. With this perspective, I will review a recent social literacy program organized and implemented in the Central Prison of Cyprus by a local institution of higher education. The data for my analysis are the following: first, the documentation of the program from the educators (Ioannidou, Kiourti & Christofidou, in press); second, interviews that I conducted with the educators; third, field notes from my experience as instructor of psychology in prison settings. Social literacy education approaches texts as 'meaning-making' semiotic sources that enable one to reflect on social roles and power relations. The curriculum of the social literacy program was based on critical theory approaches, and Paulo Freire's work on the education of the oppressed was one of the central pillars (1970). By conducting a series of interviews with educators who participated in the social literacy program, I aimed to initiate a discussion on epistemic disobedience from the educator's point of view that could help one aspire to self-questioning and epistemic humility.

For the purposes of my interviews and the analysis that follows, I used narrative analysis, a type of qualitative research that focuses on narrative as a process of knowledge-making with political and epistemic consequences (Labov & Waletzky, 2003). I conducted three unstructured interviews, prepared the transcript and then shared the collected data with the interviewees for further discussion. The participants were all educators in the social literacy program mentioned above. Furthermore, the interview data was enriched by narrative analysis from data collected during my tenure as a psychology instructor at the Central Prison of Cyprus (2010–2015). Notes taken from that period are used mostly as an amplifier to describe the process of theorizing the experience of learning from prison. Prisoners talked a lot about the benefits of the social literacy program and I decided to conduct a more detailed exploration of the program by asking the educators how they made sense of the project and how their own identities fit into the equation. My purpose was to initiate a process of theorizing through their experiences and to combine their epistemic tools with the epistemic tools of my discipline. By doing so, I allowed them to express their feelings and ideas, while I worked more *in and against interpretativism and psychologization*.

Maria is an academic in an institution of higher learning in Cyprus.[10] Niki is special teaching personnel at the same university, and Rebecca is a PhD student. Maria was coordinating the program, but the three worked as a team in close collaboration. The narrative analysis used is based on Connelly and Clandinin, who argue: "We restory earlier experiences as we reflect on later experiences so the stories and their meanings shift and change over time" (Connelly & Clandinin 1990, p. 9). What interested me specifically is the idea of collaborative stories. Using this approach, the finished document is a synergy combining the stories of the participants and the researcher.

A prison within a prison: the lack of education services for non-Greek-speaking inmates and the implementation of the program

The Central Prison of Cyprus was built in 1887. It is a colonial building with the capacity to house 700 prisoners. Out of those 700, 50 are currently female. Discussions of the corrupt penal system appear very often in the news. In addition, specific boards, such as the parole board, are notoriously dysfunctional. As Taylor (2009) mentions, post-colonial prisons remain undisciplined institutions, very often 'pre-modern,' and their transformation to modern institutions is only partial and temporary.

The women's prison is a prison within a prison. Female guards and inmates are housed in a separate wing from male prisoners. Because of this situation, prison officers in the female prison wing don't have keys and must call prison headquarters to get outside. The female wing also lacks many facilities, such as culinary, health and educational services. Based on my experience working in the prison, this gap was never questioned by the female guards or by the inmates. Female prisoners rarely described their condition as one of inequality or institutional violence.

In Cyprus, those classed as 'foreigners' (those without Cypriot nationality) make up 49 percent of the prison population and 76.3 percent of the female population (Statistical Service of Cyprus, 2014). According to a report from the European Committee for the Prevention of Torture (CPT) on the Nicosia Central Prison, "more than 50 percent of the inmate population were foreign nationals and yet little was done to address their specific needs" (Council of Europe, 2014, p. 42). The lack of access foreigners have to education, work, and mental health services and activities is underlined by the report.

In Cyprus, people from racial or ethnic minorities or from East Europe are very difficult to locate in prison statistics. Fassin (2016) suggests that for countries that have a history of race problems, such as the United States and Britain, the over-representation of racial and ethnic minorities can be observed and reported more easily. In Britain and the United States, recognition of this overrepresentation of minorities has led to research that aims to explain it, public debates that call it into question, social activism seeking to correct it, and even some changes in penal and prison policy (Fassin, 2016).

That systemic blindness which Fassin observes in French prisons, in contrast to prisons in the Britain and the United States, appears in the Cyprus penal system as well. Prison administration doesn't hold data in relation to minorities. Until now, there is no pressure from NGOs or other activist circles to address this problem. So, it is easy to trace types of crime from national statistics, but more difficult to verify the origin of the prisoners. Yet even if tracing the ethnicity or racial background of the prisoners is difficult, it is still possible to trace the double standards of prison practices toward people from racial or ethnic minorities. In fact, for the five years (2010–2015) I was working there, very few educational programs were designed for non-Greek-speaking prisoners. As a result of the above, the social literacy program was piloted only with Greek-Cypriot women first and then on Greek-Cypriot male prisoners, except for rare situations when foreigners attended the lessons in Greek language and someone from the class was translating.

The social literacy program was implemented February 2014 to June 2015. The program itself was divided into two phases. For the first six months, the educators taught only female prisoners. For the remainder of the year, they taught both men and women. The idea was born after careful consideration and some prison visits at a time when serious inmate disorders spiked and there had already been five inmate suicides. Understandably, the prison administration was looking for ways to open paths of communication with the prison community. Maria, an academic with an ethnographic and linguistic background, visited the prison school, first the male wing and later the female wing. She said of her experience,

> When I visited the women's wing, I realized that it was necessary to go there to do something. I visited a sad exercise area with two exercise machines and they told me that it was the classroom for the female prisoners. The reason I decided to get involved was because I remembered the male prisoners' classroom had a library, education facilities, and interactive boards.

(Maria, academic, 42 years old)

Maria's theoretical background was based on critical approaches to education, and linguistic and epistemological approaches to literacy as a social practice. The curriculum of the social literacy program was based on poems, digital material and literature. The idea was to create a space where female prisoners could explore literature and write, and through these means discover their own voices.

Entering an unknown territory

The three educators did not have previous experience of teaching prisoners. Two of them did not have any experience in teaching marginalized groups. What they did have was a strong background in critical approaches to pedagogy and sociolinguistics. The first lessons in the women's wing had been running successfully when suddenly the inmates did not show up for their class. One of them told the educators that they were teaching without taking into consideration their backgrounds and their experiences. The inmate was referring to the previous lesson in which the educators gave her a poem called "The World of a Woman," by M. Takvam (Ioannidou, Kiourti & Christofidou, in press). The poem is about a woman struggling to find a way to get out of a man's custody. Some of the female inmates refused to come to that lesson because they had been convicted of murdering their partners. Their life histories thus blurred with the class material and bent the boundaries of the educators. Rebecca, an educator, commented on this:

> And just like that one of the female prisoners, Sonia, said that she wasn't coming again and that was a shock for us because we thought we knew how to deal with the fact that we were teaching in a women's prison.
>
> *(Rebecca, educator, 32 years old)*

At that moment, the educators came face-to-face with the ambiguities and difficulties of teaching in a prison setting. Ethical dilemmas were emerging. Should educators meet prisoners with prior knowledge of their crimes? If yes, wouldn't that information cloud their opinions and thus affect their ability and willingness to teach? However one chooses to answer these questions, the fact remains that educators, when operating within the prison culture, need to rethink their own ideas and beliefs. They must learn and 'un-learn,' a process that demands non-linear thinking, patience and understanding (Spivak, 1993). Parker et al. believe that to sustain a decolonial classroom within the university, a radical openness is necessary.[11] A decolonial classroom requires a disrupting of research norms and a coalition on the production of knowledge. Part of that radicality means engaging with emotions, feelings and cognitive processes (Parker et al., 2017). Our transactions with the interviewees support the idea that the radical receptivity we exercised in prison settings could be applied to university settings as well. In both these cases, and in any situation where a decolonial approach is used, one must also accept the vulnerability of the teacher. That acceptance signals what Lugones (2008) has called the shift from the neutrality of Western knowledge to an engagement with a way of knowing/ learning and teaching that focuses on embodiment.

Teaching women and men in education settings: socialized sexual differences

In a conversation with Gina Dent, Davis argues that the homogeneity of female prisons all over the world challenges our assumptions about women and feminism (Davis & Dent, 2001). She therefore identifies a gap between feminist theories and women who are incarcerated. According to Davis, a strong gender attachment is often encountered in female prisons, which contradicts feminist readings of essentialism discourses. For example, in order to problematize assumptions in relation to female agency, Davis asserts that if the expression of agency against domestic violence is leaving the relationship we know that women in prison present a further challenge to us (Davis & Dent, 2001). Davis mentions this because very often women in prison experienced domestic violence at the hands of their partners but rarely ended the relationship. Dent, in turn, argues that prison realities challenge mainstream feminist theories and call for an embodied theory that also considers agency and the equality/difference debate (Davis & Dent, 2001).

Feminist scholarship has engaged thoughtfully with the equality/difference debate in the past (Scott, 1986). In prison scholarship, Gelsthorpe (2004) argues that for women the path to crime often includes specific elements in their pasts that lead them in that direction. In particular, it appears that women who have committed crimes often face financial difficulties, have the responsibility of raising children as single mothers, face domestic violence and have been subjected to high rates of child abuse. At the same time, some researchers suggest that all of this is gender-neutral and that male prisoners are susceptible to the same financial and social deficits (Genders, Player & Johnston, 1989). Loucks (2010) discusses all the above, noting that suicide attempts, the widespread use of psychopharmaceuticals and difficult social situations are also very often observed in male inmate populations.

Davis' reflections on these ideas challenged my own assumptions and made me wonder not only how gender, space and materiality constitute subjectivities in prison settings, but also how we can understand similarities without falling into the trap of essentialism. The educators in Cyprus admitted that the two spaces (men's and women's wings) were totally different and that these differences shaped the embodied consciousness of prisoners. On the other hand, the three were careful to avoid putting an essentialist spin on the different ways their teaching methods were received by male and female prisoners. Maria said, "No, I can't say that it was one hierarchical difference between male and female prisoners in their responses to the material . . . In some cases, when I was giving the same material, the comments were similar" (Maria, 42). Niki maintained a slightly different position when she argued: "Women were more difficult, men were more comfortable in prison settings, more happy and positive and they had a strong desire to work with the literature" (Niki, 32).

What emerges from their narratives is not a hierarchical difference but rather a negotiation with gender and place in different terms. Therefore, it is important to suggest here that in attempting to understand the different responses and positionalities of women and men in prison education and within prison settings in general, we need to avoid the kind of feminist discourse which takes performativity of gender and patriarchy as a non-historical wholeness. Thus, Rosalba Icaza and Rolando Vásquez (2016) follow Lugones and argue that we need to develop a historically situated understanding of gender as a socialized sexual difference. With such an understanding, we can reveal that the mechanisms of coloniality that have constructed the female criminal identity are based on differences and thus shape the socialized sexual differences that exist within prisons today. As previously mentioned, Gelsthorpe cites Lombroso, a proto-criminologist, as the first to connect female criminality to woman's sensitive nature, supporting the notion of a "double deviance" (Gelsthorpe, 2004, p. 16). Female offenders, according to Lombroso, fail to live up to their natures or to comply with their expected social roles. Coming from a totally different point of view (feminist criminology), Gelsthorpe argues that women often internalize their guilt and, because they are women and they are being criminalized, they feel it doubly. From my experience in teaching, and from the educators' narratives themselves, it emerged that women in prisons were in a more difficult position than men. This inequality exists for several reasons. Explanations for this inequality, however, may fall into the traps of essentialism or interpretivism. If we accept Gelsthope's argument that female offenders very often internalize their guilt, and then combine it with the absence of feminist activism in mainstream politics in Cyprus today, then we can understand why nobody has questioned the lack of educational and other facilities in the women's prison. That condition of inequality is taken for granted. In the beginning of this chapter I mentioned that we can observe the naturalization of violence against women and a general mentality of passivity in Cyprus. If this is in fact the case, then we need to shift from mainstream feminist theories to a situated historical understanding of the gender differences toward crime, punishment and political condition if we want to understand how these differences mentioned by the educators constitute different subjectivities.

A different currency of knowledge

According to Mignolo (2011), university institutions have three missions: training new obedient members,[12] controlling who enters and which knowledge is allowed or rejected. Having that in mind, a double perspective on university education and teaching in prison settings could reveal what Mignolo writes about submissive learning and the necessity for questioning hegemonic knowledge. In our discussions, the educators agreed that teaching in university and in a prison setting was a totally different experience. For example, Niki said:

> [University] students usually don't find a point to studying. They're complacent, sometimes even lost in university. It was like you have some people with open minds and they can discuss anything. Then you have students who can't discuss anything in a critical way, . . . the students who are locked into a certain way of seeing certain issues. It was very difficult to make them think otherwise.
>
> *(Niki, 32)*

So, students are already obedient toward accepted knowledge, learning and thinking, and toward the politics of knowledge and beyond. Prisoners, on the other hand, have an entirely different perspective. Maria mentioned that prisoners are outside the system and have a more radical way of being: "My students' answers and discussions, when I gave them the same material (a poem or some literature), were more stereotypical. The prisoners have a more raw and progressive discourse" (Maria, 42). That said, we must avoid romanticizing prisoners and thus aestheticizing violence, which is very often visible in places like prisons, without dismissing the feelings of the educators, who found that prisoners' engagement with their material was more critical than university students' engagement.

LoCi and Wittenberg University Writing Group (2016) writes about a similar initiative in a collaborative writing project from the Inside-Out Prison exchange in the United States, inspired by the work of Medina (2013) on epistemologies of the oppressed, arguing in favor of epistemologies of incarceration. Medina's basic argument, which is in turn based on Foucault, is that there is a "subversive lucidity" that is very often found in people who are oppressed (Medina, 2013, p. 45). That knowledge has certain epistemic characteristics: modesty, rigorousness/curiosity and open-mindedness. McHugh underlines that that subversive lucidity is not something that every person who is oppressed has, but that it is a positive reaction that demonstrates the will to knowledge (LoCi and Wittenberg University Writing Group, 2016). The educators all agreed that prison and the teaching experience they had there was a transformative experience. Specifically, they understood that they had learned from the margins and that the experience reshaped the way they looked at life and academia. In Niki's words, "Their life stories were amazing. Each one of them taught you something about life, about yourself" (Niki, 32).

Western universities and the coloniality of modern time are interrelated. Academics have an obligation that at times veers into an obsession to be productive. Notions of excellence, innovation and originality create a link between universities, neoliberalism and temporality. In Mignolo's words, "Success is the companion of moving fast, coming in first, and being the winner" (2011, p. 177). Maria also noticed this tendency when she recalls,

> A colleague [from] where I work asked me why I was going there [to the prison] and said I was wasting my time. I should sit down and write papers . . . The truth is that I spent many hours and precious time preparing the lessons at the prison, but I don't care. I received much more in return and I feel that I am stronger academically.
>
> *(Maria, 42)*

Maria refers here to what Lugones calls the historical embodied experience (2008). The experience of teaching prisoners supports the importance of shifting from an abstract way of knowing/learning/teaching to a particular situated embodied experience. The result, as Maria explained, strengthened her academic career.

The educators of the social literacy program mounted a double disobedience against the mainstream disciplines by challenging prisoner identity construction. They also challenged their own understanding of their roles as educators and of institutional expectations to accept and work with epistemic humility with people who had committed serious crimes. The result was a project that attempted to reject the hegemonic claims of Western knowledge and served as an epistemological challenge that applied border teaching, thinking and learning.

As a record of that experience, this chapter contributes to the discussion of decolonial options in and across academia from the point of view of prison education. Specifically, it presents the implementation of a social literacy program that advocates for disobedience and shows how it can work. Moreover, this research is an intervention from the periphery situated in a particular geographical and cultural context. Cyprus is a very small country with a complicated history and present. On the Greek-Cypriot part of the island to which I'm referring, acts and discourses of political or epistemic disobedience or of resistance toward coloniality are rare. I have tried to explain how this passivity influences both the politics of punishment and the politics of knowledge. Still, it is only a beginning. Much work remains to be done if we want to learn from prisons using decolonial pedagogical practices, and if we want to explore education and punishment from the perspective of the university instead of from the perspective of prison settings.

I would like to conclude with some suggestions towards achieving the goals listed above. First, we must learn from the margins instead of studying the margins. Second, we should be receptive to a radical openness and a way of learning/teaching that focuses on embodiment. Third, we need to rethink coloniality of gender as a historical, situated and epistemological process. At the same time, it is very important to acknowledge that the vulnerability of the educator/academic is a strength, not a weakness. Finally, following Dussel and Mignolo, we need to search for theoretical and practical ways to break the dipole of education/punishment in order to de-link the production of knowledge from modernity/European epistemological assumptions. To successfully de-link knowledge production from these modes of knowing, it is necessary to start practicing and giving meaning to epistemic disobedience across disciplines and within disciplines.

Acknowledgments

I thank the editors (Sara de Jong, Rosalba Icaza Garza and Olivia Rutazibwa) for their valuable comments and support. I also thank Stavros Karayanni, Rebecca Billström, Max Sheridan and Magda Andreou for their feedback.

Notes

1 For example, the Diagnostic Statistical Manual V (DSM-V) contains 297 disorders. The manual's shortcomings are well documented. The following are only a few: it exports disorders and the discourse surrounding them from the US to the rest of the world; the

number of disorders increases in every edition; the manual is considered to be the 'bible' of mental disorder without any critical justification for that label.

2 When referring to Cyprus, I refer mostly to the parts of Cyprus that have been under the sovereignty of the Republic of Cyprus since 1974.

3 I am following here an analysis of border thinking from Icaza as "a physical sensual experience" with the element of homelessness (Icaza, 2017, p. 26).

4 An exception is the LGBT rights movement, which has seen a boom in activism on the island in the past few years. The first pride parade took place in 2014 and it was one of the largest marches to have taken place in the South in recent history.

5 For a discussion on epistemic violence in Universities, see Heinemann do Mar Castro Varela (2017).

6 Zurn (2016) considers the notion of failure in relation to prisons. He argues that prisons fail in five ways: discursively, structurally, deconstructively, systemically and productively.

7 According to Kogan and Hanney the availability of criminology courses is growing in the UK (as cited in Earle, 2007). Also, from available reports: "about 150 journals and 120 conferences are presently dedicated exclusively to criminology and about 405,000 articles are published yearly on the current trends in criminology." (www.omicsonline. org/criminology-journals-conferences-list.php)

8 Recently the University of Harvard rejected a female ex-prisoner from enrolment as a PhD student. www.nytimes.com/2017/09/13/us/harvard-nyu-prison-michelle-jones.html

9 Names are fictional to secure the anonymity of the participants.

10 This recalls what Kuhn writes about the training of normal scientists.

11 Convict criminology is an exception. This is a field where ex-convicts with PhDs or who are in the process of earning PhDs write and challenge the mainstream production of prison knowledge. For more information about the group, visit www.convictcriminology. org/about.htm.

12 Follow bell hooks (1989) for an in-depth analysis of the concept of radical openness in pedagogy.

References

Adriany, V., Pirmasari, D. & Latifah Umi Satiti, N. (2017). Being an Indonesian feminist in the North. *Tijdschrift voor Genderstudies, 20*(3), 287–297.

Andreou, M. (2015). Cyprus the transition from Ottoman to British rule (1878–1922): Social and Political Changes, PhD thesis, Panteion University. Athens.

Argyrou, V. (1996). Tradition and Modernity in the Mediterranean: The Wedding as Symbolic Struggle. New York: Cambridge University Press.

Carrier, N. (2010). Anglo-Saxon sociologies of the punitive turn: critical timidity, reductive perspectives, and the problem of totalization. *Champ Pénal/Penal Field, 7.*

Cisneros, N. & Dilts, A. (2014). Political theory and philosophy in a time of mass incarceration: introduction to Part I. *Radical Philosophy Review, 17*(2), 395–402.

Connelly, M. F. & Clandinin, J. (1990). Stories of Experience and Narrative Inquiry. *Educational Researcher, 19*(5), 2–14.

Council of Europe (2014). Report to the Government of Cyprus on the visit to Cyprus carried out by the European Committee for the Prevention of Torture and Inhuman or Degrading Treatment or Punishment. Strasbourg: Council of Europe, retrieved from: https://rm.coe.int/1680695601

Davis, A. & Dent, G. (2001). Prison as a border: a conversation on gender, globalization, and punishment. *Signs: Journal of Women in Culture and Society, 26*(4), 1235–1241.

de Jong, S., Icaza, R., Vázquez, R. & Withaeckx, S. (2017). Decolonising the university. *Tijdschrift Voor Genderstudies, 20*(3), 227–231.

Deleuze, G. & Guattari, F. (1986). *Kafka, Toward a Minor Literature*, Vol. *30* (D. Polan & R. Bensmaïa, trans.). Minneapolis: University of Minnesota Press.

Dussel, E. (1993). Eurocentrism and modernity (introduction to the Frankfurt Lectures). *Boundary 2, 20*(3), 65–76.

Earle, R. (2011). Prison and university: a tale of two institutions? *Papers from the British Criminology Conference, 11*: 20–37.

Fassin, D. (2016). *Prison Worlds: An Ethnography of the Carceral Condition* (R. Gomme, trans.) Hoboken, NJ: John Wiley & Sons.

Foucault, M. (1995). *Discipline & Punish: The Birth of the Prison* (A. Sheridan, trans.) New York: Vintage Books.

Freire, P. (1970). *Pedagogy of the Oppressed* (M. B. Ramos, trans.). New York: Bloomsbury.

Gelsthorpe, L. (2004). Female offending: a theoretical overview. In G. Mclvor (Ed.), *Women Who Offend* (pp. 13–37). London: Jessica Kingsley Publishers.

Genders, E., Player, E. & Johnston, V. J. (1989). *Race Relations in Prisons*. Oxford: Clarendon Press.

Gibson, M. (2002). *Born to Crime: Cesare Lombroso and the Origins of Biological Criminology* (S. M. Di Scala, ed.) Westport, CN: Praeger.

Grosfoguel, R. (2013). The structure of knowledge in Westernized universities: epistemic racism/sexism and the four genocides/epistemicides of the long 16th century. *Human Architecture: Journal of the Sociology of Self-Knowledge, 11*(1), 73–90.

Hadjipavlou, M. (2010). Cypriot feminism: an opportunity to challenge gender inequalities and promote women's rights and a different voice. *Cyprus Review, 22*(2), 247–268.

Harcourt, B. E. (2006). From the asylum to the prison: rethinking the incarceration revolution. *Texas Law Review, 84*, 1751–1786.

Heinemann, A. M. & do Mar Castro Varela, M. (2017). Contesting the imperial agenda: respelling hopelessness. *Tijdschrift voor Genderstudies, 20*(3), 259–274.

hooks, b. (1989). Choosing the margin as a space of radical openness. *Framework: The Journal of Cinema and Media, 36*, 15–23.

Icaza, R. (2017). Border thinking and vulnerability as a knowing otherwise. In M. Woons & S. Weier (Eds.), *Critical Epistemologies of Global Politics* (pp. 26–45). Bristol: E-International Relations Publishing.

Icaza, R. & Vásquez, R. (2016). The coloniality of gender as a radical critique of developmentalism. In W. Harcourt (Ed.), *The Palgrave Handbook of Gender and Development* (pp. 62–73). London: Palgrave Macmillan.

Ioannidou, E., Kiourti, E. & Christofidou, C. (in press). Literacy education in prison: developing a social literacy program in the Prison School of Cyprus. *Research Papers in Education*.

Katsourides, Y. (2013). 'Couch activism' and the individualisation of political demands: political behaviour in contemporary Cypriot society. *Journal of Contemporary European Studies, 21*(1), 87–103.

Klein, D. (1973). The etiology of female crime: a review of the literature. *Issues in Criminology, 8*(2), 3–30.

Labov, W. & Waletzky, J. (2003). Narrative analysis: oral versions of personal experience. In C. B. Paulston & R. G. Tucker (Eds.), *Sociolinguistics: The Essential Readings* (pp. 74–104). Malden, MA: Blackwell Publishing.

Liska, A. E., Markowitz, F. E., Whaley, R. B. & Bellair, P. (1999). Modeling the relationship between the criminal justice and mental health systems. *American Journal of Sociology, 104*(6), 1744–1775.

LoCi and Wittenberg University Writing Group. (2016). An epistemology of incarceration: constructing knowing on the inside. *philoSOPHIA*, *6*(1), 9–25.

Loucks, N. (2010). Women in prison: research highlighs in social work. In J. R. Adler & J. M. Gray (Eds.), *Forensic Psychology: Concepts, Debates and Practice* (pp. 142–158). New York: Routledge.

Lugones, M. (2008). Colonialidad y Género. *Tabula Rasa*, *9*, 73–101.

Maculan, A., Ronco, D. & Vianello, F. (2013). Prison in Europe: overview and trends, *European Prison Observatory*, retrieved October 6, 2017, from www.prisonobservatory. org/upload/PrisoninEuropeOverviewandtrends.pdf

Mathiesen, T. (2005). *Prison on Trial*, 3rd ed. Winchester, UK: Waterside Press.

Mavratsas, C. (2003). National Unity and Political Pluralism: The Atrophy of Greek Cypriot Civil Society at the Beginning of the 21st Century. Athens, Greece: Katarti Publications.

Medina, J. (2013). The Epistemology of Resistance: Gender and Racial Oppression, Epistemic Injustice, and Resistant Imaginations. Oxford: Oxford University Press.

Mignolo, W. D. (2011). *The Darker Side of Western Modernity: Global Futures, Decolonial Options*. Durham, NC: Duke University Press.

Nilsson, R. (2003). The Swedish prison system in historical perspective: a story of successful failure? *Journal of Scandanavian Studies in Criminology and Crime Prevention*, *4*(1), 1–20.

Parker, P. S., Smith, S. H. & Dennison, J. (2017). Decolonising the classroom. *Tijdschrift voor Genderstudies*, *20*(3), 233–247.

Pont, J., Stöver, H. & Wolff, H. (2012). Dual loyalty in prison health care. *American Journal of Public Health*, *102*(3), 475–480.

Quijano, A. (2000). Coloniality of power and Eurocentrism in Latin America. *International Sociological Association*, *15*(2), 215–232.

Ruggiero, V. & Ryan, M. (2013). *Punishment in Europe: A Critical Anatomy of Penal Systems*. New York: Palgrave Macmillan.

Santos, B. (2016). Epistemologies of the South and the future. *From the European South: A Transdisciplinary Journal of Postcolonial Humanities*, *1*, 17–29.

Scott, J. W. (1986). Gender: a useful category of historical analysis. *American Hirstorical Review*, *91*(5), 1053–1075.

Shor, I. & Freire, P. (1987). *A Pedagogy for Liberation: Dialogues on Transforming Education*. Westport, CN: Bergin & Garvey.

Spivak, G. C. (1993). *Outside in the Teaching Machine*. New York: Routledge.

Statistical Service of Cyprus. (2014). *Criminal Statistics 2011*. Nicosia: Statistical Service of Cyprus, retrieved from www.mof.gov.cy/mof/cystat/statistics.nsf/populationcondition_ 27main_puparchive_en/populationcondition_27main_puparchive_en?OpenForm &yr=2014

Taylor, C. S. (2009). Tensions of colonial punishment: perspectives on recent developments in the study of coercive networks in Asia, Africa and the Caribbean. *History Compass*, *7*(3), 659–677.

Trimikliniotis, N. & Bozkurt, U. (2012). *Beyond a Divided Cyprus: A State and Society in Transformation*. New York: Palgrave Macmillan.

Verloo, M. & QUING Consortium. (2011). *Final QUING Report*. Institute for Human Sciences, Vienna: QUING.

Wacquant, L. (2009). *Punishing the Poor: The Neoliberal Government of Social Insecurity*. Durham, NC: Duke University Press.

Yaşın, M. (2000). *Step-Mothertongue: From Nationalism to Multiculturalism: Literatures of Cyprus, Greece and Turkey*. London: Middlesex University Press.

Zurn, P. (2016). Work and failure: assessing the Prisons Information Group. In P. Zurn & A. Dilts (Eds.), *Active Intolerance: Michel Foucault, The Prisons Information Group, and the Future of Abolition* (pp. 75–91). New York: Palgrave Macmillan.

13

POST-IT NOTES TO MY LECTURERS

Roselyn Masamha

In these post-it notes to my lecturers and fellow students, I attempt to strike the very delicate balance of achievable changes/steps which can be done fairly easily, while at the same time avoiding 'sticky plaster' solutions to what are clearly complex issues that warrant depth of consideration. In keeping with my aim to engage those who are directly affected by colonial dynamics in the international classroom, these Post-it notes are presented as an educational toolkit for the benefit of all involved. They draw on my own experience as a Zimbabwean nursing student in the UK, as well as on suggestions from my research participants, who are now qualified nurses reflecting on and sharing their experiences as Zimbabwean students who undertook nursing education in the UK.

> As teachers, do not always seek to control and remove tension, instead learn to value it as an aspect of learning. This particularly includes occasions when other students may make ill-informed derogatory comments that reinforce stereotypes, not challenging these, suggests collusion.

Expand your reading lists to include 'othered' voices, there are many important theories put forward by non-western intellectuals.

Get to know your students; there is nothing more inclusive than making specific time to connect with students.

Ask questions, even when you feel uncomfortable asking questions. How else are you going to know?

In case of 'fear of causing offence', ask anyway – people generally know when your questions are coming from a good place.

Share some of your vulnerabilities, this humanises relationships and redresses some of the power balances and creates moments of connection that have an impact on students reciprocating this to the benefit of future teaching and learning exchanges

Please learn my name.
In this overwhelming sea of newness where everything else is constantly shifting, it is sometimes the only fixed identity I can use as my anchor.

I cannot begin to tell you how it feels to have even that taken away...

Unpick what people understand is meant by what you may consider to be obvious terms – you will be amazed that sometimes when you think we are on the same page, we really aren't!

Be cautious of student deficit models! It is a tempting comfort zone to retreat into, which saves you from reflecting on your own input and often the need to change.

Take a respectful interest in other cultures rather than pathologizing them. It will help you understand certain classroom behaviours more accurately and thus be in a better position to respond to them more effectively and appropriately.

When putting together your scenarios and case studies, please do not limit your characters to only Anglo-Saxon names.

Include some more diverse names (I can give you many simple examples if you ask).

These relatively minor points of departure create important little points of connection that serve to make me feel less alienated. It is important for me to see that people like me can exist in your texts.

A word of CAUTION though – please do not make these diverse characters the HIV positive single mother with 5 children on the brink of starvation.

The best question I was ever asked was, "How best do you learn?"

Many more lecturers/teachers would do well to ask this!

Be prepared to reconsider positions that you may have assumed your whole life and make room for new knowledges, new insights, new understandings.

Not everything is about language problems; there are many issues that affect international students beyond language proficiency...

Actively explain particular approaches to teaching and learning whilst taking on board other experiences of the same.

As appropriate, evaluate my performance against a background of unfamiliarity as opposed to lack of knowledge.
Being judged on the basis of being new is very different from being judged on the assumption that you have no relevant knowledge.

Engage us as partners and resources in the teaching and learning exchange. It's much easier to participate in something that you have made a contribution to and can identify with.

A sense of belonging is central to being able to participate, allow me to be a part so I can take part!

Africa is also progressive, just in different ways and not ones that are usually broadcast. Let's make the classroom one of those places where we dispel myths!

Reflect on what you deem important:
It's easy to get hung up on the minor details, which in the greater scheme of things are fairly insignificant - meanwhile other issues that critically affect students are overlooked.

Embrace fresh perspectives that different students bring. The fact that they may not fit into the established norm does not make them wrong, neither is it grounds for their rejection.

Create an environment that enables the recovery & validation of suppressed knowledges, you will be amazed just how many precious nuggets of knowledge you can find in your seemingly quiet students.

Be clear about expectations, this includes defining in very clear terms what student and teacher roles are. Not all pre-university schooling is informed by the same ideas…

Ask your students to produce some brief interest inventories, they will help you to relate learning to students' lives, to build on their background knowledge and draw on their personal experiences thus making your teaching more relevant to their learning. It's a win-win!

Move away from using local examples all the time that rely on people being familiar with a historical context, research some global examples that still enable you to make your point. Not only does that give all students an entry point, it enriches all your students with a knowledge of the world beyond their doorstep.

PART IV
Disciplines

14

INTERVENTION

Sixteen participants of the "Crossing Borders" conference in Lesbos, Greece, July 2016

This is a collective statement[1] co-drafted by sixteen participants – some of whom wish to remain anonymous – as a response to the conference organization and proceedings of the "Crossing Borders" conference in Lesbos, July 2016.

We are here to read a communiqué that was collectively written by a group of participants in the "Crossing Borders" conference, both panelists and audience members. We do not intend for our intervention to close down any discussions, but rather to open up a new space of self-critique. We observe that a number of borders have been (re)produced by this conference itself.

1. *Linguistic border* – one of our limitations is that we're giving the statement in English when one of our issues with the conference is that there has been no Arabic or Farsi translation or interpretation and apparently no invitation issued to migrants/refugees to participate in meaningful ways in the conference.

2. *Epistemic border* – the Eurocentric, modern/colonial enlightenment ideology valorizing Western, heteropatriarchal rationalism marginalizes other ways of knowing or other knowledges. We see here a division being reproduced between those who speak and those who listen, those who have an authoritative voice and those who are silenced. Actually, we feel that the kind of theorization that is taking place contributes to the social death of refugees and is at least indifferent to their ontological death. We object to collapsing the "refugee issue" into the debt issue, collapsing the "refugee issue" into the Brexit issue, or instrumentalizing the current situation in the service of a macrological analysis that delegitimizes the lived experiences of people directly affected by the borders the conference claims to be addressing.

3. *Activism border* – we feel that this conference has tended to ignore and actively erase various political movements both in Lesvos and elsewhere in relation

to the camps and the criminalization of migration by not having a collective conversation about what the relationship of the conference to this system of 'migration management' is or should be—we are positioned as the "good Samaritans," "good internationals," by being invited to go to visit the detention center at Moria. Going to the detention center as a conference is validating the detention center. We feel this is a form of voyeurism, taking pleasure in, or enhancing our epistemic authority about the suffering of others. There is a transnational and a local history of activism against borders, detention and deportation that has been suppressed here. In general, refugees were not invited to give an analysis of their own situation; when they were "brought in," they were asked to perform a spectacle of suffering for experts to analyze, which is objectifying and infantilizing.

4. *Methodological border* – throughout the conference, borders were being produced, constructed by who gets the right to speak, rather than borders being occupied and defied collectively. We oppose the othering and representation of "refugees" by people positioned as experts and believe that any discussion of refugees/migrants and borders should center on refugees/migrants' own accounts, analyses and political movements. The fact that the conference did not have as its goal to be a collaborative effort with refugees raised irony when people were making well-intentioned critiques of the "othering" of refugees, yet were in fact reproducing their exclusion and marginalization. Furthermore, the juridical category of "refugee" has been used unproblematically, while it is in fact an externally imposed classification that constitutes part of the oppression of people whose movement across borders is criminalized and violently controlled.

5. *Political border* – we see this conference as engaging in politics from "above" rather than in politics from "below." Representatives or leaders of political parties are given a platform to "market" their position or to rally supporters for electoral politics. Our movements prefer to engage with the politics from "below" and to the "left," rather than the politics from "above."

6. *Relevance border* – there are issues of life and death that require practical interventions and commitments that call upon us to devote time and energy. This conference, however, has not addressed practical issues or organized us to consider how we are going to practically contribute to transforming the situation on the ground. We demand that the conference take a concrete position on the EU-Turkey deal, the Evros fence, the implementation of hotspots and mandatory detention, as well as the deportation regime. We appreciate the anti-war, anti-imperialist analysis that has been articulated, but we want to hear concrete positions and commitments with respect to reception, relocation and freedom of movement across open borders. By focusing on the relationship of the so-called "refugee crisis," to wars in Afghanistan, Iraq and Syria, we risk erasing South Asian and African migration which has been criminalized for decades. We also reduce the responsibility for migrants' deaths in the Mediterranean to United States imperialism, rather than consider how

empires and peripheral client states collaborate in the war against migration. We are opposed to a re-inscription and valorization of national sovereignty which is not only racializing and racist, but also reproduces the very system that oppresses refugees.

7. *Historical border* – we feel very uncomfortable with the term "refugee crisis" and believe that the crisis is produced by the borders themselves. The construct of "refugee crisis" has been used unproblematically in ways that conceal the histories of coerced and criminalized migration to this continent, making it seem that this is a recent or sudden phenomenon. We call for an abolition of all borders rather than their reification through discourses that locate the problem in migration rather than in national sovereignties.

8. *Internalized borders* – the conference failed to conceive of "the border" as something other than a physical geopolitical reality; yet, "the border" is something that we have all internalized in various ways and that many of us have tried to challenge in our intimate and affective relationships. Lesvos, where this conference was held, is a space where borders of all kinds have been inhabited and contested, and also where multiple efforts to "de-border" have been criminalized by the state (resulting in arrests of, and charges against, activists engaged in rescue or welcoming activities). We wanted to know more about this situation, and feel that this could have been an opportunity to hear from legal experts what possibilities there are for resisting the criminalization of solidarity.

We want to stop speaking now, and open this space to an assembly for all who are gathered here to participate together. We decided to take this space to invite people to tell us why you are now here in Lesvos and what motivates you to engage with issues of borders, migration and violence. How do we – methodologically, linguistically, theoretically and practically – cross the various borders we have named (and others we have not)? We would like to transform this "roundtable" into an open assembly that takes clear positions on the above issues, on the proposed visit to the Moria detention center, and on the practical questions of how to proceed collectively.

Note

1 A video of the intervention can be accessed here: www.youtube.com/watch?v= JXW2NULQV9g. The video was uploaded by one of the participants of the conference.

15

ON BABIES AND BATHWATER

Decolonizing International Development
Studies[1]

Olivia U. Rutazibwa

Introduction

> Sussex Development @SussexDev
>
> Recalling a conference on post development where it was asked 'After 4 decades of postdev critique, how come we still have the international #aid and #development sectors?' @o_rutazibwa began to think about the relation between teaching international development & the sector

In June 2015, DEVESTU, the Finnish Graduate School in Development Studies, organized a workshop titled Post-Development as a Paradigm, at the University of Helsinki. Consciously mixing junior and senior interlocutors – academics/ activists/practitioners – in keynote addresses[2] and break-away sessions, the question was raised by one of the post-development pioneers how it was possible that, after four decades of post-development critique, we were still stuck with the all-in-all same aid industry. I remember that the question, put forward in that consciously de-hierarchized space, bridging histories and continents, imprinted a sense of urgency in my mind, to the need to foreground, more systematically, the institutional implications of all scholarly deconstruction and critique.

I was reminded that part of the answer to the question was linked to the fact that, as long as we institutionally keep offering International Development Studies as a career path that intertwines students' financial and personal investments, as well as our own careers, it is very unlikely, however critically and pedagogically soundly we engage with coloniality in class, that it will magically dissolve unless we address the organizational and institutional architecture of development.

> **Sussex Development @SussexDev**
>
> As long as we still teach international #development and cultivate it as a career path, despite our critique in the classroom, it is unlikely that we will disrupt or destabilize the international #aid and development industry – @o_rutazibwa @IDS_UK #SussexDev

It is this realization that I seek to reiterate here. There is scope for connecting the critical scholarly insights that have been developed over the years in critical studies, dependency and world-system theories, feminist approaches, post- and decolonial thinking, and how they are timidly entering and altering what we teach, with how our institutional setup of both research and education needs to be rethought.

Today's calls to decolonize International Development Studies in the global North appear at an interesting temporal and spatial conjuncture.

On the one hand, we see both profound and sustained attempts to disrupt the colonial status quo. We see that previous understandings of what passes as knowledge and ethical behavior, often projected as universal, are being questioned and fought against through an invocation of the colonial. In university circles alone, one could think of the different movements, known via their hashtags: #WhyIsMyCurriculumWhite, #FeesMustFall or #RhodesMustFall connect academic activism in South Africa and the UK; the less publicized #GandhiMustFall call in Ghana illustrates how even the global icons of morality are being rescrutinized.

These calls within the academy have not developed in isolation. Apart from the many struggles in the past, they have been inspired by and are developing hand in hand with similar demands for radical changes by varied groups and movements in societies at large: such as the Boycott Divest and Sanctions (BDS) movements against the continued apartheid system and colonization of Palestine and its peoples; the Occupy movements, the so-called Arab Springs, the North Dakota Access Pipeline (NoDAPL) water protectors' activism, Black Lives Matter and the Women's Marches, to name but a few. This clearly partial and unfinished list points at the multidirectional and multi-issue nature of what is being challenged. Yet, in one way or the other, one can trace the protests as linked to a desire to undo and heal the breaches, fractures or *dis*-memberings (Ndlovu-Gatsheni, 2018a, 2018b) of a colonial system of governance – characterized by a *colonial matrix of power* (Quijano, 2000, 2007), interlocking and perpetuating systems of power based on patriarchy, racism, hetero-normativity, ableism, sexism, gender-binarism, . . . ; a system of governance that is too often still considered as belonging to the past. Taken together, these movements point at a growing collective realization that with the formal ruptures with colonization in the 1960s, decolonization has been partial, and very much unfinished in the present.

Sussex Development @SussexDev

#Decolonising #Development must be approach against a dual background of (a) optimistic anticolonial pushbacks like #RhodesMustFall & (b) renewed, frantic & violent attempts to hold on to the 'white man's world' – @o_rutazibwa opens the last #SussexDev lecture of 2017 @IDS_UK

On the other hand, we see our times as marked by frantic and violent attempts to hold on to the colonial status quo: racist, patriarchal hetero-normative and secular colonialities in particular (see, for example, Anievas, Manchanda & Shilliam, 2015; Muppidi, 2012; Rutazibwa, 2016). At first glance, they might seem exceptional, or expressions of a sudden rise of extremisms. If, instead, we are informed by the knowledges and lived experiences of marginalized and racialized peoples, they appear as colonial continuities; as responses to the anti-colonial pushbacks described above, from those that seek to stay meaningful in a changing context, by forcefully re-affirming and re-articulating their privilege. From the alt-right movements in the US that have penetrated the highest offices of government, to anti-immigrant sentiments, violence and voting behaviour in continental Europe and the UK[3] alike, we see a renewed vigour to protect the "white (man's) world". It is against this dual, mutually constitutive background that I want to paint my reflections concerning decolonizing International Development Studies.

In its most generous reading, the development aid sector (including university departments of International Development Studies) is – even in a global context imbued by coloniality – the site where ideas and intentions of solidarity and concerns for others' well-being are voiced and institutionalized.

An anti-colonial reading of aid and development, though, locates its actions and thinking firmly in the continuation of the coloniality that it is supposed to tackle; a coloniality that continues to carve up humanity and the other sentient beings into deserving and undeserving, human and sub- or non-human. By inscribing itself in this logic of a-historical "generous" superiority, the aid business is complicit in reproducing, invisibilizing and legitimizing the ills of poverty, conflict, deprivation, diseases, environmental degradation and exploitation of the colonial project.

Ultimately, when we speak of decolonizing International Development Studies, the question at hand is the extent to which Development Studies is complicit, partakes in or even embodies coloniality of power. Sabelo Ndlovu-Gatsheni, building on articulations by Maldonaldo-Torres (2007) and Mignolo (2007b), describes it as follows:

> Coloniality is an invisible power structure that sustains colonial relations of exploitation and domination long after the end of direct colonialism. Coloniality of power works as a crucial structuring process within global imperial designs, sustaining the superiority of the Global North and ensuring the perpetual subalternity of the Global South using colonial matrices of power.
> *(Ndlovu-Gatsheni, 2012, p. 48)*

In a blogpost engaging with my talk, former University of Sussex International Development Studies (IDS) student and development worker Agnes Otzelberger put it even more poignantly:

> The colonial world order has never actually had the rupture it is believed to have had in the 1960s. It seems a bit like a zombie wrongly believed to be dead that continues to haunt the living world, including – and perhaps especially so – the world of international development.
>
> *(Otzelberger, 2018, para. 3)*

It is at the intersection of these two readings that we need to locate the call and need to decolonize development. It is here that the question of its possibility or impossibility presents itself. If development is a continuation of a colonial mindset of inferiority and superiority, as this gift of progress by the superior societies to the others, should it be salvaged at all? Whose interests are served when we try to do so? What do we keep? What do we get rid of?

Sussex Development @SussexDev

This talk will address Western European understandings and practices of #development and how they have been shaped. #Decolonising Development discussions in previously colonised spaces may rightly come up with a different set of priorities – @o_rutazibwa @IDS_UK #SussexDev

---

The enormous task of decolonizing development cannot be thought of in the abstract – it is both inspired by and needs to be tailored to concrete contexts of international development teaching, research and practices. Mindful of this need to avoid abstractions and universals, I here specifically speak from and to contemporary western European understandings and practices of development.[4] I concentrate on the specific 'us' of development educators, researchers, knowledge producers, and other practitioners that epistemologically hail from the global north. Again, this unitary category does not exist in the world out there as, for one, there are so many variations within it – here, it serves the purpose of addressing a comparatively hegemonic positionality in the analysis of colonial power embedded in international development thinking and practices with a particular focus on the academic context. There are indeed differences between continental Europe (e.g. my country of birth and education Belgium) and the United Kingdom (my current country of residence and employment). In the former, postcolonial thought is often still either absent or timidly emerging as a critical disciplinary lens or even a topic of discussion in society at large. In the latter, there seems to be an understanding that postcolonialism has been engaged with and embraced, and that now it is time to move on to something else. I put it here in slightly simplified terms, the purpose being that comparative analyses might be instrumental in working towards a more comprehensive understanding of the challenges at hand, all the while not forgetting to re-translate them to their specific context.[5]

I turn to the "babies and bathwater" trope to conceptualize the challenge at hand. Ndlovi-Gatsheni (2012) reminds us of the stakes of decolonizing development: it is not merely about altering the content but also very much the terms on which we are having the conversation. The decolonial one, then, aims to "engage with the crucial issues of epistemology, being, and power that maintain the present asymmetrical global relations" (p. 51). In what follows I will make two points: first, that development as a system of ideologies, studies, institutions and practices is the bathwater. As such we need to find ways to go beyond critiquing and deconstructing it, and seriously considering getting rid of it. I will argue that we need to fight the desire to hold on to Development Studies, cut the umbilical cord with this discipline, even if it is the one that has given us our professional and personal identities, our status, including our pay cheques; and second, that the baby in this story, the ideas, desires and energies worth keeping and fighting for, are those pertaining to global justice, solidarity and reparations, as in righting past and present wrongs, and contribute to the "good life in the pluriverse", i.e. a world in which many worlds are possible.

Sussex Development @SussexDev

The 'bathwater' here is #development as a system (ideologies, institutions, practices) which we may need to get rid of; we need to fight the desire to hold on to 'development studies' even if it has given us our professional identities (and paychecks) @o_rutazibwa #SussexDev

---

It is important to foreground that by deploying the "babies and bathwater" trope, I do not mean to imply that we need to look for uniform, universal or even fixed ways of decolonizing development. If anything, the trope raises more questions than answers. Hence, rather than one-size-fits-all decolonial propositions, I will offer a framework of reflection, based on decolonial insights for both deconstructive and reconstructive strategies to address the implications of the decolonial invitation, option (from the original idea of Zulma Palermo (for example, 2010); see also Icaza, 2017, p. 27; Mignolo & Escobar, 2013)), or imperative, even (e.g. Grosfoguel, 2018). The concrete examples I use will invariably be partial, simplifications or even exaggerations. The invitation is to use them as lenses through which to read what we are doing in practice, differently.

Sussex Development @SussexDev

Drawing on these insights, @o_rutazibwa puts forward a threefold #decolonial strategy inspired in part by the work of @MeeraSabaratnam: a strategy that addresses Ontology, Epistemology and Normativity #SussexDev @IDS_UK

The framework addresses issues of ontology/temporalities, epistemology, and normativity, and stresses the need to actively resist separating discussions on representation from materiality. As such it is presented as a triptych – for analytical purposes, not because these different entry points of reflection are distinguishable or could be observed separately.

The decolonial strategic framework[6] that I offer here is an attempt at bringing together all these insights and tying them simultaneously to these different layers of development studies: the classroom, our research agendas and the institutional environments in which these take place. It is not necessarily to box decolonial thinking into a unitary mode of thinking, as theories are supposed to do, but, while acknowledging its contextual nature and ever-changing features, to make the insights workable, thinkable and applicable to the varied aspects of research and pedagogy we are confronted with when trying to decolonize our social worlds.

The need to "de-mythologize"

The first leg of the strategic framework addresses ontology, or the study of what "is". It is most easily captured by thinking of it as a *what* question: "How do we understand our social reality, the world to be, to have become?" In the particular context of International Development Studies, this question pertains to our understanding of the origin of wealth and poverty, of global inequality and what the role of the "international community" and its institutions is in mitigating it.

Sussex Development @SussexDev

Firstly, Ontology – this pertains to the myths that structure development thinking (and which are not acknowledged/recognised as myths): it is very difficult to conceive of a space in development that is outside of a Western present - @o_rutazibwa #SussexDev

---

One way to conceptualize the decolonial call in this context is the need to *de-mythologize*[7] in line with iterations like those of Césaire (1955, p. 84), when he points at "the fundamental European lie" at the heart of the understanding of the civilizing mission or Grosfoguel and Cervantes' (2002, building on earlier insights by Enrique Dussel and Walter Mignolo, engagement with the mythology of the Eurocentric.[8]

What does this mythology in the context of International Development Studies and the way we (are taught to) understand the world consist of? Before turning to three general points through which to engage with de-mythology, I offer two short examples of "mythology" to illustrate the ontological question at hand.

One: every new academic year, I ask my first-year undergraduate students to brainstorm some of the reasons for suffering in the global South and in Africa in particular. One of the recurrent reasons offered is that of "corruption". The other popular contenders – especially when they choose to zoom in on the situation of women – are: "their culture" or religious beliefs. What these answers have in common is the absence of "us"/the global North, a glaring absence of the past and an implicit assumption that the South's future success or good life is contained in emulating Western-style development.

Two: in the classroom and public debates alike, when we ponder how to respond to large-scale loss of human life – be it in the context of armed conflict (e.g. in Syria) or natural disasters (e.g. the earthquake in Haiti), or large-scale health emergencies (e.g. the Ebola crisis in West Africa), few would contest that "we must do something"; even fewer, that "doing more" is by definition the most ethical option. Yet again, there is a glaring absence of the North in the creation or exacerbation of the issues, of the past, and of the endless variety of avenues to address the problems – or even a debate on who is to set that agenda. So, ultimately, the main mythological element of development thinking might well be the idea that the betterment of other people's life cannot be thought of outside of a Western presence. Jyotirmaya Tripathy and Dharmabrata Mohapatra phrase it as: "Central to development studies is the ontology of underdevelopment, which requires some kind of external intervention" (2011, p. 96). Decolonizing development would therefore entail an overall imperative to de-link solidarity from the idea of Western incursion, however defined.

Sussex Development @SussexDev

We need to think about Origin, Fragmentation & Euroscentrism. Thinking about Origins: where do we start our #development courses? Truman's Speech (trumanlibrary.org/whistlestop/50 . . .) or Fanon (en.wikipedia.org/wiki/Concerning . . .)? @o_rutazibwa #SussexDev

---

Building on insights from post-development, postcolonial and decolonial (feminist) approaches, one could identify three[9] recurring issues that help us detect, understand, as well as break with, the perpetuation of these mythological reflexes in our reading of global North/global South relations: (1) point of origin or departure, (2) Eurocentricsm and (3) fragmentation.[10]

So, first, the issue of the point of departure or origin: *Where do we start the story?* At its core – there, where most syllabuses start, in its overall degree structure and lesson plans, in its various research agenda and funding schemes and priorities, but also in its consultancies and other collaborations with the "outside world" (Krishna, 2001), International Development Studies is constitutively defined by colonial amnesia. International Development Studies is not the only discipline to suffer from this, but these recurrent blind spots and institutionalized erasures are all the more remarkable and unacceptable, given that the enslavement/colonial encounter is what created the need for Development Studies, or international solidarity, in the first place.

Sussex Development @SussexDev

Eurocentrism: we need to respond to thinkers like Dipesh Chakrabarty and the idea of provincializing Europe, and think about what a #development research agenda that doesn't follow/respond to European present would look like – @o_rutazibwa #SussexDev

---

Second, we cannot but consider the most insidious of all biases in the modern understanding of the world: Eurocentrism. "What would our understanding of global relations look like if (the idea of) Europe/the west, ceased to be its benchmark or center?" There is not enough space and time to go over all the rich engagements with the idea of Eurocentrism (see, e.g., Amin, 1989; Chakrabarty, 2000; Grosfoguel & Cervantes-Rodriguez, 2002; Hobson, 2012; Quijano, 2000; Sabaratnam, 2013; Wallerstein, 1997). It is nevertheless worthwhile reiterating – especially when we are addressing critical pedagogy in a Western context – that the problem with Eurocentrism is less that it exist as *a* place from which to understand the world, than the fact that it has been projected as the neutral, objective and universal one. Equally important is the concealment (Dussel, 1993) of this universalizing move. Useful scholarly antidotes to this are calls for de-/re-centring historically silenced spaces to reconfigure our understanding of the whole global picture. As a partial, minimum yet insufficient condition we have Chakrabarty's (2000) call to provincialize Europe; equally important, and insufficient, is the concomitant call to de-provincialize Africa, for instance, and how this is different from inclusion or "adding to the mix" (see, e.g., Ndlovu-Gatsheni, 2018a). Again, Eurocentrism is not an ill that only befalls International Development Studies. But it is even more remarkable and unacceptable, given that the object of study is so clearly the non-Western condition and its supposed aim – its betterment.

Sussex Development @SussexDev

Fragmentation: We need what @GKBhambra calls connected sociologies. This means not thinking about Europe/development only appearing on the scene as 'firefighters' (as when you start courses with Truman's speech), but thinking about colonial background of development 'problems'

Third, we need to pay attention to the level of systematic and recurrent fragmentation in our storytelling: "Which parts of the story that belong together, do we keep on telling separately; chopping up in separate bits and pieces that have seemingly nothing to do with one another?" The intervention on modernity/coloniality (Quijano, 2000), i.e. the fact that modernity cannot and should not be thought of outside of its constitutive flipside coloniality, is an invaluable insight for International Development Studies, in particular. Gurminder Bhambra's (2014) work in global social theory on connected sociologies/histories is helpful in trying to imagine how fundamentally our stories change if, rather than replacing Eurocentrism with another centrism, we start from an idea of co-creation and relationality (see, e.g., Icaza, 2017; Rojas, 2016; Sarr, 2017) in time and space. Bhambra (2015) applied these ideas very insightfully to the refugee 'crisis' in Europe, and showcased how, again, it is not an issue of adding on or including, but how a connected histories approach fundamentally changes the conversation. It becomes difficult to hold on to ideas of "us" and "them", to distinctions between refugees and migrants, citizens and non-citizens, when the connected histories of all the people involved, of the creation of wealth and poverty, conflict and peace, are considered. The research agenda at hand can then not be confined to the present; the policy options, from a European point of view, not to one of more or less generosity. A decolonial approach to this so-called crisis[11] cannot fall short of re-centering the discussion on the issues of borders and unequally distributed freedom of movement embedded in the international society of states – the real reason certain groups of people (not the expats) die *en masse* while on the move.

Before looking at the concrete implications of de-mythology in the classroom, in our research agendas and the university as an institution, let us briefly recapitulate the issues to which the need to demythologize draws our attention. It is only through sustained colonial amnesia in knowledge production in our society at large that the ills in the global South are systematically and almost exclusively attributed to the "now" and the local (over there). Similarly, when we try to address questions of humanitarian interventions and emergency assistance, we tend to start the story in the "now" and locate the problems in isolation "over there" and the solutions with ourselves.[12] Even in its "grassroots, bottom-up, local ownership" post-Liberal version, within the International Development Studies framework, we still feature as those that unlock or facilitate these local solutions and potentialities to emerge. This point surely deserves a more sophisticated elaboration, but, simply put, International Development Studies, in the way it is conceived, what it chooses to focus on, and what it is supposed to do, is not equipped to see the world but through the eyes of the saviour, facilitator, intervener, . . . out there – physically, financially, epistemologically, policy-wise, . . . In the absence of that gaze upon the Other, its raison d'être dissipates.

Sussex Development @SussexDev

Looking at the institutions in which we generate knowledge: we need to think about decoupling #solidarity from international #development & #aid institutions – and if we do that, the rationale for International Development departments may disappear @o_rutazibwa #SussexDev @IDS_UK

There is very little engagement with the relational (de Jong, 2013) and connected history nature of any given emergency issue that places us as a natural aid-partner on the scene. It allows for a sustained – against all odds – presentation of ourselves (Rutazibwa, 2010, 2013, 2014), i.e. Western actors, as the natural firefighters, without engaging with the idea that both in the past and today and more often than not, we are also very much the arsonists, the pyromaniacs.[13] Institutionalized colonial amnesia allows for this. A de-mythological recalibration of the brief illustrations I offered before would first and foremost foreground the transatlantic slave trade and the colonial encounter as the sites from which any thinking about development-related issues need to be addressed. Not to merely dwell in the past for the sake of it, but because it is the only way to make sense of the current global inequalities in a way that does not perpetuate the power imbalances.

Our colonial amnesia is in no way a random one – it is one that allows for a continuation of the Western self-image as the "good guys" of history (with the exceptional hiccups). It is only via a systematic occlusion and erasure of the enslavement/colonial encounter and North-South coloniality in the present that the idea of not just material, technological, but also moral superiority of the global North makes sense, thus legitimizing the aid sector and International Development Studies as they exist today. Starting the story somewhere else, reconnecting histories and relationality, provincializing Europe/de-provincializing the places at hand: if we were to turn to the earlier examples, a whole different picture of engagement would emerge.

A de-mythologized understanding of the world provides at the same time an invitation to revisit our sources of knowledge, as well as the rational for our knowledge production in the first place. Let us now turn to our knowledge sources in International Development Studies.

The need to "de-silence"

Sussex Development @SussexDev

Sussex Development @SussexDev

On to Epistemology, the 2nd #decolonial strategy, @o_rutazibwa looks at how myths persist despite critique. There are questions about who gets to speak & who gets to be an expert, we must address Silencing, Hierarchised Binaries, & the Absence of Space for other forms of knowing

The second leg of the strategic framework zooms in on epistemology or the study of how we know, a concern that we could formulate as a series of *how* questions: "How do we know what we know about the world? Who has the microphone? Who gets to speak, as experts, and not just as empirical side-kicks, and more importantly, who systematically not? Who is invited around the expert table and who systematically not? What do we consider expertise and what systematically not? And who gets to decide all of this – and who systematically not?"

From these questions, it is immediately clear how this issue of epistemology is in no way entirely detached from the ontological question. Indeed, how is it that colonial amnesia and Eurocentric fragmentation – the "mythological" – can persist, is maintained and invisibilized, even in a context of sustained critical scholarship, of attempts at deconstructing and critiquing what we already know?

Sussex Development @SussexDev

Silencing: we need to ask how much of our work is implicated in what do Santos calls 'epistemicide'. There's no need for an *intention* for work to kill off other knowledges; this also happens through overrepresentation & hyper-visibility of certain groups @o_rutazibwa #SussexDev

Decoloniality, in line with similar calls in postcolonial and feminist scholarship, calls for the need to *de-silence*. Similar to the engagements with Eurocentrism, the literature on silencing is vast and not confined to one approach or theoretical school. Most famously attributed to Gayatri Spivak's work on the subalterns in (feminist) postcolonial studies, (black) feminist engagements with situated knowledge or standpoint theory (e.g. Haraway, 1988; Hill Collins, 2009) as well as decolonial scholars' turn to epistemologies from "the South" (e.g. Santos, 2014), all engage in more or less explicit ways with the question of silencing. Given the difficulty to do justice to the richness of the existing engagements with silencing here, I will briefly touch on two aspects of it, contained in these two questions: (1) "Who are (not) the experts?" (and connect this question to the ways in which silencing manifests itself); and (2) "What do we (not) consider expertise?" (to engage with the systematic exclusion of the vast majority of other knowledges or ways of knowing).

> ### Sussex Development @SussexDev
>
> Hierarchised Binaries: so much #development thinking takes place through hierarchized binaries, ideas like 'capacity building', where North-South equality only appears possible after a convergence in the future @o_rutazibwa #SussexDev @IDS_UK

So, first, silencing presents itself through invariably hierarchized representations; the systematic bias comes to us at times through oppositional binaries, over-representation/hyper-visibilizing (e.g. the "crime/terrorism–Muslim men" combo), neglect or literal silencing (#WhyIsMyCurriculumWhite) or oversimplification ("Africa is a country"), vilification, criminalization ("corrupt African leaders") or victimization (global South women in general). Again, this type of silencing is not limited to International Development Studies. What is of interest to highlight here, though, is the fact that these biases occur in a context where equality and partnership are being foregrounded as both the goal and the premise of the encounter (Baaz, 2005), a context in which the epistemological hierarchized binaries are institutionalized and perpetuated through seemingly innocuous concepts and practices like (unidirectional) "capacity-building".

The question of what we consider expertise is of course not detachable from whom we deem experts, i.e. who we invite around the table, in our syllabi, as colleagues next and with us to co-create knowledges on international solidarity. It is nevertheless useful to consider them both explicitly, as the implications for thinking about what we consider expertise show that decoloniality cannot be equated or mistaken with a "multiculti plussing-up" exercise of inviting more of the silenced voices around the existing table. The question of who is *not* around the table in International Development Studies, taken seriously, inevitably leads to the question of why this is so (the concept of epistemicide, i.e. the eradication of colonized people's knowledge systems, is a productive way to look at it (e.g. Santos, 2014) and what purpose it serves (Dussel (2008) helps us conceptualize this through the distinction between "will to power" over "will to live"). Yet again, these issues far transcend International Development Studies, and are part of a discussion on colonial knowledge production.

Sussex Development @SussexDev

Absence of Space: need to make space for e.g. embodied knowledge as something taken seriously not just used to make classes interesting! After @RobbieShilliam we need to think of knowledge *cultivation* not knowledge production & invite #unlearning into the classroom #SussexDev

---

Shilliam (2015) invites us to think about knowledge cultivation instead of the linear, speed, 'originality' and quantity-obsessed features embedded in the idea of knowledge production. It is worthwhile citing him at length:

> To my mind, decolonial science cultivates knowledge, it does not produce knowledge. Using the Latin roots of these words, we could say that to produce knowledge is to lengthen, prolong or extend, whereas to cultivate knowledge is to till, to turn matter around and fold back on itself so as to rebind and encourage growth. Knowledge production is less a creative endeavour and more a process of accumulation and imperial extension so that (post)colonized peoples could only consume or extend someone else's knowledge (of themselves) (Chatterjee, 1998). In short, a colonial science produces knowledge of and for subalterns. Alternatively, knowledge cultivation is a necessarily creative pursuit as it requires the practitioner to turn over and oxygenate the past. Most importantly, cultivation also infers habitation, which means that knowledge is creatively released as the practitioner enfolds her/himself in the communal matter of her/his inquiry. What is more, this constant oxygenation process – a circulatory one – necessarily interacts with a wider biotope, enfolding matter from other habitations. To cultivate knowledge of deep relation can therefore be understood as "grounding".
>
> *(Shilliam, 2015, pp. 24–25)*

The image of knowledge cultivation allows understanding knowledges as always already there, to be unearthed, bound back differently, for different reasons, by anyone, into knowledges. Similarly, we could consider which place we make for the transcendental, for non-binary engagements with gender and sexuality, for the situatedness of knowledges, for non-linear temporalities, and what the classroom, research-agenda and institutional consequences would be if we were to do so. From a decolonial tradition, the idea of the pluriversal is productive in this respect (Mignolo & Tlostanova (2006, p. 219), following the Zapatistas' call for a world in which many worlds co-exist; Henderson (1995, p. 42)).

The imperative to (*anti*-colonially) "de-colonize"

> ### Sussex Development @SussexDev
>
> Finally the 3rd #decolonial strategy, 'Normativity': we must have the guts to detach our teaching & research from the idea of objective knowledge production, which is often knowledge that serves the status quo. How do we produce knowledge that is not in service of a 'will to power'?

Finally, the third part of the triptych turns to normativity or the *why* question: "Why are we producing knowledge? What project of society does our engagement with knowledges serve? The colonial status quo (Triparty & Mohapatra, 2011, p. 95) or does it foreground the need to break away from it? For radical alternatives, for thinking the world *otherwise*?" Decoloniality calls here for an explicit move away from the pretence of the possibility of objective and neutral knowledge production. It calls for knowledge-cultivation that consciously places itself at the service of (im) material de-colonization. This call is one that is not merely relevant to International Development Studies, but as a discipline that derives its rationale and legitimacy from a more or less explicit will "to help people", it is especially well placed to take on this task more seriously and explicitly. The task at hand is to investigate how the discipline, its ontological and epistemological inclinations have and continue to contribute to coloniality. It is also the place where, for some, the distinction between some efforts of postcolonial scholarship towards the inclusion of silenced voices and peoples and the decolonial imperative presents itself. Julian Saurin, writing about IR, rightfully raises the following question: "Is it not unimportant, then, to ask whether the call to decolonize is a call to postcoloniality or a call to anticolonialism (or anti-imperialism)" (2006, p. 38). An accessible image to this effect is that of the game of musical chairs, a game of elimination when the music stops, with one fewer chair than there are players. The strategies presented so far could be deployed to merely negotiate the right to participate in the game. Instead, this third leg of the strategy underscores how decoloniality is about rejecting, about changing the rules of the game, which has as its premise that there is not enough for everyone to play.

How do we concretize this challenge? Building on Dussel, Grosfoguel and Ndlovu-Gatsheni, one way to conceptualize the imperative of knowledge-cultivation for *anti-colonial* decolonization, is distinguishing between teaching and learning that contribute to the will-to-power vs those that foreground the will-to-live. An even more evocative one is Julia Suarez-Krabbé (2015): deployment of the Colombian Nasa people's concept of the "Death Project" to conceptualize that death invariably accompanies the colonial encounter and its contemporary corollary in international development and human rights thinking and practices.

> ## Sussex Development @SussexDev
>
> Even if wrapped in good intentions, most #development institutions are animated by a will to power. Thinking about how our knowledge production can *not* be in service to a will to power, we may start by thinking of #aid as reparations, not aid – @o_rutazibwa #SussexDev @IDS_UK

Will-to-power vs will-to-live and the Death Project are ways to make sure that our attempts at decolonizing go beyond the merely representational by engaging with the materiality of being, and the systems that produce life and death. It is at the same time a way to understand the co-constitutive nature of the material and the immaterial. Re-conceptualizing aid and development as reparations, i.e. moving from the idea of generosity and superiority to one of restitution and justice, is much more than a discursive trick – taken seriously, it is a decentring and displacement of power epistemologically, while at the same time foregrounding the material, those tangible issues that allow or prevent (quality of) life.

To anti-colonially decolonize in this sense means pushing back against the TINA (There Is No Alternative) beliefs that permeate and frame many of the International Development discussions. Liberal market democracy, even if not always explicitly framed as such, continues to be the benchmark and ultimate goal of successful development. At this moment in time, and especially in the global North, decolonizing International Development Studies cannot but critically and radically engage with capitalism and neo-liberalism. Institutionally speaking, it is here that we encounter the impossibility of true decolonization inside the neo-liberal university and, in that context, the impossibility to de-link International Development Studies Departments from the will-to-power, if there is no real room created, engage with the impossibility in its current form to contribute to this good-life-beyond-borders without reproducing coloniality. Yet – in the meantime – it should not prevent us from more systematically engaging with the pressing research, pedagogical and institutional question of "what we are cultivating the knowledge for".

To what extent do we displace power in the choices that we make about research agendas? To what extent do our choices contribute to the possibility of even imagining these other possible worlds? How much is our research invested in the continuation of the world as it is? How much of our career is dependent on our deconstructive work only, on talking back? In our pedagogy, what are we preparing our students for? For a sustained critical engagement with a colonial world? For a career in the aid and development sector? As most departments today seem to be doing both, how do we ethically navigate that they are mutually exclusive? In the UK, for instance, it is our students' tuition fees – attached to the promise of a career in the sector – that allow for the critical discussion in the first place, and at the same time this link is the reason that, similar to the discussions within the sector itself, it won't lead to a fundamental overhaul, discontinuation of it.

It might well reveal itself as impossible, but seriously engaging with this norma-tive strategy, will help us not to lose sight of the need to radically break with certain institutions and practices if our aim is to *anticolonially* decolonize our global ethical engagements. My contention here is that International Development Studies is one of those.

Our classroom, research agenda and institutions revisited

What are the implications of de-mythologizing and de-silencing for our pedagogy and the classroom, our research agendas or the institutional environment in which we offer and engage in International Development Studies? The answers to these questions are endless and need to be formulated collectively and in context. Here I provide some sketchy examples, framed as questions, from my own experiences as an educator and researcher in a UK university.

In the classroom: rather than reproducing US president Truman's 1949 speech on international aid as a watershed moment for the aid and development sector, my students now start their module by reading *Discourse on Colonialism* by Aimé Césaire (1955). It foregrounds not only where the need for international aid originates, but exposes the readers immediately to the myth embedded in the hegemonic under-standing and practice of so-called aid, through his engagement with the civilizing mission. The text also reconnects the horrors of the Holocaust to the violences perpetrated against the colonized people, by those who – at that time and still today – are framing themselves as the "good guys" of World World II. The text, moreover, shows what a non-Eurocentric engagement with the world might look like in practice: it is not the absence of Europe or its thinkers in the narrative, but a de-naturalizing of the white European vantage point as the only experience from which to theorize reality.

In the classroom, de-silencing most straightforwardly forces us to look at the composition of our syllabi. By whom are they populated? What is the order of the different approaches? Which new themes emerge, which are pushed back or out, when we foreground those voices and insights from a locus of enunciation of those on the imagined receiving end of our solidarity-beyond-borders thinking? For one, it is here that a fundamental reconceptualization comes to the fore, presenting itself as urgent and unavoidable maybe: both "aid" and "development", concepts that are steeped in a hierarchized understanding of the world, reveal themselves as highly problematic and inadequate to organizing our thinking on the betterment of people's lives. Reparation and global justice, for instance, seem to be doing a much better job in this respect.

De-mythology in international development *research* can take different shapes and forms, depending on one's current specializations. In my own research, inspired by the arsonist/firefighter insight, I have started to consider the need for a research agenda that focuses on international absence rather than assuming that Western presence is a prerequisite for the attainment of the "good life" (e.g. Rutazibwa, 2013). Overall, by de-naturalizing ideas of Western superiority and the location of the solutions and the problems in International Development Studies, a more sustained engagement with what needs further research and fixing in the global North could be considered more systematically. The Ebola crisis invited us, naturally, to think about emergency relief and solidarity; it should more systematically and concomitantly make us question structural adjustment policies and patent and intellectual property laws – considerations that show that decolonial solidarity does not per definition place the "helping" actor physically or epistemologically in the global South.

Sussex Development @SussexDev

#decolonising epistemology in #development also means being prepared to close down certain research areas for ourselves, refusing for instance to be a 'country expert' – whatever that may mean!
@o_rutazibwa #SussexDev @IDS_UK

In our own research, engaging with this two-level de-silencing, the following questions arise. In our bibliographies, where do we locate theory, abstract and conceptual work? How do we engage with the need for self-reflexivity and positionality, without being merely self-referential? How do we truly think about the implications? Can we, for instance, be country experts without speaking a language? Or, more importantly, without considering the fact that our vested interest in a place or issue might be light years away from our colleagues that live it, there? Can we engage with this insight without turning to extractive knowledge production practices? Can we part with our own career needs and refuse to be branded country experts, whatever that might mean?

If we consider the university as the *institutional* environment in which both teaching and research take place, de-mythology would invite us to look for the concrete instances in which the university participates in institutionalized Eurocentrism. It raises the big questions of the placement years through which we attract many students to choose International Development Studies. De-mythology invites us to revisit the racialized power relations that are perpetuated in sending inexperienced 20-something-year-olds to take up responsibilities overseas that we would never give them at home, let alone to visitors that do not speak our language. It is an attitude that is perpetuated in the aid business outside academia. The decolonial invitation, here, is to rethink these global North/South encounters in a radically different way (see, e.g., Vázquez, 2015, where, building on Lugones' idea of "world-travelling", they are understood as relating to the world, rather than "consuming" or "saving" it),[14] and maybe have the courage to suspend them until we manage to do so; to push more seriously for ways to make these encounters a mutual, two-way street affair; and to embed solidarity work also, or first, in one's or the university's immediate environment.

De-mythology also takes us to the administrative nitty-gritty of academic life. This can go from funding schemes, to something as seemingly innocuous as the composition and requirements of ethics committees or the questions raised in insurance and risk assessment forms for fieldwork travel outside the global North: they are invariably raised around the racist trope of the white civilized development researcher venturing out in places of potential danger, the "wilderness". Ethics boards do rarely account for the skills that global South researchers bring to their fieldwork or how on many occasions pulling out consent forms during fieldwork is not necessarily the way to guarantee ethical research. On the contrary. These very brief examples show how the scope for investigating the practical implications of de-mythology is endless – the explicit invitation of this intervention is that we need to foreground it more as a central, integral part of our deconstructive critical work. Engaging with the content of our syllabi also raises institutional questions linked to the university. What is the institutional support for educators to fundamentally review their material? How much space do we have in our classrooms – literally – and marking and examination strategies – figuratively – to take on the value and necessity of embracing the idea of situated knowledge and collective knowledge cultivation instead of knowledge production? How much willingness is there to rename our departments, knowing that the saviour-complex trope is in and of itself a student magnet, and as such intimately linked to the corporate interests of our universities in a neo-liberal context?

Conclusion

The question I wanted to address here was the following: against the dual background of continuity and disruption of coloniality in the present, how do we formulate – scholarly and pedagogically first and foremost – a politics of solidarity and justice that does not reproduce the coloniality of development thought and practices as we know them today; an aid sector that, in spite of the myriad of well-intentioned peoples it contains, we can read as a direct continuation of the civilizing mission idea that was constitutive and a necessary condition for the mere possibility of the colonial enterprise?

What do we keep, and what do we chuck out? How do we hold on to the baby of solidarity, shared responsibility and care, but get rid of the colonial bathwater of continued fantasies of superiority, homogeny and violent universality, civilizing the Other and the age-old white man's burden? How can we think and enact a decolonization of International Development (Studies)?

Apart from the contention that we should at the very least be willing to consider abolishing our departments of International Development Studies, as I announced in the introduction, I have not offered any straightforward, ready-made, universally applicable answers to the question of how to decolonize international development. Instead I offered, building on decolonial (feminist) and post-development approaches, a framework that speaks to questions of (a) ontology – how we *see, understand* the world; (b) epistemology – how we *learn* the world; and (c) normativity – *why*, that is, for what material and immaterial purposes we want to know the world, to navigate the decolonial option, invitation or imperative. The hope is that it is specific, yet loose enough to be adaptable to the space from which one tries to think through its (im)material implications.

Sussex Development @SussexDev

In closing the #SussexDev lecture: we cannot commit to anti or #decolonial global justice, reparations & solidarity while there is a colonial international #development industry fed by our (profitable) int dev departments – @o_rutazibwa #SussexDev @IDS_UK

My contention here was that we have to make sure we (a) move beyond deconstruction but engage in both epistemic deconstruction as well as push forward with more urgency the need to translate deconstruction into its tangible, institutional implications; and (b) move beyond "plussing up", i.e. adding voices and experiences to the existing, or "talking back", making space for thinking, seeing and connecting with radical alternatives towards solidarity-beyond-borders and justice *otherwise*. By definition, this path goes via the concept and enactment of reparations, rather than the phantasy of the "gift" and the copy/paste mentality embedded in the aid and development infrastructures. The decolonial strategic framework offered here, conceptualized these challenges respectively in the need to (a) *demythologize, desilence* and (b) *anti-colonially decolonize*.

If development – with its assumption of the need for Western presence; its superiority and systematic partial storytelling; partial understanding of who the experts are (and who are not); what counts as expertise, with its built-in epistemicidal features; its push towards a homogenized, de-politicized "developed" future – is the bath water, we need to find a way to part with it. The implications of the decolonial strategies presented here vary depending on whether they seek to address our institutions, our learning and teaching or research agendas; all the while, the discussion above showed how they are closely linked, within the academy as well as the aid sector "out there".

The challenge is to de-link solidarity and global justice from the bathwater of the ideas, institutions and practices of development. Our departments of International Development Studies, for which career opportunities in the existing aid industry is the underlying promise, and the belief in linear development and Westernized superiority, even when disavowed, its constitutive philosophy, are decolonially untenable. Hence discussions about their dismantling should be more systematically embraced in our discussions of decolonizing International Development Studies. More importantly, maybe, in the spirit of paying more attention to the reconstructive side of the decolonial challenge, the real task ahead rests in combining our energies to reinforce the study, ideas and institutions at the service of the baby of decolonial solidarity: reparations and global justice for a pluriversal coexistence.

Notes

1 This chapter is a reworked version of a talk given at the University of Sussex on 7 December 2017 as part of the Decolonising Development Lecture Series, www.youtube. com/watch?v=qdVUBYlYtF4. The textboxes throughout this chapter are a selection of the tweets by Paul Gilbert (@paulrgilbert) during that evening.
2 For details, see http://blogs.helsinki.fi/devestu-school/closing-workshop-2015/. Among the keynote speakers were Arturo Escobar, Eduardo Gudynas, Wendy Harcourt, Sumi Madhok and myself.
3 More or less explicitly, a considerable amount of the campaigning around Brexit and its subsequent success can be understood in this sense.
4 Decolonizing development discussions in other settings – for example, within formally colonized spaces and countries – might well come up with a different set or ranking of priorities. In discussions about decolonizing the mind, epistemologies and in casu development with colleagues and friends in Kigali, Rwanda, for instance, have taught me that we might be discussing the same historical system of domination and imposition, but the priorities to countering them are not the same at all times. The diasporic positionality (in my case, of a second-generation Rwandan in a global northern academic context) makes the multi-directional, if not schizophrenic, nature of the decolonial imperative almost palatable. More often than not, I – and many with me, I suspect – find myself seemingly having different conversations, foregrounding different points, receiving different questions or push back, depending on whether I am interacting in, with and from a global northern context or a (Westernized) context in the Global South.
5 I speak from my experiences as an international relations scholar/former journalist and Africa desk editor in Belgium and Italy, as well as my more recent experiences as an International Development Studies lecturer in the Anglo-sphere, in the UK and Portsmouth, in particular. In all this, my lenses are informed by a diasporic positionality as a second-generation Rwandan born and raised in Belgium, as well as a hypermobile academic with the "right" (European) passport – a real and material privilege that is nevertheless periodically pierced and questioned at the different border crossings in this world, the passport being carried by the "wrongly" racialized and gendered body.
6 Thinking of decoloniality in terms of research strategy is, among others, inspired by Meera Sabaratnam's (2011, 2017) work.
7 It is important to highlight here that pointing at the need to de-mythologize does not imply that there is an inherent problem with myths and mythology in knowledge production. On the contrary: it is rather an imperfect attempt at conceptualizing the problematic premises on which colonial knowledge is being produced, all the while not upholding its own "standards" of objectivity, rationality, and universally applicability.
8 For a poetic engagement with this Eurocentric mythology, see Robbie Shilliam in this volume (Chapter 17).
9 These points are in no way meant to be exhaustive; they merely offer a framework from which to think about coloniality in our knowledge production systematically.
10 This list is nowhere near exhaustive, does not necessarily need to be considered in that order, and – again – its three points are not necessarily observable independently of each other.
11 It is undoubtedly a crisis with regards to the unacceptable loss of life and lack of sustained public outrage and swift policy response. It is not to the extent that it is something particularly new or sudden that befalls the peoples concerned, nor when it comes to the number of people that Europe is supposed to accommodate – especially not when we compare it to the relative and absolute numbers of people on the move that countries in the Global South take in.

12 Mahmood Mamdani (2010), for instance, speaks about how debates about the Responsibility to Protect (R2P) reveal a bifurcation of the world into the capable and incapable.
13 See, for example, de Jong (2013) for a relational reading of the global citizen along these lines.
14 Many thanks to Rosalba Icaza for pointing this out to me.

References

Amin, S. (1989). *Eurocentrism*. New York: New York University Press.
Anievas, A., Manchanda, N. & Shilliam, R. (2015). *Race and Racism in International Relations: Confronting the Global Colour Line*. London: Routledge.
Baaz, M. E. (2005). *The Paternalism of Partnership: A Postcolonial Reading of Identity in Development aid*. London: Zed Books.
Bhambra, G. K. (2014). *Connected Sociologies*. London: Bloomsbury Academic Press.
Bhambra, G. K. (2015). The refugee crisis and our connected histories of colonialism and empire. *Sicherheits Politik-Blog*. Retrieved from www.sicherheitspolitik-blog.de/2015/10/01/the-refugee-crisis-and-our-connected-histories-of-colonialism-and-empire/
Césaire, A. (1955). *Discourse on Colonialism*. New York: Monthly Review Press.
Chakrabarty, D. (2000). *Provincializing Europe: Postcolonial Thought and Historical Difference*. Princeton, NJ: Princeton University Press.
Chatterjee, P. (1998). Talking about our modernity in two languages. In *A Possible India: Essays in Political Criticism* (pp. 263–285). Calcutta, India: Oxford University Press.
de Jong, S. (2013). Intersectional global citizenship: gendered and racialized renderings. *Politics, Groups, and Identities*, 1(3), 402–416.
Dussel, E. (1993). Eurocentrism and modernity (introduction to the Frankfurt Lectures). *boundary 2 20*(3), 65–76.
Dussel, E. (2008). *Twenty Theses on Politics*. Durham, NC: Duke University Press.
Grosfoguel, R. (2018). *[Talk] Ramon Grosfoguel @UoP II: Epistemic Racism/Sexism in the Westernized Universities*, retrieved February 13, 2018 from https://youtu.be/LoIrDlIgDjU?list=PL8GqlYPiRldnu3OtU36MempXDPB9mV0lx
Grosfoguel, R. & Cervantes-Rodriguez, A. M. (2002). Introduction: unthinking twentieth-century Eurocentric mythologies: universal knowledge, decolonization, and developmentalism, in *The Modern/Colonial/Capitalist World-System in the Twentieth Century: Global Processes, Antisystemic Movements, and the Geopolitics of Knowledge* (pp. xi–xxix). Westport, CT: Praeger Publishers.
Haraway, D. (1988). Situated knowledges: the science question in feminism and the privilege of partial perspective. *Feminist Studies*, 14(3), 575–599.
Henderson, E. (1995). *Afrocentrism and World Politics: Towards a New Paradigm*. New York: Praeger Publishers.
Hill Collins, P. (2009). *Black Feminist Thought: Knowledge, Consciousness, and the Politics of Empowerment*. New York: Routledge.
Hobson, J. M. (2012). *The Eurocentric Conception of World Politics: Western International Theory, 1760–2010*. Cambridge: Cambridge University Press.
Icaza, R. (2017). Decolonialfeminism and global politics: border thinking and vulnerability as a knowing otherwise. In M. Woons & S. Weier (Eds.), *Critical Epistemologies of Global Politics* (pp. 26–45. Bristol, UK: E-International Relations Publishing.
Krishna, S. (2001). Race, amnesia, and the education of international relations. *Alternatives* 26(4), 401–424.
Maldonado-Torres, N. (2007). On the coloniality of being. *Cultural Studies 21*(2–3), 240–270.

Mamdani, M. (2010). Responsibility to protect or right to punish? *Journal of Intervention and Statebuilding*, 4(1), 53–67.

Mignolo, W. (2007a). Delinking: the rhetoric of modernity, the logic of coloniality and the rammar of de-coloniality. *Cultural Studies 21*(2), 449–514.

Mignolo, W. (2007b). Introduction: coloniality of power and e-Coclonial thinking. *Cultural Studies, 21*(2–3), 155–167.

Mignolo, W. & Escobar, A. (2013). *Globalization and the Decolonial Option*. London: Routledge.

Mignolo, W. & Tlostanova, M. (2006). Theorizing from the borders: shifting to geo- and body-politics of knowledge. *European Journal of Social Theory 9*(2), 205–221.

Muppidi, H. (2012). *The Colonial Signs of International Relations*. New York: Columbia University Press.

Ndlovu-Gatsheni, S. J. (2012). Coloniality of power in development studies and the impact of global imperial designs on Africa. *Australasian Review of African Studies, 33*(2), 48–73.

Ndlovu-Gatsheni, S. J. (2018a). Against bringing Africa "back-in." In *Recentering Africa in International Relations* (pp. 283–305). London: Palgrave Macmillan.

Ndlovu-Gatsheni, S. J. (2018b). Racism and blackism on a world scale. In O. U. Rutazibwa & R. Shilliam (Eds.), *Routledge Handbook of Postcolonial Politics* (pp. 72–86). London: Routledge.

Otzelberger, A. (24 January 2018). Five questions you need to ask yourself if you (want to) ork in International development. *The Good Jungle* [blog], retrieved from https://medium.com/the-good-jungle/five-questions-you-need-to-ask-yourself-if-you-want-to-work-in-international-development-79b32b8c8f6d

Palermo, Z. (2010). La Teoría como Proyecto Político. Otras Memorias, "Narrativas Otras." *De Signos y Sentidos, 1*(11), 177–192.

Quijano, A. (2000). Coloniality of power and Eurocentrism in Latin America. *International Sociology 15*(2), 215–232.

Quijano, A. (2007). Coloniality and modernity/rationality. *Cultural Studies 21*(2–3), 168–178.

Rojas, C. (2016). Contesting the colonial logics of the international: Toward a relational politics for the pluriverse. *International Political Sociology, 10*(4), 369–382.

Rutazibwa, O. U. (2010). The problematics of the EU's ethical (self) image in Africa: the EU as an "ethical intervener" and the 2007 joint Africa-EU strategy. *Journal of Contemporary European Studies, 18*(2), 209–228.

Rutazibwa, O. U. (2013). What if we took autonomous recovery seriously? A democratic critique of contemporary western ethical foreign policy. *Ethical Perspectives, 20*(1), 81–108.

Rutazibwa, O. U. (2014). Studying Agaciro: Moving beyond Wilsonian interventionist knowledge production on Rwanda. *Journal of Intervention and Statebuilding, 8*(4), 291–302.

Rutazibwa, O. U. (2016). From the everyday to IR: in defence of the strategic use of the R-word. *Postcolonial Studies, 19*(2), 191–200.

Sabaratnam, M. (2011). IR in dialogue . . . but can we change the subjects? A typology of decolonising strategies for the study of world politics. *Millennium, 39*(3), 781–803.

Sabaratnam, M. (2013). Avatars of Eurocentrism in the critique of the liberal peace. *Security Dialogue, 44*(3), 259–278.

Sabaratnam, M. (2017). *Decolonizing Intervention: International Statebuilding in Mozambique*. London: Rowman & Littlefield International.

Santos, B. d. S. (2014). *Epistemologies of the South: Justice Against Epistemicide*. New York: Routledge.

Sarr, F. (2017). *Habiter le Monde: essai de politique relationelle*. Montréal, Quebec: Editions Mémoire d'Encrier.

Saurin, J. (2006). International relations and the imperial illusion; or, the need to decolonize IR. In B. G. Jones (Ed.), *Decolonizing International Relations* (pp. 23–42). London: Rowman & Littlefield.

Shilliam, R. (2015). *The Black Pacific: Anti-Colonial Struggles and Oceanic Connections*. London: Bloomsbury Publishing.

Suarez-Krabbe, J. (2016). *Race, Rights and Rebels: Alternatives to Human Rights and Development from the Global South*. London: Rowman & Littlefield International.

Sylvester, C. (1999). Development studies and postcolonial studies: disparate tales of the "Third World." *Third World Quarterly 20*(4), 703–721.

Tripathy, J. & Mohapatra, D. (2011). Does development exist outside representation? *Journal of Developing Societies 27*(2), 93–118.

Vázquez, R. (2015). Decolonial practices of learning. In J. Friedman et al. (Eds.), *Going Glocal in Higher Education. The Theory, Teaching and Measurement of Global Citizenship* (pp. 92–100). Middelburg, The Netherlands: University College Roosevelt.

Wallerstein, I. (1997). Eurocentrism and its avatars: the dilemmas of social science. *Sociological Bulletin, 46*(1), 21–39.

16

"STRAIGHT FROM THE HEART"[1]

A pedagogy for the vanquished of history

Asha Varadharajan

An anecdotal beginning . . .

Caught the retrospective of *60 Minutes* the other day and was struck by a moment in otherwise unexceptional tributes to Morley Safer and Ed Bradley.[2] Safer was described as the epitome of a gentleman while Bradley earned the epithet of the coolest guy around. I wondered why the epithets couldn't have been reversed and how long it would take for even a man as cultivated and mannerly as Ed to become a gentleman in public opinion. The image of Oroonoko's demise flashed in my inward eye – the mocking doffing of the accoutrements of gentlemanliness that make the moment of his bodily dismemberment so poignant and so appalling and, yes, so cool (Behn, 2004). Why does (even colloquial) representation linger in a seemingly transcended colonial/slave past?

Back in kinder, gentler, America,[3] or my home and native land, Canada, I had an equally wrenching encounter with the racialization of rage and disappointment, fear and abjection. I was standing at one of those awkward pedestrian crossings where the walk light comes on at the same time when cars that want to turn the corner are allowed to do so. Anyway, a man started walking just as a car at the corner began to move. The driver braked smartly but the (white) pedestrian banged on the (South Asian or Caribbean-Canadian) driver's window and yelled, I mean screamed, "Fuckin' watch where the fuck you're goin' you dumb fuck!" The driver recoiled and cowered and caught my eye in baleful recognition. Would the pedestrian have pulled a gun in the US, I wonder? I'm sure the pedestrian's anger was partly a result of fear and of being jolted into awareness of his surroundings because he could, theoretically, have been hit or run over. It was just one of those driving errors in judgment that had a happy ending, thankfully. Was the pedestrian's string of colorful curses racially charged? Would he have reacted the way he did if the driver had not been a person of color? If I had seen him in any other context, he would have appeared to be a perfectly innocuous man, huddled against the cold and disappearing without a trace. Why is such a moment still shocking in Canada? And why doesn't it occur to me to think about a widespread repressed rage or just plain disappointment in one's existence unless it comes up close and grabs my eye or kicks me, so to speak, in the gut? How would I raise this in my classroom and how does my professing of literary studies, of the world of representation, make this event more than an occasion for narration, or for reflexivity on the encounter with difference? As the proverbial bystander in this scenario, how would I translate witnessing into pedagogy? Is pedagogy only ever a witnessing rather than transmission or dissemination? What kind of learning curve would this pedagogical moment ascend?

The other day at the bank, I was trying to organize a transfer of funds from my account to one in India. The polite and helpful (white) teller suggested I could avoid coming in to the bank in person every month by setting up an arrangement with one of the bank personnel "I trusted" (his words) whom I could call or email to arrange the transaction. I agreed that was a smart and convenient solution and waited for him to hand me a card with the contact details of the branch employee (himself or one of the several tellers at work that day) who would help me out each month. Instead, he introduced me, after keeping me waiting for a while, to an employee who was also South Asian Canadian and whom, presumably, I would "trust." I don't wish in any way to impugn his thoughtfulness or the trustworthiness and willingness to help of the employee to whom he introduced me; however, I found the situation unexpectedly instructive in the context of this chapter. Desire, as René Girard always maintained, is mimetic (Girard, 1976); I was intrigued both by the white teller's assumption that I was unlikely to trust him and by his resort immediately to someone "just like me" in whom I was likely to place my trust without protest or hesitation. As someone who has never understood why my friends and family in India would measure my comfort in Canada on the basis of ready access to a steady diet of *masala dosa* and Bollywood hits, I have been equally puzzled by attempts to defend "other" literatures "as looking-glasses possessing the magic and delicious power of reflecting the figure" of their like (not like-minded) readers at exactly their natural size (my apologies to irresistible Virginia Woolf [Woolf, 1989]). In other words, are both mimesis and interpretation dependent on the detection of likeness and the abjection of difference? To use a more colonial and colloquial example, reading works in English growing up in India, I didn't care that I had never seen a daffodil (Wordsworth, 2008, p. 303) or consumed any of the goodies in an Enid Blyton picnic that she described with such gusto.[4] Of course, there is a more complex argument to be made about colonial enchantment and Macaulay's children of whom I am one.[5] Nevertheless, reading a text in which it was impossible to be reflected, about characters with whom I could not identify, made it possible to dream and imagine without surrendering my self or my habitat. Being lured *out* of my self was precisely the point, as was comprehending the virtues of both proximity and distance in the pleasures of reading. The struggle against stereotypical notions, for example, is futile if reading and writing are always a matter of recognition rather than of defamiliarization.

In the film *Legally Blonde* (Luketic, 2001), one of my guilty pleasures, a mock-admissions committee at Harvard admits the protagonist, Elle Woods, into its august midst because the institution has always wanted to encourage "diversity" and the major in Fashion Marketing who created faux-fur bikinis for an environmentally conscious charity counts just as easily in that regard.[6] The gentle mockery in this scene has teeth, however, because it reveals how the proliferation of diversity and inclusivity remains anodyne with little or no effect upon the hegemony of institution, the imperviousness of power, or the entrenchment of prejudice. Harvard, in other words, graciously *accommodates* diversity without so much as needing to brush lint off its stylish cloak of customary privilege and exclusivity.

Disturbing complacencies

I like to think of my intellectual career as both unsettled and unsettling. As a scholar who resides in a settler nation/culture, I intend all the connotations the word "settle" conjures: the "anxious proximities" (Lawson, 2004) that constitute the settler imagination, the ambiguity, illegitimacy, and historical violence of inhabiting territory that one can neither claim nor disavow, and the fraught and still underexamined relations among indigenous, migrant, and refugee populations within the contested terrain of the nation-state. These are, equally, concerns that haunt the invention and consolidation of national literary culture that must negotiate the local and the global, the vernacular and the cosmopolitan, "mass civilization" and "minority culture" (Leavis, 2008 [1930]), and cultural capital and the financialization of the globe. I want to develop the implications of a simultaneous attention to proximity, intimacy, and distance for reconceiving pedagogy within the domain of English. My aim is to reinvent literary studies but also to discern and embrace its resilience. I think it has too often been described as either dead or decaying, beleaguered or behind the times or, paradoxically, as imperious in its smugness and patrician in its disdain for the instrumentalization of knowledge and cultural value(s). My argument about these knotty problems is on guard against what Cynthia Enloe describes as "a cynical form of knowing" that "dulls curiosity" and resists surprise (2004, p. 18), and is conducted in the spirit of Raymond Williams' assertion that "It is then in making hope practical, rather than despair convincing, that we must resume and change and extend our campaigns" (1989, p. 209).

The name of my university, Queen's, with its possessive apostrophe, tells its own modest tale of Empire.[7] Its campus is flanked by a park in which the statue of Sir John A. Macdonald abides, bearing the inimitable inscription, "A British subject I was born/A British subject I will die."[8] If belatedness characterizes colonial modernity, Queen's has made a rather charming habit of dragging its feet – an impossibly bland Charles and a supremely bored Princess Diana graced our sesquicentennial celebrations, and "God Save the Queen" still resounds through our Convocation ceremonies. This is not, perhaps, surprising in a nation which continues to issue "domestic" stamps featuring images of the world's longest-reigning monarch, Queen Elizabeth II, and in which an attempt to remove this benign imperial countenance from our stamps was met with a hue and cry worthy of a dominion, replete with a Governor-General, rather than a nation-state. No citizenship ceremony is complete without swearing allegiance to the Queen and her unremarkable progeny. And, of course, William and Kate's visits to this colony with the friendly natives are accompanied by TV shows that regale us with tales of "Prince William's Africa" – there's that pesky possessive again! I even remember the outrage the authors of *The Empire Writes Back* provoked when they refused to stand for the playing of "God Save the Queen" during the award ceremony for the Commonwealth Writers' Prize (Ashcroft, Griffiths & Tiffin, 2002). As if the British Empire wasn't the real outrage!

While I don't deny that I write these words with glee, my intention is only partially facetious or an example of provocation for its own sake. Queen's University has been and is in the throes of a conscious and determined effort to decolonize and to diversify, to think in terms of cultures of "isms" and phobias, and systems of entrenched and pervasive inequalities, unfreedoms, and injustices. The changes, if they achieve their desired aims, will be radical and rejuvenating. As a professor who has spent most of her academic career within its limestone and ivy walls, I have witnessed all the ways in which the institution, like Orwell's elephant, both resists and surrenders to change and, in terms of curriculum and pedagogy, to what Toni Morrison describes as the claim of others upon canonical values (Morrison, 1988; Orwell, 2009). I will return to Morrison's experiment with "cannon fodder"; for now, I want to emphasize that all the recent hubbub about decolonization at my institution and on the Canadian scene must be thought with and against the grain of a longstanding historical amnesia. I also want to underline that pedagogy within such a terrain thrives on rather than transcends the contradictions and overdeterminations within it. Put another way, I have spent my pedagogical and intellectual career using the master's tools to dismantle the master's house (Lorde, 1984 [2007]) and making impossibility the condition of faith and hope. I can't get Yeats' "the fascination of what's difficult" out of my head (1994, p. 75); if decolonization were easy, I wouldn't want, understand, or appreciate it.

Anishinabe artist Rebecca Belmore's *Quote, Misquote, Fact* contains three pieces in which a rubbing taken from the inscription at the base of Sir John A. Macdonald's statue progressively loses words, such that in the final version of the inscription only the words "I was born/I will die" remain (2003). In the label attached to the exhibit, Belmore's smudging, even effacement, of the inscription is described as shifting its meaning from a declaration of Macdonald's "political identity" as Canada's first Prime Minister to an "emphatic declaration of the inevitable 'fact' of subjective existence." This is no doubt an accurate interpretation which effectively explains how Belmore takes "Johnny Mac" down a notch or two while simultaneously making him all too human or no more than (a) mortal. I'd like to suggest, however, that Belmore's "misquote" is also a nod to a biopolitical regime that gave the likes of Johnny Mac the power of life and death over indigenous populations, the right to dispose and render disposable. Belmore, it seems to me, implies an invisible "you" haunting the "I" in the declaration "I will die" such that the shift in focalization reverses the dispossession of indigenous populations and transforms a self-possessed assertion into an (indigenous) injunction – "you will die" – to which the British Macdonald becomes subject.

I allude to Belmore's angry and poignant work because she honors the legacy of contention and agency in the quest for sovereignty and in the struggle against what Arthur Manuel calls "extinguishment" (Manuel & Derrikson, 2015, p. 59). Belmore's dissolution of assertion and inscription, dissemination of meaning, and performance of the transmutation of death into life and life into death, resist the self-possession and territoriality that underwrite claims to identity, colonial or otherwise. Decolonization for her is a palimpsest of traces, an unfinished process of excavation and rewriting, and a necessarily asymmetrical mapping of power and resistance. Hers is an act of epistemic disobedience, as Walter Mignolo might describe it (2011), an opening onto a new and different order of *becoming* rather than being. Belmore shows that such delinking might be an aspiration but is certainly not an accomplishment within a regime *and* an episteme that remains resolutely settler-colonial. The decolonial subject exists not as the new but the not-yet. To put it simply, she needs the complete inscription for her de-scription to appear.

Her rewriting of history and her reinvigoration of "the relation between texts and social action" (Sara Ahmed's phrase [2006, p. 105]), however, must be distinguished from the speech act that has now become routine in ceremonies and institutions, including my own. I become uneasy whenever a sober and meaningful gesture or ritual becomes merely customary or habitual and absorbed easily into the quotidian life of the institution. I refer here to the opening of ceremonies and occasions with a verbal acknowledgment that the lands upon which the buildings in question stand were once indigenous. To my mind, these words and the gesture they imply, function like a non- rather than a failed performative. As Sara Ahmed explains, performatives "fail" or are "unhappy" when conditions are not in place that would enable the action to succeed (2006, p. 105). They are nonperformatives because they "fail to bring about what [they] name" (2006, p. 105) – "the issuing of the utterance" *displaces* "the performing of an action" (J. L. Austin's phrases, as quoted by Ahmed [2006, p. 104]). Their reiterative and citational function (both Austin [1975] and Judith Butler [2006] have noted this aspect of performatives) reinforces the irony (paradox?) that Ahmed highlights: these performatives "['work'] *because* [they] fail to bring about what [they name]" (2006, p. 105; italics in original). As Ahmed is aware, these non- and failed performatives have hope invested in them of a better future, but such hope cannot be realized without exposing the gap between ideals and actions, words and deeds (2006, pp. 124–125). For indigenous populations, these performatives do not contain a promise of repatriation; they are a double whammy not only because they fail to bring about what they name but also because the conditions that are required for them to produce the action they utter do not exist. This acknowledgment may indeed be preferable to a blunt form of settler entitlement, but it is not exactly an admission of culpability or conquest either: it presents the settler as both conscientious and gracious and ensures that indigenous witnesses to such scruple and recipients of such grace remain quiescent.

While I have some reservations about Tuck and Yang's now classic essay "Decolonization is not a metaphor" (2012), I can extrapolate from their argument to perceive why performatives such as these only serve to "resettle," as they put it, to "[extend] innocence to the settler, [and to continue to] entertain a settler future" (2012, p. 3).

I consider it my pedagogical duty first to indicate to my students the historical shift from ignorance and impunity to admission of historical wrongs that must be righted that these nonperformatives represent; however, I don't allow such pleasurable self-flagellation to last. I make sure that I elaborate upon why these nonperformatives also make me squirm. Kam'ayaam/Chachim'multhnii (Cliff Atleo, Jr.)'s "*Unsettling Canada*: A Review" (2016) helps illuminate my affective response (2016). His interpretation of A. Manuel and R. M. Derrikson's *Unsettling Canada: A National Wake-Up Call* (2015) outlines the manner in which apologies and "awake" admissions are actually designed to "funnel" indigenous "governance systems, economies, and right to exist" through "state-centric processes" (Kam'ayaam/Chachim'multhnii, 2016, p. 72). In applauding the program for indigenous political and economic autonomy that Manuel derives from his experiences as a residential school survivor and band chief, Atleo writes that he has never seen governments "actually *negotiate*" (2016, p. 75); instead, indigenous peoples continue to suffer the consequences of "justifiable infringement" of aboriginal title (2016, p. 76) and, post 9/11, of the State's monopoly on the legitimate use of violence (2016, p. 74). This means that indigenous peoples no longer have the right or the duty to protect or defend their lands and the Supreme Court of Canada's definition of justifiable infringement, which includes agriculture, forestry, mining and hydroelectric power, contravenes the United Nations Declaration on the Rights of Indigenous Peoples. Because such "infringement" cannot proceed without their free, prior, or informed consent, but does, indigenous peoples are denied political and economic autonomy by the State. For this reason, nonperformatives are not only travesties of justice and autonomy but actual obstacles to reconciliation and repatriation, because, as Ahmed explains, they claim to have overcome the conditions that necessitated them in the first place.

When I have pedagogical occasion to address questions of entitlement and dispossession in the context of indigenous land claims, I prefer to introduce my students to 13-year-old Tenelle Starr of the Star Blanket First Nation in Saskatchewan, Canada, who came to school on January 14, 2014, wearing a sweatshirt with the words "Got Land? Thank an Indian" emblazoned on its front and back, respectively.[9] Starr was well aware that her sweatshirt supported indigenous treaty and land rights based on agreements with the Crown, and defended her actions by indicating she was doing no more than reinforcing what history lessons had already taught her and her classmates – that "Indians were on this land first." After receiving complaints, school authorities first asked Starr to refrain from wearing the sweatshirt or wear it inside out (a nice irony there reproducing the dishonoring of Crown treaties), before relenting and letting her don it again. Starr's youth and pizzazz, her pride and joy, are instantly appealing to the teenagers I teach, of course, but I choose her for a more sobering reason. Her age signifies *indigenous* rather than settler futurity and her action serves as a testament to the aims of Arthur Manuel and Kam'ayaam/ Chachim'multhnii (Cliff Atleo, Jr.), who consider their "sacred obligations to protect the land" inextricable from "the birthrights of future generations" (2016, p. 72). Besides, Starr's classmates accused her of being cheeky and rude, a welcome alternative, in my view, to the albeit telling melancholia that pervades Belmore's art or the endurance demanded of those subjected to the ritual of nonperformatives. More to the point, the words on Starr's sweatshirt emphasize the illegitimacy of settler occupation rather than treat it, like the nonperformative does, as a version of "too bad, but the land is ours now." These words are an exhortation as well as a mischievous evocation of a gift economy rather than an (unequal) exchange economy/treaty. The sweatshirt transforms invasion and occupation into a munificence on the part of "Indians." I believe this is what Manuel and Atleo mean when they refuse to discount historical agency both during and after the occupation of sovereign lands and demand resistance that is not merely a nuisance and inconvenience but proceeds to "rock the boat" (2016, pp. 75–76). Atleo concludes his review by calling for the centering of "the voices of Indigenous women" and I could not agree more (2016, p. 77).

Save the World on Your Own Time[10]

Departments of English seem victims of a perennial angst or crisis of identity, heroes of a *Bildungsroman* in which the project of self-realization is doomed to failure or in which protectionist gestures designed to consolidate identity are continually mediated by epistemological and methodological shifts and the simultaneous encroachment upon and dissolution of disciplinary boundaries. Peter Osborne is skeptical of this tale of woe and erosion, arguing, instead, that "English" embodies a hegemonic form of disciplinarity that incorporates new developments into a radically expanded version of its former self (2015). Thus, both the departmental structure and the nationalist ethos have remained virtually unchanged. In settler colonies such as Canada, the English literary tradition, with only occasional nods to Scots or Irish or Welsh interlopers, still has pride of place, and its increasing usurpation by Canadian and U.S. literary canons only reinforces the struggle between nations rather than undermines a nationalist ethos. The urge to indigenize, while both welcome and long overdue, may well serve to demarcate national boundaries further, even if such nationality is contested by both the debates over sovereignty and the desire to think indigeneity across the boundaries of nation and culture. Postcolonial literatures, for their part, particularly Anglophone ones, need either the canon or the political economy of settlement, slavery, and capital to write back to, which means the British Empire, Europe's civilizing mission, and the "universal" logic of modernity and development can continue to sit pretty, except this time as violent and soul-destroying rather than as the standard of value and the measure of the human. A corollary to this predicament is the persistence of periodization, both as "the dominant mode of literary specialization" and as "an organizing grid [for curricula] that is able to survive repeated, sweeping transformation of its content" (Underwood, 2013, p. 3) and a movable feast of critical methods. As Underwood explains, periodization allows great works to retain their explanatory function and permanent exemplary value (2013, p. 15). It seems remarkable to me that both the conservatism of canon and curriculum and the radicalism of the current struggle against expertise and information result in an identical conception of the humanities as "the conscience and consciousness of society" (Chandler, 2004, p. 357).

Global English

This perennial identity crisis, however, rarely contends with the phenomenon of the globalization of English, not only as a consequence of the imperial past but as the virulent engine of a neoliberal present. Departments and schools of English no doubt have to conceive of this linguistic universe as their natural habitat and ingrained habitus, but the hegemony of English has to be thought simultaneously with its global pseudopodia, its *deterritorialization* rather than its reterritorialization. As Robert Phillipson remarks with excoriating irony, Goethe's remark, "*People who know no foreign languages know nothing of their own*," has been glibly transformed into "*Whoever knows English has no need of other languages*" (2017, p. 316; italics in original). Phillipson argues that, along with racism, classism, sexism, and speciesism, what he dubs *linguicism* operates in tandem with the Europeanization and Americanization of the globe. Recent studies of this phenomenon reflect on the privatization and Anglicization of education in which the British Council and Pearson Publishing, among others, play a crucial role: there is little to choose between Macaulay and recent policy documents issued by the British Council, for example. While I don't have the space here to discuss the implications of the emergence of "World Literature" – the teaching of literatures from many parts of the world that have been translated into English – it does seem to participate in the insidiousness with which English masquerades as worldliness itself. This new field rejects the "vivid [differentiation and particularization of] vanished eras" (Underwood, 2013, p. 3) that resulted from periodization and revives "an anthropological theory of literary development" (2013, p. 12), "distant reading" and the "[graphing of] macroscopic trends" (2013, p. 16) more common in Comparative Literature instead. Works lucky enough to circulate in the global literary market and wise enough to conform to recognizable genres or to be recognized as doing so become representative of their national cultures in populating syllabi in World Literature. Moreover, the apparatus of local knowledge required to decode them and the vicissitudes of translation ensure that they also become unwitting tributes to those cultivated and cosmopolitan enough to read and disseminate them. As an inoffensive alternative to the anxiety and deracination the encounter with difference and incommensurability usually provokes, the ascendancy of World Literature is hardly surprising.[11] The panoply of Englishes in former colonies as well as the rebuke to standardization in the form of abrogation and appropriation in postcolonial literatures may not always be liberatory, because they too contribute to the persistence of English in the periphery. As for English departments, they may well be hospitable to postcolonial and indigenous studies and welcoming of inter-and multicultural transactions of various kinds, but arguments such as Phillipson's are salutary reminders that the encounter with the other, in every sense of the word, is still disciplined and disciplining. No wonder even the savvy scholar finds herself in a pickle in these confusing times.

Giving life and making free[12]

I understand the import of Tuck and Yang's asseveration – "Decolonization is not a metaphor" – but what does it signify? They worry that decolonization has become an empty signifier and want to fix its signified as an "elsewhere" (2012, p. 36) that has no synonym. In other moments, they object to decolonization being "punctuated by metaphor" (2012, p. 35) and call for "the demetaphorization of decolonization" (2012, p. 10). And, in still other moments, they declare that it is "not a metonym for social justice" (2012, p. 21) and "incommensurable" (2012, p. 31), and insist that it be thought "as material, not metaphor" (2012, p. 59). Based on these examples (although the semantic variation in each of these formulations has to await another occasion for more exacting analysis and might contradict their claim that they no longer wish to trifle or have truck with signifying), Tuck and Yang stand by decolonization as literal, as historical rather than symbolic, as a break from rather than only an ephemeral subversion of the colonial condition, and as designed to "[unsettle] everyone" (2012, p. 7). I doubt anyone would disagree with the spirit of these claims, but would the incommensurability of their stance be perceptible outside the system of differences within which signifiers acquire linguistic value in relation to what they are not and without a prior act of translation that could find no equivalent to the decolonization they envision? And, while I have every sympathy for the fatigue their passionate essay exudes, I cannot grasp decolonization without the signifying chain of substitution and displacement (metaphor and metonymy) in which it is (dis)located. Call it my professional blindspot – I teach literary studies – but my pedagogy has always been animated by not only the principle that words matter, that literacy is the product of examining "the historical semantics of culture,"[13] but also that law and politics might be, as Patricia J. Williams muses in *The Alchemy of Race and Rights* (1992), "a matter of words" (1992, p. 13). Tuck and Yang open the door to my meditation here when they write: "poetry is giving a name to the nameless" and that "freedom is a possibility that is not just mentally generated; it is particular and felt" (2012, p. 20). If one followed their argument to its logical conclusion, the incommensurable would be unnameable; in the slippage in this sentence between the unnameable and the nameless resides the promise of decolonization.

Anyone who knows me knows that I quote T. W. Adorno's "one must have tradition in oneself to hate it properly" (1951 [2005], p. 52) to anyone who will listen. This aphorism encapsulates why postcolonial scholars are surprisingly the most conservative of creatures, entrusted with the task of "provincializing" the Europe

(Chakrabarty, 2000) by which they remain haunted and which they both love and repudiate. I have taught across cultures, geographies, and histories, often disdaining periodization in an attempt to produce critical genealogies of concepts such as race and cosmopolitanism, or to generate contrapuntal readings of culture and imperialism – Hegel and Haiti (Buck-Morss, 2009) or Tabish Khair and Wilkie Collins.[14] In an age when "popular consciousness" displays "a confident presentism that reduces the past to retro style" (Underwood, 2013, p. 15), I feel more compelled than ever to trace "a causal, continuous" history (2013, p. 13) precisely in order to discern moments of rupture and discontinuity and to communicate to students how historical difference has shaped the world they experience (2013, p. 15). The split enunciation of the colonial subject, "divided to the vein" (Walcott, 2007, p. 6), and for whom language is always and never anguish (Philip, 1989), defines me. Neither authenticity nor solidarity has ever cast a spell, however, which is why I don't specialize in Indian Writing in English or, unless pressed, write on the diasporic condition which I inhabit. Critique, not community, drives me.

In the remainder of this chapter, I outline a pedagogical experiment – a seminar in literary interpretation focused on Toni Morrison's *The Bluest Eye*. I cannot do justice either to what occurred or to the brilliant complex of affect and insight my students demonstrated, or indeed to the curiosity, wonder, and generosity their writing, art, and video evinced. I include, with her permission, a painting my student Hamdah Shabbir created as a glimpse of the "decolonization" that occurred. I shall explain why solidarity, as it is usually understood, was not my aim, nor I believe was it Morrison's, in the writing of this, her finest novel.

FIGURE 16.1 'Black and Blue' by Hamdah Shabbir

In her afterword to the novel (it appears in a slightly different variation in her Tanner Lectures), Morrison describes her subject as "racial self-loathing" (1970 [1994], p. 210). The singularity and extremity of Pecola's predicament was also the means by which Morrison could communicate "the aspects of her woundability [that] were lodged in all young girls" (1970 [1994], p. 210). My class was racially differentiated – European or Anglo-Canadian, Iranian, Pakistani and Vietnamese Canadian, South African-Australian, and mixed race – but none of them were exclusively African Canadian or African American. They had, in other words, to contend with singularity before they could recognize universality. Thus their comprehension of the novel did not rely merely on what Tuck and Yang describe as sympathy and suffering, on the infinite substitutability of the "everybody hurts"[15] model, but on exploring the curious mix of beauty and horror, desire and perversion contained in Pecola's desire for blue eyes. The title of the novel suggests the idealization of whiteness Morrison has spent her career battling, and its concomitant connotations and denotations of blackness. Here, Morrison *requires* metonymy to do the work that metaphor can't; Tuck and Yang's dismissal of both metaphor and metonymy seems too hasty, in my view. That is, whiteness is an impossible object of desire that nevertheless wounds deeply. For students accustomed to thinking of racism as prejudice attributable to not quite "with it" individuals, Morrison's novel is a profound experience in defamiliarization. By their own admission, it had never occurred to them to think about the *internalization* of racial self-loathing and the violence and harm that African-American characters do to each other as a result. As Morrison puts it, "seeing oneself preserved in the amber of disqualifying metaphors" made her novel imperative (1970 [1994], p. 216); she could not write "race-free" prose without "race-specific" prose (1970 [1994], p. 211). Thus, students are unlikely to decolonize their imaginations without understanding how "racial hierarchy and triumphalism" work (1970 [1994], p. 211), without engaging the "demonization of an entire race" (1970 [1994], p. 210) that precedes them. That demonization is precisely an effect of language, of the weight of words.

Morrison also challenges the rhetoric of survival and testimony by shaping "the void that is Pecola's 'unbeing'" (1970 [1994], p. 215). Pecola hallucinates rather than sees a self. This aspect of the novel was the most devastating for my students because they could comprehend a fragmented self but not the impossibility of wholeness. I deployed Lady Gaga's performance at the 2016 Oscars, clad all in white and seated at a white grand piano, awaiting the survivors of abuse to emerge from the shadows. While she has indicated that hers too was a story of survival and I agree that the moment was a powerful one of consciousness raising and solidarity, I wanted my class to perceive the depth of Pecola's voicelessness and invisibility, the failure of her community to sustain her, and Morrison's rejection of the pat narrative arc of the *Bildungsroman* in which suffering is both redeemed and transcended. Rather counter-intuitively, perhaps, but oh so meaningfully, Morrison defines narrative as that which gives shape and texture to silence and nonentity rather than expresses voice or self-consciousness. It is this quality that communicated to my students the embeddedness of racism and the intractability of power. All of them said that their own helplessness, their inability to do something to "save" Pecola, was the hardest thing to bear. Claudia signifies hope in the story because she lives to tell the tale, but the very division of the narrative into a failed past and uncertain present and future speaks volumes.

Morrison also opts for "co-conspiracy and intimacy" and deliberately fails to offer "a distancing, explanatory fabric" (1970 [1994], p. 215). I asked my students why Morrison eschewed the comforts and grit of social realism, forcing them instead to piece together cause and effect in a narrative that could only begin to utter how, not why, the events unfolded the way they do. In a novel steeped in the erotic and disturbing dimensions of spectacle, my students understood Morrison's reluctance to turn them into voyeurs, on the outside looking in on the quaint and salacious habits of African Americans. The effect of her work relies on the shock of intimacy without safety, a novelty in the current institutional climate of safe spaces and trigger warnings. It is intimacy, not incommensurability, that my students found unsettling, what Morrison describes as her simultaneous capacity to expose and sustain the painful secret at the heart of the narrative. It is an intimacy they eventually embraced, however, acknowledging the necessity of a learning curve that was based on having nowhere to hide and nothing to console them.

I concluded the seminar, however, with the moment when Morrison sabotages "the despising glance" (1970 [1994], p. 211) with race-specific prose that is also, miraculously, race-free: "[The baby] was in a dark, wet place, its head covered with great O's of wool, the black face holding, like nickels, two clean black eyes, the flared nose, kissing-thick lips, and the living, breathing silk of black skin" (1970 [1994], p. 191). I commented on how the "O's" are both aural and visual, the hole that is the womb from which emerges a w(h)ole baby, the mouth open in wonder at this new life and the exclamation of joy that escapes it, the curls implied by O as a metaphor for roundness, and the subtle transformation of the description of Pecola earlier in the novel as an emptiness, a "nothing/ no thing to see" into the mother of an O that is substantial: kissing-thick lips, an abundance of curly hair, and living, breathing skin. As Tuck and Yang indicate, one must feel to act; this is why Morrison writes works that not only touch, but move, us (1970 [1994], p. 191). That the baby is dead and only alive in Claudia's mind's eye motivates the reader to realize what Claudia can only intuit or dream. Morrison's afterword expresses her doubts about whether her first novel achieved what she set out to accomplish. If my students' rich responses to it are any indication, she did, because she showed how language can both debase Black American culture and become worthy of its complexity and wealth (1970 [1994], p. 216).

Afterword

I wrote this chapter in a single sitting – thus, I had no choice but to let its momentum guide me. Years of teaching and unforgiving post-mortems of its "successes" and "failures" no doubt contributed to this unwonted inspiration! I did eschew familiar discursive logic rather deliberately, setting out to produce something more fractured and fractious and truer to the manner in which pedagogy is both in and of the moment. Besides, the space of the classroom is what I wished to foreground, its safety and familiarity as well as its vitality and dynamism. As all students and teachers are only too aware, however, what happens in the classroom overflows its bounds, lingers in memory, haunts writing and action, and returns to bite or reinvigorate.

I wanted my writing to emulate and encapsulate my pedagogical style and personality – the mix of anecdote, musing, speculation, humor, passion, spontaneity and analytical rigor – that I hope my students find ebullient and exhilarating and that I know they occasionally also find enigmatic, polemical, difficult, and discomfiting. A head full of quotations and allusions is the hallmark of a colonial sensibility, in my view, an illustration of the manner in which a colonial subjectivity harbors that which is strange or makes intimate that which estranges her from herself. By definition, these quotations and allusions will resonate with some and not others, but they serve to articulate a self-fashioning that is both inherited and made. I make it a point to communicate this to my students desirous of authenticity, otherness, or color in an otherwise drab palate. It is worth noting how colonial education and tastes in reading prove remarkably similar across inhabitants of colonies in the British Empire, particularly in India, Africa, and the Caribbean, and Australia – a disturbing version of universality, no doubt! Sometimes, however, quotations say things with more flair and point than I can; I don't intend my students or readers to pore over their provenance or significance if this is the case, but the expression and its author may well introduce them to someone or something they may be delighted enough by to investigate. There are also threads that are not woven seamlessly into the argument in part because of limited space and time, but I also like to make glancing references and raise questions that I hope will invite and provoke any given audience to pursue or consider on their own terms and at leisure. My pedagogy and writing, therefore, are always unfinished, quests rather than their fulfillment, and evocations of a restlessness of mind and spirit.

It has probably been obvious that I have avoided the usual forms of self-positioning common to critical practice these days. While I have been careful to introduce historicity in moments of self-reckoning throughout, I remain committed to contradiction and overdetermination in subject formation such that the self emerges in any given critical, historical, and geographical conjuncture, its intersectionality capable of both instability and metamorphosis, and its identity determined rather than determining. In this chapter I am by turns (post)colonial, migrant-settler, Canadian citizen, liberal-bourgeois, educated elite, radical pedagogue, conservative and erudite scholar, racialized, heterosexual, feminist, pop culture aficionado, anti-whatever. I am, in short, all of these things and none of them, except when they trip me up or presume to name and categorize. Since this chapter is concerned with the dangers of nonperformatives, I wanted to avoid an empty self-positioning that merely ensures rather than challenges business as usual or that remains sentimental rather than skeptical. Such fluidity and self-invention may well be a function of privilege, but merely acknowledging that to be the case isn't going to improve matters either. My nod to Cynthia Enloe is my quick way to make this point – I don't ever want to sacrifice curiosity to complacency or surprise to the consolations of knowledge or belief. Or to refer to an anti-colonial analogue, at the end of an excoriating critique of the white masks worn by and imposed on black bodies and subjectivities, Frantz Fanon ends on a note of prayer and promise that nevertheless continues to celebrate doubt – he asks to be made not only a man but one who questions.

Finally, a word about Tuck and Yang's "Decolonization is not a metaphor." I admire its political scruple, its courage in identifying the complicity of otherwise marginalized migrant populations in settler colonialism, and its uncompromising demand for indigenous sovereignty and futurity (2012, p. 35). My analysis of non- and failed performatives is intended to supplement and endorse their contentions about settler innocence. I am also on board with their rejection of loose or casual or ubiquitous uses of the word "decolonization" without substance and their reintroduction of conflict and contention in exercises in coalition-building and in affirmations of solidarity. My chapter, however, objects to the title of the essay – "Decolonization is not a metaphor" – by arguing that decolonization cannot not be one, as the multiple connotations of their own use of the word signifies, and by the very intractability of settler colonialism they set out to dismantle, but also to *represent* and *communicate*. They contradict their central claim by resorting to poetry as invoking the elsewhere they imagine, which means that figurative language is crucial to their enterprise. I also challenge their emphasis on incommensurability even as I recognize its necessary provocation in the self-congratulatory bubble they puncture. I deploy Toni Morrison's *The Bluest Eye* to demonstrate how minds and bodies, as well as states and nations, need to be decolonized before a new order can emerge. Tuck and Yang rather unceremoniously and unconvincingly dismiss metaphor and metonymy, both of which Morrison wields as weapons against the gaze that belittles and despises blackness. Morrison exposes all the damage language has wrought as well as all the wonder it can conjure, and she does so by plunging her readers into intimacy rather than holding them at bay with incommensurability. To return to the world of Tuck and Yang, unsettling innocence and restoring indigenous futurity cannot begin, let alone be accomplished, without decolonizing the mind and the language that bespeaks it. Morrison, for her part, does not abandon metaphor but cajoles, caresses, persuades, and demands that it speak in the name of blackness and for the imagination of beauty.

Dedication

For Tim, my goad and inspiration.

Acknowledgments

Sara de Jong's patience and luminous intelligence and Robyn Carruthers' strategic research eased the path to the writing of this chapter.

Notes

1 Bryan Adams released "Straight from the Heart" in 1983. His global success as a singer and songwriter has not merited the critical acclaim accorded artists such as Joni Mitchell, Neil Young, or Leonard Cohen or been deemed as edgy as that of his fellow Kingstonian, Gord Downie of *The Tragically Hip*. He is a considerably talented photographer and is also well-known for his humanitarian and philanthropic interests and work on behalf of animal rights. I chose him because he was born in Kingston, where Queen's University is located and, like many of its students, is smart, liberal, and concerned. The line from his song says what I mean.

2 *60 Minutes* debuted on CBS, a U.S. television network, in 1968 and still retains its reputation for investigative reporting and journalistic integrity. Morley Safer was "white" and Ed Bradley "black"; both served as hosts and correspondents on the show and died in 2016 and 2006, respectively. Interestingly, Safer was born in Canada. My point here has to do with how the retrospective remembered them with all-too-familiar tropes; I respect Safer's reporting on the Vietnam War and Bradley's work on Cambodian refugees among other stellar examples of their courage and insight. Aphra Behn's *Oroonoko: or, the Royal Slave* was published in 1688. It concludes with the execution of its eponymous hero, an African prince who is tricked into slavery. The scene of his dismemberment, partially self-inflicted, occurs simultaneously with his donning and doffing of gentlemanly attire and with his nonchalant smoking of a pipe. The blend of farce and horror highlights the *incongruity* of blackness with gentlemanliness, an incongruity still prevalent in the tribute to Bradley.

3 I'm referring here to George H. W. Bush's goal of making the United States a 'kinder, gentler nation.'

4 Enid Blyton (1897–1968) was a popular English author of children's fiction and a staple in the reading habits of children in the colonies.

5 Thomas Babington Macaulay (1800–1859) was a British politician and historian deeply committed to the idea of 'progress.' His "Minute" (1835) called for creating "a class of persons Indian in blood and color, but English in tastes, in opinions, in morals and in intellect." See www.columbia.edu/itc/mealac/pritchett/00generallinks/macaulay/txt_minute_education_1835.html for further details.

6 *Legally Blonde* (2001), starring Reese Witherspoon, was directed by Robert Luketic and distributed by Type A Films, Marc Platt Productions. My summary of it seems self-explanatory.

7 Queen's University, founded in 1841, is located in Kingston, Ontario, Canada.

8 John A. Macdonald (1815–1891) was the first Prime Minister of Canada, holding office from 1867 to 1873 and again from 1878 to 1891.

9 CBC News (2014). See also Anthony J. Hall and Gretchen Albers, June 6, 2011, www.thecanadianencyclopedia.ca/en/article/aboriginal-treaties/, for a detailed account of treaties as "the constitutional and moral basis of alliance between indigenous peoples and Canada" (last edited September 11, 2017).

10 Fish (2012).

11 See also Landry and Matz (2015) for a skeptical, but more sympathetic account, of the travails of aspiring to globality in the teaching of World Literature.

12 The epigraph to *The Bluest Eye* reads: "*To the two who gave me life and the one who made me free*"; Morrison (1994 [1970]; italics in original). What follows is a meditation on how pedagogy mediates between and negotiates those options. Morrison tells the story of a black girl on the threshold of adolescence who yearns for blue eyes that she might

witness beauty and not ugliness, who is the victim of incest because her father cannot love without hurting, and whose broken body and fragmented psyche at the end of the novel take the form of a hallucinated self endowed with blue eyes. Pecola is the silence and unbeing at the heart of the novel. Morrison's narrator is Claudia, Pecola's friend, and witness to her suffering, who lets the story unfold in retrospect and who comprehends the significance of Pecola's predicament. She embodies strength, hope, and clarity because she feels rage rather than succumbs to shame and despair.

13 Heath (2016).
14 See Buck-Morss (2009); Collins (1997); and Khair (2010).
15 R.E.M., *Automatic for the People*, 1992. The full line is "everybody cries/And everybody hurts sometimes." The song exhorts one to "hold on," which is of course an impossibility for Pecola. By the way, I love R.E.M.!

References

Adams, B. (1983). Straight from the Heart. *Cuts Like a Knife*. A&M.

Adorno, T. W. (2005 [1951]) *Minima Moralia: Reflections on a Damaged Life* (E. F. N. Jephcott, trans.). New York Verso.

Ahmed, S. (2006). The nonperformativity of antiracism. *Meridians*, 7(1), 104–126.

Ashcroft, B., Griffiths, G. & Tiffin, H. (2002). (Eds.). *The Empire Writes Back: Theory and Practice in Post-Colonial Literatures*. New York: Routledge.

Austin, J. L. (1975). *How to Do Things with Words* (J. O. Urmson & M. Sbisà, eds.), 2nd ed. Cambridge, MA: Harvard University Press.

Behn, Aphra. (2004). *Oroonoko; or the Royal Slave* (J. Todd, ed.). New York: Penguin. (Originally published 1688.)

Belmore, R. (2003). *Quote, Misquote, Fact*. Graphite on vellum. Agnes Etherington Art Centre, Queen's University, Kingston, Ontario, Canada, retrieved from www.rebeccabelmore.com

Buck-Morss, S. (2009). *Hegel, Haiti and Universal History*. Pittsburgh, PA: University of Pittsburgh Press.

Butler, J. (2006). *Gender Trouble: Feminism and the Subversion of Identity*. New York: Routledge.

CBC News. (2014). Message on First Nation teen's sweatshirt deemed offensive by school officials. January 15, retrieved from www.cbc.ca/news/canada/saskatchewan/first-nation-teen-told-not-to-wear-got-land-shirt-at-school-1.2497009

Chakrabarty, D. (2000). *Provincializing Europe: Postcolonial Thought and Historical Difference*. Princeton, NJ: Princeton University Press.

Chandler, J. (2004). Critical disciplinarity. *Critical Inquiry 30*(2), 355–360.

Collins, W. (1997). *The Moonstone*. Ware, UK: Wordsworth Classics.

Enloe, C. (2004). *The Curious Feminist: Searching for Women in a New Age of Empire*. Berkeley: University of California Press.

Fish, S. (2012). *Save the World on Your Own Time*. New York: Oxford University Press.

Girard, R. (1976). *Deceit, Desire, and the Novel: Self and Other in Literary Structure*. Baltimore, MD: Johns Hopkins University Press.

Hall, A. J. & Albers, G. (2011). Treaties with indigenous peoples in Canada. *The Canadian Encyclopedia*. Toronto: Historica Canada. Retrieved from www.thecanadianencyclopedia.ca/en/article/aboriginal-treaties/ (last edited 2017).

Heath, S. (2016). Raymond Williams and Keywords. *Keywords Project*. University of Pittsburgh and University of Cambridge, retrieved from http://keywords.pitt.edu/williams_keywords.html

Kam'ayaam/Chachim'multhnii (Cliff Atleo, Jr.) (2016). Unsettling Canada: a review. *Decolonization: Indigeneity, Education & Society 5*(1), 71–78.

Khair, T. (2010). *The Thing About Thugs*. New York: Houghton Mifflin Harcourt.

Landry, T. & Jesse Matz, J. (2015). Small college, world literature. *Pedagogy: Critical Approaches to Teaching Literature, Language, Culture, and Composition, 15*(2), 253–269.

Lawson, A. J. (2004). The anxious proximities of settler (post) colonial relations. In J. Rivkin & M. Ryan (Eds.), *Literary Theory: An Anthology* (pp. 1210–1223). Malden, UK: Blackwell Publishing.

Leavis, F. R. (2008 [1930]). Mass civilization and minority culture. In J. Storey (Ed.), *Cultural Theory and Popular Culture: A Reader* (pp. 3–30). New York: Routledge.

Lorde, A. (2007 [1984]). The master's tools will never dismantle the master's house. In C. Clarke (Ed.), *Sister Outsider: Essays and Speeches* (pp. 110–114). Berkeley, CA: Crossing Press.

Luketic, Robert. (Dir.) (2001). *Legally Blonde*. Type A Films/Marc Platt Productions.

Macaulay, T. B. (1835). Minute by the Hon'ble T. B. Macaulay, dated the 2nd February 1835. Retrieved from www.columbia.edu/itc/mealac/pritchett/00generallinks/macaulay/txt_minute_education_1835.html

Manuel, A. & Derrikson, R. M. (2015). *Unsettling Canada: A National Wake-Up Call*. Toronto, Canada: Between the Lines.

Mignolo, W. D. (2011). *The Darker Side of Western Modernity: Global Futures, Decolonial Options*. Durham, NC: Duke University Press.

Morrison, T. (1988). Unspeakable things unspoken: the Afro-American presence in American literature, 7 January 1988. *The Tanner Lectures on Human Values*. Ann Arbor: University of Michigan Press.

Morrison, T. (1994 [1970]). *The Bluest Eye*. New York: Plume.

Orwell, G. (2009). *Shooting an Elephant*. New York: Penguin.

Osborne, P. (2015). Problematizing disciplinarity, transdisciplinary problematics. *Theory, Culture & Society, 32*(5–6), 3–35.

Philip, M. N. (1989). *She Tries Her Tongue, Her Silence Softly Breaks*. Charlottetown, Canada: Gynergy Books/Ragweed Press.

Phillipson, R. (2017). Myths and realities of "global" English. *Language Policy, 16*(3), 313–331.

R.E.M. (1992). Everybody hurts. *Automatic for the People*. Warner Bros.

Tuck, E. & Yang, K. W. (2012). Decolonization is not a metaphor. *Decolonization: Indigeneity, Education & Society, 1*(1), 1–40.

Underwood, T. (2013). *Why Literary Periods Mattered: Historical Contrast and the Prestige of English Studies*. Stanford, CA: Stanford University Press.

Walcott, D. (2007). *Selected Poems* (Edward Baugh, ed.). New York: Farrar, Straus and Giroux.

Williams, P. J. (1992). *The Alchemy of Race and Rights: Diary of a Law Professor*. Cambridge, MA: Harvard University Press.

Williams, R. (1989). *Resources of Hope: Culture, Democracy, Socialism* (R. Gable, ed.). New York: Verso.

Woolf, V. (1989). *A Room of One's Own*. San Diego, CA: Mariner Books.

Wordsworth, W. (2008). *William Wordsworth – The Major Works: Including "The Prelude"* (S. Gill, ed.). Oxford: Oxford University Press.

Yeats, W. B. (1994). The fascination of what's difficult. In *The Collected Poems of W. B. Yeats*. Ware, UK: Wordsworth Editions Ltd.

17

NOTES ON EUROPE AND EUROPEANS FOR THE DISCERNING TRAVELLER

Robbie Shilliam

Europe has the only classical tradition that is also considered modern.

Europe claimed Greece as its ancestor. But not anymore.

Europe once turned a Black god white.

Once upon a time Europe decided that it was a family of nations. This decision is commemorated as the beginning of international law.

Because indigenous peoples were not mentioned in a very old book, Europeans wondered if these peoples were human.

Some of the Europeans who cleared lands of their indigenous peoples liked to represent themselves as indigenous princesses.

Europeans once thought that if they left Europe they would degenerate. To this day they view their cousins over the seas with suspicion.

European scientists once found a way to break up human beings into a set of quantum parts.

Europe is proud of freeing itself from metaphorical chains.

Europe got rich out of African slavery. Then it freed the slaves.

Europe was so concerned with slavery that it colonized the African continent.

In Europe you can baptize yourself so as to be born again with a humanitarian soul.

Some of Europe's top philosophers were bigots and racists, even for their own time.

Europeans were so fascinated with primitives that they created a space in the brain called the unconscious.

Europeans say that Unconscious bias is regrettable but that it doesn't make a person bad.

Europe prefers to narrate its eras of global war as eras of 'long peace'.

Europe once had a big war with itself when some Europeans started to practice in Europe what they had been practicing in their colonies.

Algeria was a part of Europe. But Algeria was not part of the pax-Europa.

Anyone can be European so long as you tell Europeans where you come from.

Europeans can only trust women who show their whole face. Exceptions apply.
Europe never said thank you to Muslim scholars.
The Mediterranean is currently the deadliest sea crossing in the world.
Europeans are experts on Africa, Asia and Oceania.
Europeans prefer to learn about Africa, Asia and Oceania from other Europeans.
Europe is the only cosmopolitan that is allowed to keep its own adjective.
Europe believes that if it wasn't written down it didn't happen.
Europeans like to write about themselves.
Only Europeans can know Europe.
Once Europe was narcissistic, but Europeans fixed that by turning the mirror into
   a window onto the world.

This text was originally published in *The Disorder of Things*, 24 February 2015
(https://thedisorderofthings.com/2015/02/24/notes-on-europe-and-europeans-
for-the-discerning-traveller/).

INDEX

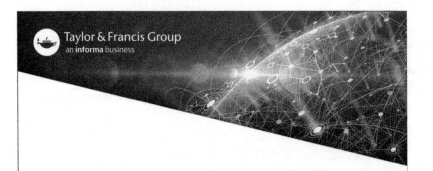